Zimbabwe in Crisis

This book covers not only the political situation in Zimbabwe, but its international context and those areas of privation, exclusion and silence within the country that are beneath the everyday face of politics.

Written by either a Zimbabwean or an internationally acknowledged expert on aspects of Zimbabwe, all the chapters agree that the silences in and surrounding the African state cannot continue. This volume utilizes the perspectives of diplomacy, health, law and literature written in both English and Shona, and of those deeply concerned with democratization in Zimbabwe and its surrounding region.

Zimbabwe and the Space of Silence will be of interest to students and scholars of African studies, African and Third World politics and international law.

This book was previously published as a special issue of the Journal *The Round Table*.

Stephen Chan is a Professor of International Relations in the University of London and Dean of Law and Social Sciences at the School of Oriental and African Studies.

Ranka Primorac is a Research Associate at the School of African and Oriental Studies, University of London.

Zimbabwe in Crisis

The International Response and the Space of Silence

Edited by Ranka Primorac and Stephen Chan

To Mervyn
Happy Birthday!
Stephen and [signature]

 Routledge
Taylor & Francis Group

LONDON AND NEW YORK

First published 2007 by Routledge
2 Park Square, Milton Park, Abingdon, Oxon OX14 4RN

Simultaneously published in the USA and Canada
by Routledge
270 Madison Ave, New York, NY 10016

Routledge is an imprint of the Taylor & Francis Group, an informa business

© 2007 The Round Table Ltd

Typeset in Times New Roman by KnowledgeWorks Global Limited, Southampton, Hampshire, UK
Printed and bound in Great Britain by MPG Books Ltd, Bodmin, Cornwall

British Library Cataloguing in Publication Data
A catalogue record for this book is available from the British Library

Library of Congress Cataloging in Publication Data
A catalog record for this book has been requested

ISBN10 0-415-41549-7
ISBN13 978-0-415-41549-1

Contents

Introduction: The Spaces of Silence'

The decline of Zimbabwe continues to haunt African, Commonwealth and wider international relations. As this book goes to press, inflation in Zimbabwe is estimated at almost 1000% and rising. The opposition party is fragmenting, rural malnutrition is continuing, the victims of urban destruction have not been rehoused, and the off-on availability of petrol and diesel has played havoc with transport, communications, and the servicing of such infrastructure as remains. Even though Kofi Annan has called upon African leaders to condemn misgovernment in Zimbabwe, the African response has been, even up to now, tentative, timid, and largely unwilling to criticize, let alone condemn, Robert Mugabe's Zimbabwe.

Richard Dowden's *Times* article of 16 May 2005 hung over the discussions at the Britain Zimbabwe Society 2005 Research Day, held on 11 June at St Antony's College, Oxford, under the title *Zimbabwe, Africa and the World*. What viable alternative is left to the British Government, Dowden wrote, but to talk to Mugabe? Silence in place of talks had created a space where only further decay was possible, and progress out of it unlikely. Talking to Mugabe was not a palatable option, but there were few others. What also hung over the Research Day, however, was the impact and aftermath of Operation *Murambatsvina,* the razing of huge areas of Zimbabwe's 'illegal' urban settlements and the rendering of their inhabitants homeless in the middle of the Zimbabwean winter. The suddenness and heartlessness of the operation made many Research Day participants wonder how any meaningful talks could take place. In the face of such callousness, what would, or could, Mugabe and Blair talk about? This question continues to echo in the first half of 2006. In an updated version of his article published in this volume, Richard Dowden asks it himself.

The papers presented at the Research Day, which was organized by Ranka Primorac, were all revised and reviewed for a special issue of *The Round Table* (Issue 384, April 2006). The Dowden end-piece is not a direct by-product of the Day, but it is closely connected to its discussions. The paper by Robert Martin is also a later addition, and recounts a history of Zimbabwean judicial practice and possibility to nearly the present day. The stand against arbitrariness, through law and the judiciary, has had its heroic moments – but did the farm invasions of 2000 do more than seize land and erode economic production? Was judicial independence also a victim? With the exceptions of the Dowden and Martin pieces, all other papers in the special issue of *The Round Table* were based on those presented at St Antony's in June 2005. Great care was taken to retain some of the conversational flow of the debate between Hasu Patel and Stephen Chan on Zimbabwean foreign policy; the open questioning, ambivalences, and passionate pro-Zimbabwe flavour of Beacon Mbiba's presentation have also been retained in this published version. Patel, Chan,

Mbiba and Jack Spence all speak of the silences or near-silences to which Zimbabwean foreign policy has been reduced. Whereas Chan and Spence hear the hollow echoes of these silences, Patel and Mbiba detect possibilities of positive outreach. But no one is reaching out from the West to Robert Mugabe's Zimbabwe.

While Mbiba laments the reluctance or lateness of the West to help alleviate the Zimbabwean HIV/AIDS pandemic, Sunanda Ray and Farai Madzimbamuto argue strongly that much fault for the huge rise in HIV infections and fatalities lies with the prevarications and biases of the Zimbabwean government. Here, a silence grew into something literally deadly. In many ways the Ray and Madzimbamuto paper lay at the heart of the Research Day. It is a paper written by two medical activists who have seen at close quarters the devastation wreaked by the pandemic and the decline of living standards and health-care in Zimbabwe. In this paper in particular, passion shines through – and the editors were extremely careful not to excise it. Nothing represents better the catastrophic decline of Zimbabwe than the human tragedy related to HIV/AIDS – a disease whose very name was until very recently cloaked in silence. An earlier, more positive and compassionate set of government policies could have done much to prevent it.

The internal malaise of official denials and self-justifications has not escaped the attention of Zimbabwe's writers. Here, the Research Day sought to illuminate the public condition by considering how a range of writers, texts and genres addresses and interrogates the Zimbabwean silences and denials. Unlike most 'Postcolonial Literature' panels, the Research Day presenters deliberately turned their attention not only to established writers in English, but also to popular, non-canonical and indigenous-language texts. In the tryptich of literature-related contributions to this volume, recurring themes and preoccupations overlap and interweave. Drew Shaw uncovers a web of transgressive innovations in Zimbawean authors' representations of sexuality: many can be read as challenges to the official government stance on 'deviant' desire. Shaw's chapter helps to highlight the extent to which the work of Dambudzo Marechera – the maverick author all too often treated by critics as a Zimbabwean literary *exception* – is in fact embedded within his nation's literary traditions. Ranka Primorac draws attention to the cultural importance of post-independence popular literature in English, produced by black *and* white writers, and thus far almost completely un-researched. Underpinning her Research Day presentation was the claim that Zimbabwe's popular writings have long been engaged in a wide-ranging debate about the nature of the nation, which readers and researchers can no longer afford to ignore. Maurice Vambe's analysis of key Shona novels' attitudes to land reveals how the novels' plot-lines and characters resist land reappropriation by corrupt and powerful *black* actors as much as its earlier ownership by white ones. Vambe's treatment of a Shona novel written in 2005 and set in the middle of contemporary land seizures is particularly revealing. The three papers on literature and Ray and Madzimbamuto's paper on HIV/Aids place a particular emphasis on issues related to gender and sexuality.

The editors sought a volume which would go beyond a mere condemnation of Robert Mugabe and a lament about Zimbabwe's decline. In summing up the Research Day, Diana Jeater (Britain Zimbabwe Society's Chair) pointed out that, in many contexts, the problem with Zimbabwe was simply that wrong things were being perceived as threatening by various parties, and this makes dialogue difficult.

Often (as in the case of popular literature), Zimbabwe appears to be talking to itself; in other respects (as in the case of AIDS), it is as if the curse of a confession-demanding *ngozi* (vengeful spirit) prevents a national movement forward. The Research Day participants were unable to answer the questions as to whether, when, how, and about what Mugabe and Blair should talk – but they accepted that these questions must be asked. The editors wish to celebrate the heroism of activists, health workers, judges, publishers and writers who seek to remain pro-active, while the international politicians and diplomats continue to manipulate the spaces of silence.

Added to the papers collected in *The Round Table* are two further contributions to the present volume. Ken Good describes a southern African region where democracy is not always honoured in practice. He uses the example of Botswana, and this offers a comparative case alongside that of Zimbabwe. Democracy can become a silence even in the countries professing it. Brian Raftopoulos, who sought to mediate the quarrels within the MDC opposition party before it split in early 2006, here recounts how the split happened. The faults and difficulties of Zimbabwe are not located within Mugabe's government alone. The spaces of silence should not extend to the manoeuvres and mistakes of those opposing him.

The editors have incurred many debts in their work: our warm thanks to Fareda Banda, Elleke Boehmer, Richard Delahunty, David Jobbins, Gugulethu Moyo, Andy Williams and members of the Britain Zimbabwe Society Executive, for various kinds of help and participation. The 2005 BZS Research Day was facilitated by the sponsorship and grants received from Air Zimbabwe, The African Studies Association of the UK, Britain Zimbabwe Society and Oxford University's Centre of African Studies.

Ranka Primorac and Stephen Chan

Zimbabwe's Foreign Policy: A Conversation

STEPHEN CHAN* AND HASU PATEL[†]
*School of Oriental and African Studies, University of London, UK
[†]University of Zimbabwe

Hasu Patel

In my opening statement and the subsequent discussion, I will present a broad framework to understand and explain Zimbabwe's foreign policy. In 1985 I published an extended chapter entitled 'No master, no mortgage, no sale: the foreign policy of Zimbabwe' (Patel, 1985). It was later updated and expanded (Patel, 1987). The first part of the title was abstracted from official statements, and I believed then and continue to believe that it broadly captures the central character of Zimbabwe's foreign policy.

I will, first, outline the key principles that guided Zimbabwe's foreign policy shortly after independence in April 1980, discussing the symmetry and asymmetry between principles and practice. Second, I will analyse the extent to which the original principles have retained their validity and/or evolved and the new elements that have emerged. Third, I will show that since 1980 there has been an organic link between the method of independence, that is, the armed struggle (the Second *Chimurenga*) for independence, and its values and beliefs, and domestic policy and foreign policy. This organic link underpins Zimbabwe's highly active and visible foreign policy, especially since the chief maker and articulator of Zimbabwe's foreign policy, President Robert Mugabe, and other major policy makers were leaders in the armed struggle.

Fourth, I will suggest that, for a small, weak, landlocked and vulnerable developing independent country, such as Zimbabwe, the dispersal of dependence is a viable strategy to safeguard its sovereignty and independence in an historically structured international order of dependence and inequality, especially since the demise of the Cold War and its bipolar bloc system.

Key Principles of Zimbabwe's Foreign Policy

In the first official pronouncement on Zimbabwe's foreign policy principles, in May 1980, the then President Canaan Banana, emphasized non-alignment, African issues, peaceful co-existence, reordering of the international economic order, and exchange of ideas, culture and trade (Patel, 1985, pp. 228–229).

Thereafter, in a major speech at the United Nations in August 1980, Mugabe, then prime minister, expounded on the five key principles of Zimbabwe's foreign policy: 1) 'national sovereignty and equality among nations'; 2) 'attainment of a socialist, egalitarian and democratic society'; 3) 'right of all peoples to self-determination and independence'; 4) 'non-racialism at home and abroad'; and 5) 'positive non-alignment and peaceful co-existence among nations' (Patel, 1985, pp. 229–230).

It is recognized that there are overlaps between the above five principles, which also incorporate the principles of nationalism, Pan-Africanism, anti-imperialism, solidarity, non-intervention and non-interference in internal affairs, multilateralism, and the Look East Policy which has been especially vibrant during the past two years.

Centralization of Foreign Policy

One of the paradoxes of our time is that, as the attachment to and practice of democracy has increased, so also has increased the tendency towards the centralization of power in foreign policy. Zimbabwe is not an exception and this centralization has been associated with Mugabe, who was the executive prime minister from 1980 to 1987 and has been the executive president since 1987. His ideas, views and personality, and experience as an African nationalist and one of the then co-leaders of the armed struggle, have been crucial. He is an intellectual with a keen interest in foreign policy and he has been the chief maker and articulator of Zimbabwe's foreign policy.

Other official institutions having an input into or impact on foreign policy include the Politburo and the Central Committee of the ruling party, the Zimbabwe African National Union–Patriotic Front (Zanu–PF), the cabinet, the Ministry of Foreign Affairs, the Office of the President and Cabinet, other ministries, Parliament, the Reserve Bank of Zimbabwe, and parastatals.

Principles and Practice of Foreign Policy: Some Examples

Zimbabwe has fiercely guarded its sovereignty, even at great cost. For example, it was subjected to apartheid South Africa's destabilization policy during 1980–94

(Patel, 1986) and to the UK's threatened and the USA's actual aid cut, both in the 1980s. Since the late 1990s, and especially since the fast-track land reform programme beginning in 2000, it has also been subjected to Prime Minister Tony Blair's unilateral abrogation in 1997 of the UK's historical responsibility regarding the 'land question', to associated Western targeted and general sanctions, and to personalization and demonization, as part of a regime change agenda.

During the past few years, Zimbabwe's reinvigorated defence of its sovereignty as the continuation of the struggle for independence, recast in terms of the Third *Chimurenga* being fought against the UK in particular, and its Western allies, is illustrated by the official currency of phrases such as "Zimbabwe will never be a colony again", and "the land is the economy, the economy is the land", and by the characterization of the March 2005 parliamentary elections as the 'anti-Blair elections'.

In pursuit of its own sovereignty, independence, economic and strategic interests, and Pan-Africanism, in the 1980s Zimbabwe sent its defence forces to protect the Beira Corridor in Mozambique from South African attacks and later assisted Mozambique in checkmating its rebel force and the latter's South African support. Also in 1998 Zimbabwe, together with Angola and Namibia, sent its defence forces to the Democratic Republic of Congo (DRC) to protect the giant Inga Dam, which supplies part of Zimbabwe's electricity, and the government in the DRC from the invasion by Uganda and Rwanda and its rebel allies.

However, some difficulties associated with guarding one's sovereignty are illustrated by the fact that, notwithstanding its suspicion of the International Monetary Fund (IMF), Zimbabwe adopted an Economic Structural Adjustment Programme, and its successor, during 1991–2000. Further, since 2004, Zimbabwe has significantly reduced its arrears to the IMF in order to avoid expulsion from the Fund, to enhance its international creditworthiness, and to engage with the wider international community.

In pursuit of multilateralism, Pan-Africanism, good international citizenship, and peaceful resolution of conflicts, Zimbabwe participated in UN peacekeeping operations in Angola (including as UN Force Commander), Somalia (including as UN Deputy Force Commander) and Uganda/Rwanda in the 1990s. It also participated in mediation in Mozambique and Angola (1989–91) (Patel, 1993); in UN police contingents in Bosnia, East Timor, Somalia, Sierra Leone, Liberia and Darfur in the Sudan; and in bilateral and multilateral training of defence forces from the Southern African Development Community (SADC). However, in a rare disenchantment with multilateralism, Zimbabwe withdrew from the Commonwealth in December 2003 because it concluded that it was being unfairly treated by Nigeria, the 'white' Commonwealth and the Commonwealth Secretary-General.

In pursuit of peoples' right to self-determination and independence, since 1980, Zimbabwe has supported independence movements in, *inter alia*, South Africa and Namibia (but, in recognition of facts of geography and history and of its vulnerability to military attacks from South Africa, did not provide guerrilla bases and transit facilities), Western Sahara, East Timor and Palestine.

The pursuit of non-racialism at home and abroad resulted in the domestically and internationally acclaimed post-independence policy of Reconciliation (between the races and ethnic groups) and the Government of National Unity. Race has been part of Zimbabwe's history since occupation in 1890 and attempts at non-racialism are difficult at the best of times; indeed, the domestic salience of race has increased, especially since the fast-track land reform programme from 2000 onwards. Internationally Zimbabwe has pursued alliances with Africa, the African diaspora and the Third World, in line with its principles of Pan-Africanism, anti-imperialism and solidarity, as counterweights against Western 'kith and kin' attacks against Zimbabwe (Phimister and Raftopoulos, 2004).

The pursuit of a socialist, egalitarian and democratic society has had mixed results, as discussed below.

Regarding socialism, since 1980 Zimbabwe has pursued relations with the then 'Eastern Bloc', China, Cuba, North Korea, etc., both because of their support for the armed struggle and as a method of modulating its historically structured dependence on the West. In the 1980s, 'socialism' and 'Marxism–Leninism' were state policy, but with the demise of communism in Eastern Europe and the USSR, these terms have lost currency. Nevertheless, it could be argued that the indigenization and black economic empowerment policies and the fast-track land reform programme since 2000 are part of the pursuit of socialism.

In 1992 Zimbabwe had announced an 'economic thrust' to its foreign policy, which anticipated future trade, investments, joint ventures, tourists, etc. coming from the East. During the past two years the Look East Policy, involving emphasis on relations with China, especially, and with Malaysia, India, Pakistan, Singapore, Indonesia, Thailand and Iran, has acquired a high profile because of the on-going dispute and stalemate with the West.

The pursuit of egalitarianism is a never-ending exercise. The indigenization and black empowerment policies, the 1980–90 'willing buyer-willing seller' land reform programme, and the fast-track land reform programme since 2000 have resulted in an historically and morally necessary massive redistribution of income, wealth and ownership to the majority population. Nevertheless, it is also true that the past few years have witnessed increasing levels of poverty and unemployment, triple-digit inflation, chronic shortages of foreign exchange and essential commodities, falling agricultural and industrial production, and per capita income lower than in 1980.

Democracy was implemented in Zimbabwe only with independence in April 1980 and there have been regular parliamentary elections every five years and (executive) presidential elections every six years (since 1990) (Patel, 2000). Also, Zimbabwe is the only country in the region which legislatively incorporates many provisions of the 2004 SADC Principles and Guidelines on Democratic Elections. However, since 2000 the opposition Movement for Democratic Change (MDC), sections of domestic and international civil society, and Western governments, election observers, and commentators (and in 2002 also the Commonwealth) have rejected the 2000 and 2005 parliamentary and the 2002 presidential elections as flawed/not reflecting the will of the people and/or not free and fair. On the other hand, governments, election observers and commentators from Africa, the Third World and the 'East' have declared them as reflecting the will of the people and/or free and fair.

Some political space has narrowed, e.g. with the 2002 Public Order and Security Act (POSA), the 2002 Access to Information and Protection of Privacy Act

(AIPPA). Domestic and global polarization over democracy in Zimbabwe has been a feature since 2000 but, whatever the shortcomings of democracy in Zimbabwe, it is still healthier than in quite a few other countries world-wide.

In the Cold War bloc system positive non-alignment was especially relevant for the Third World's attempt to safeguard its newly acquired independence, maintain some space in and change the international order, and avoid being incinerated by superpower rivalries. Zimbabwe has been an active member of the Non-Aligned Movement (NAM); however, the end of the Cold War and the new age of the 'war on terrorism' has brought forth continuing re-examination of the relevance of the movement.

Zimbabwe has pursued peaceful co-existence both in the region and elsewhere. For example, from 1980 to 1994, when South Africa became free, Zimbabwe was subjected to severe destabilization by apartheid South Africa. However, recognizing facts of geography and history, and conscious of its vulnerability to South African military attacks, Zimbabwe maintained pragmatic relations with its neighbour. Thus, while supporting South African and Namibian liberation movements, Zimbabwe denied them guerrilla bases and transit facilities and maintained trade and consular relations, but withheld full diplomatic relations and supported UN sanctions against South Africa. Zimbabwe has consistently exhorted other nations in disputes to peacefully co-exist and settle their differences in a peaceful manner.

Stephen Chan

Hasu Patel has been the most articulate scholar of Zimbabwean foreign policy. He rightly points to his 'No master, no mortgage, no sale' (Patel, 1985) paper as capturing the central character of early Zimbabwean foreign policy. It is in the deliberate use of the qualifier, 'early', that I differ from him. The idealism implicit in the 1980s is simply not the same confused idealism apparent in the 2000s. The early idealism did not die away as soon as the 1980s ended. In a volume I myself edited (with Vivienne Jabri), Patel gave the most detailed account then written of Zimbabwean foreign policy up to 1991 (Patel, 1993), and I completely agree with him as to its courage, indeed its daring, not only in resisting South African destabilization insofar as it was visited upon Zimbabwe, but by militarily entering Mozambique in the mid-1980s. That was a huge risk for a venture of course beneficial to Zimbabwe, but also to the beleaguered government of Mozambique. The military professionalism of the Zimbabwean troops was exemplary, and very much put to shame the rag-taggle indolence, disorganization and plain cowardice of Mozambican government forces. Zimbabwe never officially mentioned the contrast, but it was never hard to find Zimbabwean officers very ready to do so privately.

The Patel account stops at 1991, but I have taken the account forward (with Moises Venancio) to 1992, and hailed the Zimbabwean contribution, indeed Mugabe's personal contribution, to the success of the Rome peace talks over Mozambique (Chan and Venancio, 1998), whereas other authors have singled out the USA (Hume, 1994) or Lonrho's Tiny Rowland (Vines, 1998) as the main breakthrough players. I think they are wrong, and attribute the success of Rome to the informal work of the Santo Egidio religious community first of all, but to

Mugabe finally. I want to say this by way of agreement with Hasu Patel, for the sake of giving credit where it is due, and to indicate that I am not a knee-jerk opponent of all things associated with Mugabe. Far too many of today's blanket opponents of Mugabe were once blanket and uncritical supporters. What I want to say is against blankets.

In this context, having said where I think Hasu Patel is correct, let me now say where he is wrong. Before that, however, let me comment on his depiction of the 'key principles' of Zimbabwean foreign policy. These are essentially direct borrowings from the foundation principles of the Non-Aligned Movement. Indeed, they were first articulated at Bandung in 1955. I want to make the simple point that 50 years have passed since then. Twenty-five years have passed since, in Hasu's account, both Canaan Banana and Mugabe rearticulated them in 1980. Very simply, we live in a quite different world in 2005. If those key principles have not been revisited in the wake of the end of the Cold War in 1989, then those principles are antique. There is no need for non-alignment when there is no gap between superpowers in which to be non-aligned. In a uni-polar world it is not old non-alignment that opposes or stands neutral to the USA, but forces with which Mugabe's Zimbabwe has no attachment. Indeed, the entire emphasis on an Afro-centralism, even an Afro-essentialism, necessarily makes no room for any other form of essentialism—or for complex emanation from essentialism.

Where then is Hasu wrong? He is right to indicate the centralization of Zimbabwean foreign policy formation. He includes the Ministry of Foreign Affairs as still being a player in the process, but it must irk him—as a particularly distinguished former High Commissioner and diplomatic doyen—privately to understand that the ministry is marginalized in policy formation. The one key and central player Hasu omits to mention is the Central Intelligence Organization (CIO). The CIO was central to Mugabe's breakthrough in Mozambique. It worked closely, ironically, with the American CIA. When Mugabe went to meet the Mozambican rebel leader, Dhlakama, in Malawi in early 1992, the Zimbabwean Ministry of Foreign Affairs had neither involvement nor even knowledge of what happened until after it had happened. That exclusion on important matters has continued. Hasu Patel will know only too well that his recall from Canberra on the eve of the crucial 2002 Commonwealth summit in Australia—the one that set into motion Zimbabwe's suspension from the Commonwealth—to be replaced, if I might not mince my works, by a party hack, did the Zimbabwean position no good at all. Unlike the military expedition into Mozambique, professionalism had no place alongside politics.

The second issue over which I think Hasu is wrong concerns the Zimbabwean intervention in Congo. He characterizes this as a contribution to the defence of Congo against Ugandan and Rwandan invasion. This is a most partial characterization, as the Ugandan and Rwandan forces, albeit with their own agenda, took their place within an essentially Congolese quarrel of factions. It was centrally a power struggle within Congo by Congolese. What the Zimbabweans did was to enter the struggle on the side of one of the factions and, in the process, to secure control of a vast swathe of mineral deposits with which Mugabe has been able to buy-off military dissent—or buy in a guarantee of senior military support for his own government during the days of the farm invasions and the resulting economic melt-down. What the Third *Chimurenga* has brought about is the semblance of authenticity and the reality of poverty.

This leads to the related third issue, where Hasu views Zimbabwean foreign policy as a defence against the British prime minister. Tony Blair has a wide range of faults, stupidities and capacities for self-righteous rashness. I am sure that British historians will judge him harshly. I count myself among the first to say outright that Blair must shoulder much blame on the Zimbabwean issue (Chan, 2003). But Blair has never sought to overturn Zimbabwe's sovereignty. Indeed, the Mugabe ploy of saying that the farm seizures were inevitable because Britain would not provide the funds for nationalization with compensation is precisely a statement against Zimbabwe's own sovereign capacity. "We didn't have the sovereign capacity to compensate; therefore, because you did not provide your funds for compensation in our country, you are against our sovereignty". There is an illogicality here, which is addressed by the rhetoric of accusation and self-justification and not by policy as it is normally understood and rationally planned.

So, fourth, when Hasu later mentions Zimbabwe's being "unfairly treated" by the "white Commonwealth and the Commonwealth Secretary-General", he is being both disingenuous and a participant in this rhetoric. The Commonwealth Secretary-General has no executive powers to mistreat anyone or anything. The Zimbabwean position at the December 2003 Abuja Commonwealth summit was not supported by Kenya and Ghana, nor by the distinctly non-white Caribbean, Pacific and Asian states. In short, it was not supported by a wide cross-section of the NAM. Zimbabwean foreign policy has a question to address here, and it is seeking to duck the question under the bogey of either Blair or Commonwealth Secretary-General, Don McKinnon.

I want to say two final things about where I think Hasu is wrong. He is wrong, fifth, in taking seriously the prospect of any beneficial 'economic thrust' in seeking to develop a 'Look East policy' involving Chinese investment in Zimbabwe. Let me put this in a stark and point-blank manner. The Chinese will not ride to Zimbabwe's economic rescue. The Chinese want to gain economic benefits from Zimbabwe. They want to use Zimbabwe as a springboard into other African countries. The Chinese cannot believe how exceptionally naïve the Zimbabwean government is being. The Zimbabwean 'Look East policy' is a sign of desperation, having trashed a long list of other foreign policy options.

Finally, I will not call it wrong in any outright sense. Let me call it an understatement. But, when Hasu says "some political space has narrowed", he has invented a polished euphemism. Notwithstanding the regularity of elections and all the superficial apparatus of a democracy "still healthier than in quite a few other countries world-wide" (and this is true), the fact remains that this 'narrowing' has been a violent and tenaciously prosecuted affair. Whatever Thabo Mbeki might say in public—and, as with Nigeria's President, Olusegun Obasanjo, it differs somewhat from what he says in private—the fact remains that the Zimbabwean affair has ruined Mbeki's effort to claim some African oversight of the New Economic Partnership for Africa's Development (NEPAD). As a consequence, the Zimbabwean affair reinforces the Western intrusion upon the pace of Africa's democratization and Africa's sovereignty. What Mugabe has done, in the name of

Africa, has been to diminish the space of international belief in Africa, and to diminish the effective nature of African sovereign space.

Let me summarize. I have been at pains both to praise and to criticize Zimbabwean foreign policy. Hasu has acted the ambassador here, which is indeed what he was—and he still retains the rank and title. I think he was the most polished and accomplished of all the ambassadors Zimbabwe has ever had. He is remembered with great respect in Canberra. Doors still open for him in Whitehall and Pall Mall. But he is seeking to represent something that has lurched beyond the pale. I conclude with reference to what is happening as we speak today in the cloisters of Oxford, and that is the wholesale demolition of entire suburbs of Harare—in the name of legality and urban cleanliness. A most middle-class cover for a policy of violence. Is this the true face of the regime? That it has all this capacity and self-organization which it uses not to build but to destroy? And now that there are almost no white farmers left, has Zimbabwe, like Saturn, taken to eating its own children?

Hasu Patel's Response

Stephen Chan's deep knowledge of Zimbabwe, over many years, as reflected in his prolific and insightful writings on Zimbabwe, makes sharing a panel with him a hazardous business. Nevertheless, I am happy to be here because we have been very good friends for about two decades.

I am most grateful to Stephen for his complimentary remarks about my academic and diplomatic lives. However, I would like to clarify a point he made. Even though I served in the Zimbabwean diplomatic service from April 1994 to the end December 2000 and I still retain the rank and title of ambassador, my participation here is as a recently retired but still practising academic; I have no authority to, nor do I 'represent' anyone but myself.

Stephen is sceptical about Zimbabwe's 'Look East Policy' (LEP). He may be proved correct but a considered judgement on the LEP's efficacy will require some time. Nevertheless, the pursuit of what I have labelled the 'dispersal of dependence' by a small, weak and poor state such as Zimbabwe is a viable option. I mentioned many countries, but both China, a rising world power, and Zimbabwe will pursue their national interests. However, where there is some compatibility between their national interests, even if the benefits and losses may be unequal but there is reasonable mutual satisfaction, then the engagement is worthwhile for both. I suggested that the LEP's contemporary roots are in the 1992 'economic thrust' to foreign policy and that, during the past two years it "has acquired a high profile because of the on-going dispute and stalemate with the West", but it would be appropriate to see the LEP as complementary, rather than as an alternative, to engaging with the West.

Regarding Zimbabwe's involvement in the DRC in August 1998, I stated the intertwining of sovereignty, independence, and economic and strategic interests. In the DRC I mentioned the protection of both the government (at its invitation) from the Ugandan/Rwandan invasion and the giant Inga Dam. Stephen adds the issues of mineral deposits and military 'buy-off' and 'buy-in', but it is still important to distinguish between the primary motivation (a combination of my above-mentioned three factors, within a Pan-African framework) and collateral or consequential benefits. Nevertheless, Zimbabwe's involvement in the DRC was financially costly, led to a sharp decline of the Zimbabwe dollar, and complicated Zimbabwe's relations with the West.

Stephen is correct in pointing out that I omitted to mention the CIO in my list of examples of official state institutions having an input/impact in foreign policy. In the example he gave there may well have been reasons, of which I have no knowledge, for the lack of knowledge by or participation of the Zimbabwean Ministry of Foreign Affairs (MFA) in the meeting in 1992 in Malawi between Mugabe and the then rebel Mozambican leader Afonso Dhlakama during Zimbabwe's mediation efforts in Mozambique. We both agree about the centralization of foreign policy in Zimbabwe, but whether this centralization and the CIO's role means the marginalization of the MFA in foreign policy formation is another matter, because reports, research, analyses and recommendations emanating from the MFA, both at Head Office and from diplomatic missions, and the MFA's personalities and their ideas and persuasive powers have an on-going important input/impact.

I stated that "Zimbabwe withdrew from the Commonwealth in December 2003 because *it concluded* [my emphasis] that it was unfairly treated by Nigeria, the 'white' Commonwealth and the Commonwealth Secretary-General". Stephen leaves out Nigeria and declares that I am "being both disingenuous and a participant in the rhetoric". One may interrogate the conclusion, without any labelling. Stephen is correct in pointing out that Zimbabwe's position was not supported by Kenya, Ghana (I had included Nigeria), and the 'non-white (non-African)' states and this needs to be addressed by Zimbabwe's foreign policy.

However, one should also address, for example, the following facts. 1) The 'white' members of the Commonwealth have been the leading, and most vocal and persistent 'bloc' in their 'anti-Zimbabwe' stance. 2) There has been a seeming 'flip-flop' by Nigeria, whose President Olusegun Obasanjo, with the concurrence of President Thabo Mbeki, wrote a letter in February 2003 to Prime Minister John Howard of Australia (as Chair of the Commonwealth Troika on Zimbabwe) recommending the lifting of the previous 12-month suspension of Zimbabwe from the Councils of the Commonwealth. The suspension issue was within the mandate of the Commonwealth Troika; nevertheless, two votes out of three could not lift the suspension! Yet, contrary to Zimbabwean expectations, Mugabe was not invited to the December 2003 Commonwealth Heads of Government Meeting (CHOGM) in Abuja, Nigeria, to present his case, as per the Report of the High Level Review Group's recommendations (concerning procedures to be adopted relating to perceived breaches of Commonwealth Harare Principles in circumstances other than an unconstitutional overthrow of a democratic government) adopted at the March 2002 CHOGM in Coolum, Australia. Further, SADC leaders were not allowed to give a press conference/s in Abuja to voice their displeasure about the treatment of the 'Zimbabwe issue' at the Abuja CHOGM (Government of Zimbabwe, 2002; Obasanjo, 2003). 3) Zimbabwe's disaffection with Commonwealth Secretary-General Don Mckinnon related to the perceived inadequate use of his 'good offices' role and, especially, his March 2003 'Commonwealth Statement on Zimbabwe', in which he declared that the Troika had agreed to continue Zimbabwe's suspension until the Abuja CHOGM in December 2003. Zimbabwe questioned his authority to make the statement and the public absence of the contents and results of his consultations with Commonwealth governments. Similar concerns were publicly raised by the SADC diplomats based in London (*The Herald*, 22 March 2003; *The Times*, 6 October 2003; Commonwealth Secretariat, 2003). 4) while primarily the 'white bloc' within the Commonwealth argued for Zimbabwe's continued suspension, Blair supported Pakistan's readmission to the Commonwealth because of 'progress towards democracy'. 5) Swaziland, the last remaining absolute monarchy in Africa, and Uganda, a 'non-party democracy', continued as members of the Commonwealth.

Stephen's statement that "Blair has never sought to overturn Zimbabwe's sovereignty" is puzzling. We are both aware of the long and tortuous history of the idea of sovereignty, and its evident difficulties in practice, especially for small, weak and poor states, but also for large, strong and rich states. However, the increasing relevance of non-state actors, the continuing role of the UN Security Council, and attachment to and discussions about 'responsibility to protect' and 'liberal imperialism' in some quarters, have not negated the fact that state sovereignty is still the basic organizing principle in the international system. Nevertheless, sovereignty may be overturned by military and/or non-military means.

In spite of the significant and continuing financial contribution from the UK (and the West in general) to Zimbabwe in a range of development areas, there *has* been an attempt to 'overturn Zimbabwe's sovereignty'. There have been targeted and general sanctions (by the UK, EU, Australia, New Zealand, Canada, and the USA with its Zimbabwe Democracy and Economic Recovery Act of 2001). There have been media obsession, travel advisories, external support for the opposition MDC and civil society, and the personalization and demonization especially of Mugabe, within the framework of regime change. However, a replication of the 'moments' in Zambia, Indonesia, Serbia, Madagascar, Georgia, Ukraine and Kyrgyzstan has not materialized. Zimbabwe's call for adequate compensation from the UK for the 'land issue' is not merely, as Stephen puts it, "a statement against Zimbabwe's own sovereign capacity" but, crucially, is a statement about the UK's responsibility as a former colonial sovereign to meaningfully contribute to redressing the colonial dispossession of land in Zimbabwe. Stephen himself has written extensively about Zimbabwe–UK relations, including the issues of land and compensation (Chan, 2003), and knows only too well that it is not simply a question of 'you don't give me compensation, then I seize the farms'.

The complicated history of the 'land/compensation issue' and the difficulties and controversies associated with the form the land distribution has taken, especially since 2000, involve many factors. Between 1981 and 1996, under the Lancaster House Agreement of December 1979, the UK contributed £47 million (considerably less than the reported mid-1970s 'Kissinger's billions of dollars' to 'buy-in' willing white farmers for a 'Rhodesian settlement') to the first land reform programme in which about 3.5 million hectares of land were purchased on a 'willing-buyer, willing-seller' basis, with full compensation for land and improvements, although about £4 million was not spent because Zimbabwe did not have the funds to match the 'pound for pound' arrangement. In the 1990s Zimbabwe 'went slow' on its land reform programme, because of the lack of its own and UK funding, and made friendly approaches in order not to upset the difficult negotiations over South Africa's transition to majority rule. Crucially, real difficulties emerged after the 1996–97 mutually hopeful land reform discussions between Zimbabwe and the UK, under the leadership of Prime Minister John Major, were scuttled by his electoral defeat in May 1997. The subsequent unilateral abrogation of the UK's historical responsibility by the incoming New Labour government of Prime Minister Tony Blair, as exemplified by the November 1997 'I am not a colonialist' letter from the Secretary of State for International Development, Clare Short (Short, 1997), to Zimbabwe caused consternation and resentment within the Zimbabwe Government. This was compounded by Blair's rebuff of Mugabe at the November 1997 Edinburgh CHOGM. And it was reinforced by ministers such as Foreign Secretary Robin Cook and Minister of State for Africa Peter Hain engaging in vitriolic personal attacks on Mugabe, just when the war veterans, through the Zimbabwe National Liberation War Veterans' Association (ZNLWVA), had become a significant political force and had succeeded, in November 1997, in gaining unbudgeted and large gratuities and pensions.

Subsequently, sporadic farm occupations began in 1998, but the occupiers were removed by the government. At the International Donors' Conference on Land Reform and Resettlement in Zimbabwe (9–11th September 1998), the government proposed a 10-year land reform plan, involving the 'market-buying' of one million hectares per year over five years (total of five million hectares, about half the 'white' agricultural land), with another five years for all infrastructure development. The total cost would be about US$1.9 billion, of which Zimbabwe would pay 35.8%; about US$541 million was allocated for 'market compensation' for both land and improvements. The conference did not result in any specific funds on the table, with the donors settling for an Inception Phase of 24 months involving 118 farms, with nebulous donor technical/or financial support (Government of Zimbabwe, 1998; Communiqué, 1998). In December 1999 the Zanu–PF National Congress resolved that the UK should pay compensation for agricultural land acquired under the land reform programme and the government would pay compensation for improvements; the resolution was incorporated in the constitutional proposals of 2000, and later given constitutional effect. Soon after the defeat of the Constitutional Referendum in February 2000, massive, often violent, farm invasions were conducted by the war veterans, which were not part of any government plan; later, fatefully, the government went along with the farm invasions. The April 2000 UK/Zimbabwe Joint Ministerial Consultations in London agreed to restart the '1998 Inception Phase', for which the UK offered only an unspecified part of an additional £36 million, over two years, for all development projects in Zimbabwe (Communiqué, 2000). The Abuja Agreement of September 2001 confirmed that "Land is at the core of the crisis in Zimbabwe and cannot be separated from other issues of concern to the Commonwealth, such as the rule of law, respect for human rights, democracy and the economy", and stated the UK's commitment to a significant financial contribution to and mobilization of other donors to a land reform fund, but without mentioning monetary figures (Commonwealth Secretariat, 2001).

Finally, Stephen states that the key principles of Zimbabwe's foreign policy, which were first articulated by Zimbabwe in 1980 and which I discussed earlier, "are essentially direct borrowings from the foundation principles of the Non-Aligned Movement" and that "we live in a very different world in 2005. If those key principles have not been revisited in the wake of the Cold War in 1989, then those principles are antique." I agree with Stephen's formulation.

However, while time is one variable, changing circumstance or context, and the intrinsic validity of any principle are other variables. Many of the key principles both predate and postdate Bandung in 1955 and Belgrade in 1961. I have already commented on the limits to the practice of many of the key principles. For example, the end of the Cold War and its bloc system has meant a re-evaluation of the continued relevance of non-alignment; socialism has lost its earlier currency; egalitarian and democratic society and non-racialism have had mixed results; while self-determination and independence has been realized for most colonial peoples, some exceptions remain; and, for all states, sovereignty and equality among nations is increasingly problematic in practice and yet has continuing attachment and relevance.

It is a mistake to assume that, for example, Zimbabwe's deep attachment to Pan-Africanism excludes other attachments. A continent deeply scarred by slavery and colonialism and continually experiencing marginalization is bound to see the relevance of Pan-Africanism, which itself has a long pedigree in Africa and in the African diaspora. But the practice of Pan-Africanism will vary among different countries, based on a mixture of variables. In a fast-changing world, with the possibilities and problems of contemporary globalization, it is a question of the proper and efficient equation between the 'local' and the 'cosmopolitan' identities, each having its relevance, opportunities and difficulties. Excessive 'localism' may be comforting but also debilitating, while excessive 'cosmopolitanism' may be liberating but also lonelier.

The Way Forward

The way forward is both simple and complex. It is intriguing to note that, while the UK has engaged in negotiations with what it may perceive as 'difficult' countries, it has been reluctant to do the same with Zimbabwe; the last time that the two parties bilaterally met at a high level was the UK/Zimbabwe Joint Ministerial Consultations in London in April 2000.

Yet all conflicts need to be ended, sooner rather than later. Put simply, Zimbabwe and the UK need to enter into discussions based on equality, mutual respect and earnestness in 'listening to each other's stories'. As Richard Dowden wrote recently, "Britain's policy of isolation and regime change has failed ... If we want Zimbabwe to survive there is no alternative: we have to talk to Mugabe" (Dowden, 2005[1]).

While the 'Zimbabwe issue' has been internationalized, and has affected Zimbabwe's relations with especially the West and also the Commonwealth, it is self-evident that at its epicentre the conflict has been between Zimbabwe and the UK, triggered by the issue of land, with its associated issue of race, both issues being historically intertwined in Zimbabwe since colonial occupation in 1890.

Both the leaders of Zimbabwe and the UK are 'conviction politicians' who are deeply committed to their own principles. Whereas New Labour sees itself as making 'new' history, Zanu – PF sees itself as the revolutionary vanguard maker and continuing guardian of an 'earlier' history (of the armed struggle for independence), which is also 'current' history.

The 'clash of histories, principles and personalities' has resulted in the increasingly dire economic situation and political polarization in Zimbabwe, the fractured

Zimbabwe–West and Zimbabwe–Commonwealth relations, and the denting of Zimbabwe's international image. The search for culpability would logically include state and non-state actors, both within and outside Zimbabwe, whose acts of commission and omission have differentially contributed to Zimbabwe's travails.

It may be worthwhile to revisit the Abuja Agreement of September 2001, which stated, in part: "Land is at the core of the crisis in Zimbabwe and cannot be separated from other issues of concern to the Commonwealth, such as the rule of law, respect for human rights, democracy and the economy" (Commonwealth Secretariat, 2001). Although Zimbabwe withdrew from the Commonwealth in December 2003, both Zimbabwe and the UK agreed to the statement. Nevertheless, it seems that the UK–Zimbabwe impasse has resulted from Zimbabwe emphasizing the prior resolution of the 'land and compensation issue', and the UK emphasizing the prior resolution of the 'rights and governance issues'. The 'circuit-breaker' may lie in depoliticizing and depersonalizing the two issues and recasting them into technical issues to be dealt with concurrently.

Robert Mugabe, who has announced his retirement at the end of his present term of office in 2008, has publicly declared his availability for a face-to-face meeting with Tony Blair, who has also announced that his current term in office will be his last. Will the latter be available?

Stephen Chan's Response

Hasu Patel has spoken cogently and made a number of meritorious points. I disagree with many of them, but they do illustrate that the Zimbabwean government has set about its recent policies with a degree of rationality or, at least, with a sense that rationalization of policy is important. There has been some intellectual work here. Not all of it, however, has been productive—so that, when Hasu launches into his exposition of processes surrounding the Abuja Commonwealth summit, he is seeking to construct a legalistic case to demonstrate that Zimbabwe was poorly treated. He knows very well that the legalisms can be argued both ways. What is important, however, is that the politics surrounding Zimbabwe's suspension from the Commonwealth were such that President Mugabe's position had lost key support. The so-called 'flip-flop' by Obasanjo was not gratuitous or sudden. Obasanjo realized, and had been trying to make this plain in his diplomatic overtures to Mugabe, that the Zimbabwean line was damaging the international relations of Africa as a whole. I have made this point earlier: in the name of African authenticity: Mugabe has actually been damaging an Africa that must live in a wider world. He has been single-handedly cancelling Africa's leverage in that wider world. And Obasanjo has far more important things to do than continue to explain and support an irascible country that has, ironically, withdrawn into a *laager* mentality and, in its own disregard for legality and legalisms, has drawn an iron fist over all its policy enactments.

This leads me to make what I hope is an obvious comment on the statement that, despite all the pressures from the West, all the (relatively mild) sanctions, and support for the opposition or civil society in Zimbabwe, there has been no democratic 'moment'. There has been no 'moment' of mass uprising against Mugabe and the Zimbabwean government—no 'moment' as occurred in Zambia, Indonesia,

Serbia, Madagascar, Georgia, Ukraine and Kyrgyzstan. Please let me say something quite directly: in the majority of those countries, when the 'moment' came, the security and police forces of those countries did not fire upon their own people. Let me now contrast that with the brutal suppressions of the 'days of action' the MDC used to hold. There was mass participation in those days—but also on those days the amount of tear-gassing, clubbing and, indeed, shooting that was directed against those feeling the 'moment' was immense. Perhaps this is indeed a point of connection with China. In 1989, of course, 'moments' came to both East Germany and China. In Berlin, the police and soldiers could not bring themselves to fire on their own citizens. In Beijing, at Tiananmen Square, they did.

Let me labour the Chinese connection a little more. Hasu has tried to portray it as a complementary foreign policy, alongside relationships with the West and the rest of the world. This may have to be the case. It is true that it very much was the case that Zanu – PF policy formulators briefly thought China could take the place of the West. This thought was premised on the recognition that China was a growing economic superpower, but it was also premised on nostalgia. In the era before the end of the 1970s China spent over $100 million (averaged out) in assistance to each sub-Saharan African country (Chan, 1985). China spent a lot of money on the Zimbabwean liberation struggle in that period—which ended precisely with Zimbabwean independence in 1980, but also with great Chinese embarrassment over the Soviet triumph in Afghanistan and its own need to invade North Viet Nam in 1979. Expensive foreign policy suddenly seemed no longer worth it. But it seems that, for all the years of independence, elements in Zanu – PF have harboured a desire once again to be in the arms of Chinese support. That support will simply not come again. The Chinese do not have the state money to do that. The Chinese capitalist momentum is precisely a capitalist momentum, and Chinese firms are no doubt grateful for the naïve reception accorded them by a recidivist socialist Zimbabwe. The Zimbabwean looking backwards, to a bygone Chinese era, to a bygone set of non-aligned principles, to a bygone era when John Major led Britain— this is a pattern of looking backwards and a bankruptcy of new ideas.

Now, having said all that, let me agree—as I already have—with Hasu that the Blair government got its Zimbabwe policy all wrong. I do not think it should have disengaged from the land compensation issue; I think it should have engaged more closely with Mugabe in the early days of the Blair premiership; I think that the Blairite response to the farm invasions was shrill and left no room for negotiation—I even agree with Hasu's implied comment that Kissinger probably got it right. I am certainly saying that Blair did not get it right. I simply ask the question: was it then right to plunge one's own country into chaos, turmoil, and precipitate decline for the sake of someone else's mistake? To augment several times over his mistake with a catalogue of one's own? To ruin a country? And, if for some future historical justification, what if that justification never comes? What if the ruins of modern Zimbabwe are all there will be for many long years to come?

Now it is precisely because of the ruins of modern Zimbabwe, and precisely because the Blair government got so much wrong, that I agree with Hasu on a difficult step for the future. Hasu has been purveying his message of a need to start talking whenever he treads the corridors of Whitehall and Marlborough House. He has been indefatigable about this on each and every visit. As Hasu says, the eminent

Africanist Richard Dowden has said the same thing: the British prime minister and the Zimbabwean president need to open a channel of communication. They need to talk, and they need to talk because people are suffering in Zimbabwe and because the region of Southern Africa will see no progress while Zimbabwe is an economic basket-case.

Having said that, about what will they talk? Can Mugabe talk to Blair without doing his own 'flip flop'? The amount of character assassination by each leader of the other has grown into a huge obstacle of psychological difficulty for them both, and of symbolic difficulty in the world of politics with the weight given to symbols. Can third-party mediators open the door inch by inch? Neither Obasanjo nor Mbeki has succeeded, nor has Kofi Annan. Must it wait until 2008 when both Mugabe and Blair will have retired, and new leaders make a new start? As Hasu has pointed out, there are fundamental difficulties about the preconditions for talks. What is prior to what? But it is not just Blair who has said that rights and governance issues take priority over the settlement of the land issue—Mbeki has tried to say that too. And for what does Mugabe seek by way of settlement of the land issue? The British government really has very little cash to spare. If it should indeed find the means to compensate the dispossessed white farmers, none of that rebuilds the ruins that have grown in the fields of seizure. And if the talk is to be simply about humanitarian relief, the recent record of how that relief has been politically biased by the Zimbabwean government is not a pretty encouragement. Frankly, there would need to be a long transition period of talks about talks, even if the two sides could agree in principle to concurrent talks about governance and land. Hasu has ended his intervention with a positive note on the possibility and desirability of talks. I end mine, albeit most reluctantly, with the negative note that, however desirable, talks will not come soon, and they will have no immediate role in saving Zimbabwe from itself.

Note

1. This article was published in many outlets, as well as its initial appearance in *The Zimbabwe Independent*, and attracted much attention. Richard Dowden has updated the piece for the present collection.

References

Chan, S. (1985) China's foreign policy and Africa: the rise and fall of China's Three Worlds theory, *The Round Table*, 382, pp. 376–384.

Chan, S. (2003) *Robert Mugabe: A Life of Power and Violence* (Ann Arbor, MI: University of Michigan Press).

Chan, S. and Venancio, M. (1998) *War and Peace in Mozambique* (Basingstoke: Macmillan).

Commonwealth Secretariat (2001) Commonwealth Secretary-General welcomes Zimbabwe agreement, Commonwealth Secretariat Press Statement, London, 6 September.

Commonwealth Secretariat (2003) Commonwealth Statement on Zimbabwe, Commonwealth Secretariat Press Statement, London, 16 March.

Communiqué (1998) Communiqué issued at the end of the International Donors' Conference on Land Reform and Resettlement, Harare, 9–11 September.

Communiqué (2000) Concluding statement of the Ministerial Consultations that took place in London, on 27 April between Zimbabwe and UK delegations, Harare.

Dowden, R. (2005) We've got to talk to Mugabe now, *The Zimbabwe Independent*, 20 May.

Government of Zimbabwe (1998) Land Reform and Resettlement, Phase II: A Policy Framework, and Phase II, project document, Harare, released in June.

Government of the Republic of Zimbabwe (2002) *The Commonwealth and the Zimbabwe Presidential Election 2002* (Harare: Government Printers).

Hume, C. (1994) Ending Mozambique's war: the role of mediation and good offices (Washington, DC: US Institute of Peace).

Patel, H. (1985) No master, no mortgage, no sale, in T. Shaw and Y. Tandon (Eds), *Regional Development at the International Level*, Volume II, *African and Canadian Perspectives* (Lanham, MD: University Press of America).

Patel, H. (1986) South Africa's destabilization policy, *Review of International Affairs*, XXXVI(877), pp. 8–12, reprinted in *The Round Table*, 303, pp. 302–310, 1987.

Patel, H. (1987) *No Master, No Mortgage, No Sale* (Nairobi: Centre for Research, Documentation and University Exchanges).

Patel, H. (1993) Zimbabwe's mediation in Angola and Mozambique, in S. Chan and V. Jabri (Eds), *Mediation in Southern Africa* (Basingstoke: Macmillan).

Patel, H. (2000) Southern Africa and democracy in the light of the Harare Declaration, *The Round Table*, 357, pp. 585–592.

Phimister, I. and Raftopoulos, B. (2004) Mugabe, Mbeki and the politics of anti-imperialism, *Review of African Political Economy*, 101, p. 385.

Obasanjo, O. (2003) Olesugun Obasanjo to John Howard, *The Herald* (Harare), 12 February.

Short, C. (1997) Letter from Clare Short, Department for International Development, to Kombirai Kangai, London, 5 November.

Vines, A. (1998) The business of peace: 'Tiny' Rowland, financial incentives and the Mozambican settlement, *Accord*, pp. 66–74.

'Point Man' on Zimbabwe: South Africa's Role in the Crisis

J. E. SPENCE OBE
King's College London, UK

Introduction

Space will not permit a detailed historical account of the relationship between South Africa and Rhodesia/Zimbabwe. What is clear from the historical record is that there has existed what Deon Geldenhuys calls a "special relationship" between the two countries based on "geographical contiguity, historical ties, economic interdependence, racial solidarity and shared political interests" (Geldenhuys, 2003, p. 102).

In this context we should note the importance of certain key events in the relationship:

- The attempts by the South African government in the early 1920s to persuade the white Rhodesian minority to accept incorporation as a fifth province in the Union of South Africa. The referendum on that issue resulted in a negative vote principally because Rhodesia's largely British population feared the impact of Afrikaner nationalism on their way of life.
- South African support for the Smith regime following the Unilateral Declaration of Independence in 1965. Pretoria helped the regime to escape the worst effects of

sanctions and provided military assistance against the liberation movements operating on Rhodesian soil. "We have blood relations over the border", claimed Dr H. F Verwoerd, South Africa's prime minister in 1965, an appeal based on racial solidarity which was to be echoed 30 years later by President Thabo Mbeki and his colleagues as they grappled with yet another crisis in their neighbour's territory. The two governments went their separate ways after the 1976 Soweto uprising, which led to mounting pressure on South Africa to disengage from Rhodesia; the consequence was the withdrawal of military and economic support (including oil supplies) paving the way for the Lancaster House Agreement and the independence of the new state of Zimbabwe. As Geldenhuys remarks "historical ties and racial solidarity gave way to a clinical calculation of (white) South African interests" (Geldenhuys, 2003, p. 106).

- During the 1980s South Africa pursued a destabilization strategy against the newly established Mugabe regime designed to weaken the exiled African National Congress presence in Zimbabwe and to weaken the government's resolve and its legitimacy via attacks on the country's infrastructure and the "manipulation of cross-border transport links and support for opposition factions in Zimbabwe" (Geldenhuys, 2003, p. 107).
- In the 1990s, after the initial euphoria generated by the establishment of the new South Africa in1994, relations between the two governments soured over a range of economic and security issues. There was growing estrangement between Presidents Mandela and Mugabe, compounded by rivalry over leadership roles in the Southern African Development Community (SADC).

What this brief excursion into the past demonstrates is that the relationship between the two states "has given South Africa—whether under white rule or black rule—leverage but at the same time constrained it in dealing with Rhodesia/Zimbabwe" (Geldenhuys, 2003, p. 102).

South Africa: An Emerging Power?

An understanding of the incentives and constraints that attend South Africa's relations with Zimbabwe requires some analysis of the country's aspirations in both continental and global terms; of its capabilities—economic, military and diplomatic; and of its role as a putative regional hegemon.

In terms of one system of state classification, South Africa may be regarded as an emerging power, the key defining characteristic of which is the aspiration to play a dynamic and constructive role beyond its borders. (In this context it bears comparison with states such as India, Brazil and Nigeria.) And to play that role requires, *inter alia*: a secure domestic base providing a high degree of legitimacy for its political process; sizeable economic capability; resources, both human and material; and a decent 'enabling environment', i.e. a set of well established political and judicial institutions, including a lively and influential civil society.

South Africa's performance scores well measured against these criteria of good governance; it is also helpful, however, in signalling 'emergence' to the international community, if an aspiring power has the inestimable advantage of an hospitable regional environment in which to exercise its authority and would-be hegemony.

And in this context South Africa is severely disadvantaged: the environment (both regional and continental) for articulation of this role is inhospitable. South Africa is surrounded by poor, weak states, most of which have frail political and economic structures. Indeed, partly because of bitter memories of the apartheid regime's destabilization strategy in the 1980s, the neighbouring states have an understandable fear of South Africa's role as a potential hegemon, despite protestations by both presidents Mandela and Mbeki to the contrary.

Nevertheless, reluctant or not, South Africa is perceived as the hegemonic power by Western governments and as having a special responsibility for providing security for the region as a whole in its role as the dominant power in the Southern African Development Community (SADC) or as a major player in the African Union (AU). However, this is a formidable task given the disparate nature of the so-called human security threats that menace the region. It is awash with weapons, the detritus of Africa's civil wars; crime flourishes (both domestic and transnational); disease, e.g. AIDS is rampant throughout the region; poverty is widespread, the result of decades of economic and political mismanagement. There is, too, the corroding impact of drugs and weapons smuggling, money laundering and enforced migration. The latter, for example, constitutes a particular threat to regional security if only because tensions within member states increase when migrants compete for jobs with indigenous peoples.

Thus, if South Africa is regarded as the lead player in the provision of regional security, it is fair to see the smaller weaker states in the region as consumers of security; their governments lack effective and sufficient hard power as well as the soft power resources to deal with the threats mentioned above. Their bureaucracies are thinly stretched; political institutions are fragile; inter-governmental cooperation via the mechanism of regional organization, for example SADC, lacks sufficient and effective bureaucratic resources and, most importantly, political will. In addition, there is division within the member states about what strategies to adopt, not least towards Zimbabwe. The region's internal and external borders are long, porous and difficult to control. The result is an influx of refugees from African trouble spots into the region, with many making for South Africa or Botswana, both seen as offering jobs and a higher standard of living.

This combination of adverse circumstances both in the southern African region and in the wider continent complicates Pretoria's attempt to foster a constructive role. Nonetheless, the view that South Africa is a hegemonic power with the means to influence acceptable outcomes in Zimbabwe and elsewhere in the region is widely held. Indeed, Mbeki has been criticized both at home and abroad for not being more outspoken on the issue. Thus, for example, H. Solomon has claimed: "it is incomprehensible that South Africa does not use this dependency (for fuel, energy and maize) for the benefit of Zimbabwe citizens by ridding the country of their tyrant that occupies State House. It is incomprehensible that . . . Pretoria continues to engage in quiet diplomacy . . . where rationality and truth have no meaning" (quoted in Schoeman and Alden, 2003, p. 16).

By contrast, Schoeman and Alden have argued that this view exaggerates the influence to be derived from South Africa's alleged hegemonic role. Indeed, notwithstanding Mandela's 1992 assertion that the "new South Africa" would treat its SADC partners with "sensitivity and restraint", Scheoman and Alden argue convincingly that South Africa "is not in a hegemonic position as far as Zimbabwe is concerned" (Scheoman and Alden, p. 17). They assert rightly that a "hegemon's ability to lead is derived as much from what it stands for as from how it seeks to achieve its goals" (Evans and Newnham, p. 221). Thus hegemony, to be effective, must enjoy legitimacy in the eyes of those over whom it is exercised. It must be capable of exercising "unchallenged leadership" (Nel and McGowan, 1999, p. 320). In other words, hard power is not enough. And the dilemma facing South Africa in this context arises from a fundamental contradiction in its foreign policy. On the one hand, the Mbeki government has made every effort to be an African power, and a leading one at that. Witness, for example, its role in helping to reconstitute the former Organisation of African Unity (OAU) and its key role in getting the New Economic Policy for Africa's Development (NEPAD) underway.

Both these developments are the product of the so-called African Renaissance, Mbeki's brainchild and designed to promote African transformation in both the political and economic realm. Supported by President Olusegun Obasanjo of Nigeria, Mbeki believes that peculiarly African solutions can and must be found for Africa's problems and that, as NEPAD produces results, sympathetic Western governments will play their role in relieving debt, increasing aid and eliminating trade barriers—an acceptable role to be infinitely preferred to one involving sustained Western pressure on South Africa to take a tough and consistent line on the Zimbabwean issue. What must be recognized is that South Africa's attitudes to Zimbabwe are not simply to be explained as an aberration from an otherwise coherent and consistent foreign policy. On one level of analysis, South Africa's policy towards Zimbabwe does, in part at least, reflect a major thrust of South African foreign policy in general, i.e. an aspiration to create a peculiarly Africanist post-liberation foreign policy—one which emhasizes the virtues of a multilateral approach to help solve Africa's difficulties. Hence the emphasis on NEPAD and the AU, on the need for African interstate cooperation.

The difficulty with this strategy is that its impact in a positive sense on the Zimbabwean situation is long-term. In the short to medium term the South African government has to impress overseas investors and traders that it is the one great African exception to decades of misrule, and underdevelopment elsewhere. And the risk is that the country is branded in the eyes of its envious African counterparts as a puppet of the West.

On the other hand, persevering with quiet diplomacy, trying to stay in line with African colleagues, hostile to intervention strategies, risks disillusioning Western liberals (and conservatives), who argue with some justice that black liberation solidarity of the kind that links Mbeki with Mugabe trumps human rights and profoundly damages South Africa's claims to be a good and influential citizen of the international community.

Yet, in the last analysis, South Africa's policy makers will put the imperative for African solidarity before any too obvious kowtowing to Western pressure; they have vivid memories of what happened when Nelson Mandela tried unsucessfully in 1955 to persuade his fellow African leaders to impose sanctions on the Abacha regime in Nigeria. Geldenhuys argues that the lesson learnt was that "to act unilaterally" was to "confirm lingering suspicions on the continent that South Africa has hegemonic ambitions and, worse still, was an agent of Western imperial interests in Africa" (Geldenhuys, 2003, p. 126).

South Africa's difficulties with regard to Zimbabwe are compounded by the peculiar nature of the Zimbabwean state. To a degree it defies attempts to classify it according to the orthodox criteria; as one writer has put the matter; "has Zimbabwe crossed a threshold and entered the slippery slope of state decay?" (du Plessis, 2004, pp. 18–19). Alternatively, "due to its non compliance with the settled norms of international contact is Zimbabwe a rogue state?". Certainly the answer to these questions must take into account the perilous state of the Zimbabwean economy: according to one authoritative source, "the last four years have seen the forced removal of many white farmers from their land; a negative fall in GDP growth from 11% in 2002, 8.2% in 2003, to 2.5% in 2004, earning the country the woeful status of the world's 'fastest-shrinking economy'". Inflation stood at 600% in January 2004; unemployment is massive; according to the same reliable source "two out of three Zimbabweans are unemployed…five million Zimbabweans are on the brink of starvation" (IISS Strategic Survey, 2004–05).

The informal economy has been badly battered by the government's so-called clean-up operation, which led to the destruction of some 20 000 shacks, with their desperate inhabitants deported to camps in the distant countryside. Adverse media publicity was reinforced by a highly critical report by Anna Tibaijuka, a UN envoy to Zimbabwe in the summer of 2005 charged with reporting on the forced removals programme.

Yet despite the appalling state of the economy, Mugabe's ZANU–PF Party won the 2005 elections comfortably with 78 seats to 41 for the Movement for Democratic Change (MDC), representing a loss of 16 seats for the latter. Presidential elections are due in 2008. Mugabe's two-thirds majority in parliament will enable him to change the constitution at will and, in effect, devise a mechanism for appointing a successor acceptable to him. The opposition MDC appears demoralized; it is unable or unwilling to challenge the government by extra-parliamentary demonstrations of 'people power' of the kind pioneered in the Philippines against the Marcos regime and which subsequently proved so successful in central and southeastern Europe in the late 1980s and latterly in the Ukraine, Georgia and Bolivia.

The Zimbabwean state retains a monopoly of power and its leaders enjoy the loyalty of the armed forces and the police. It also retains a degree of popular legitimacy as the outcome of the recent election makes clear. Moreover, the record of the security forces in dealing with dissent in the past does not inspire confidence that their commitment to maintain order would crumble in the face of a massive campaign of passive resistance. In other words, this particular avenue of peaceful process is closed in large part because of the regime's capacity for intimidation. (Indeed, in the unlikely event of such disturbances, one wonders whether the outcome might be the equivalent of Tiananmen Square in 1989 rather than East Berlin in the same year.)

In addition, by the same token more violent protest is similarly inhibited and this, too, is hardly surprising given the arduous struggle of the majority of Zimbabweans to find the bare means of subsistence. After all, revolutions are rarely made by the poor and the depressed, who have enough to do to keep their heads above the economic parapet of survival. Such implosions are often led by middle-class individuals who are making gains, but are not perceived to be making them fast enough, and because there appear to be cracks in the power structure of the state. This is hardly the case in present-day Zimbabwe. Moreover, many radical members of the middle class have been forced into exile by Mugabe's policies.

This combination of virtually untrammelled state power and a poverty-stricken economy and citizenry makes it difficult to slot Zimbabwe into one of the more obvious categories of statehood. It is certainly not an emerging power, like its neighbour South Africa. It could be described as a state in transition, but transition to what? It is not a collapsed state (e.g. Somalia) although it could be argued that it is a failing state and equally a state of concern (or rogue state) to its neighbours and the international community. Yet, while the Zimbabwean government maintains its authority over its territorial jurisdiction, as well as a monopoly of force, it is difficult to see how the country could be described as failing in the way that, for example, might be the case with respect to the Democratic Republic of Congo (DRC), where factional violence, punctuated by periods of fragile peace, is a defining feature of such political process as exists. Zimbabwe is certainly characterized by failure to deliver social and economic goods to all its citizens in reasonable quantities, but is that enough to bracket Zimbabwe with more obvious examples of state failure where there is clear evidence of impending or actual breakdown in both the political and economic dimensions of statecraft? Perhaps Zimbabwe in this context is best described as an autocratic state characterized by partial failure, but hardly ungovernable or on the move to complete collapse. However, we should bear in mind that its status (and the structure and substance of its statehood) could change rapidly as circumstances change.

Finally, it is worth noting that Zimbabwe is not a rogue state (or state of concern) in the orthodox sense of that term. Traditionally such states are defined as such because they represent a threat—usually nuclear—to both neighbours and the wider international community. Zimbabwe has no such pretensions, but its domestic policies do constitute an indirect threat to neighbours in so far as disruption of trade within the Southern African region and enforced migration across the latter's porous borders continues to have a disruptive impact on local economies.

What this analysis demonstrates is that the Zimbabwe crisis presents South Africa with a peculiarly intractable problem. And, unlike the short-term crises of the kind that were characteristic of the Cold War (Cuba 1962); or the Arab–Israeli conflicts (1967 and 1973), the Zimbabwean issue does not readily permit productive and subtle diplomatic management (coercive or otherwise) leading to a successful outcome. Estimates of the costs to the region vary. Martin Adelman, for example, argues that "the human and economic costs of the crisis have so far largely been kept within the borders of Zimbabwe" (Adelman, 2004, p. 272). Indeed he goes further and argues that "looking at other cases of state crisis in Africa, where a rapid 'Regime Collapse' led to destabilization far beyond the borders of the afflicted country, the current South African policy may well be the most rational option" (Adelman, 2004, p. 272).

Not all commentators agree, however. Linda Freeman argues that some two million Zimbabweans have fled to South Africa, with the cost of the crisis to the region as a whole amounting to £25 billion, "with South Africa being the hardest hit" (Freeman, 2005, p. 156). Faced with what appears to be conflicting evidence on the impact on the region, perhaps all one can say is that Mugabe's policies certainly have the potential to cause major long-term damage, regardless of how much has been caused in the more recent past.

Options for Change

Whatever the merits of this argument, the fact remains that the options open to South Africa and the wider international community remain severely limited. And a further constraint is the fact that Robert Mugabe has contrived to interpret criticism from Western quarters as racist-inspired, and that this anti-colonial discourse resonates positively with African audiences throughout the region. Mbeki and his colleagues have, therefore, to tread carefully in criticizing the Mugabe regime and, in any case, remain committed to a tradition of conflict resolution by peaceful, quasi-diplomatic means of the sort that was so successful in South Africa's transition from apartheid to democratic rule.

Clearly coping, indeed resolving the crisis by orthodox instruments more coercive than quiet diplomacy, e.g. economic sanctions and military intervention, offer scant chance of success. Commonwealth 'smart' sanctions have had little effect and there is virtually no prospect of increasing their scope and substance given the conservative attitudes of African members of the association. Cutting off aid, e.g. electricity supplies to Zimbabwe, might in the short term make the situation worse, leading to an implosion in the urban areas with riots and crude repression in the streets of Zimbabwe's major urban centres. Perhaps the strategy might work in the long term, but it would require extensive intervention by either SADC or the AU and/or the UN to make a precarious peace during which a new political dispensation might be negotiated. Understandably, however, South Africa's leaders and those of the neighbouring states might well feel that this is too high a price to pay. In any case it is doubtful if there is enough political will, let alone capability, to engage in what might amount to a long-term occupation of Zimbabwe.

Unilateral military intervention by South Africa to effect regime change is highly unlikely and the same would be true of a SADC or AU 'coalition of the willing'. Mbeki is, in any case, very reluctant to use military capability in peace enforcement mode. A major social explosion in Zimbabwe might force his hand and those of his SADC colleagues, but this is not probable in the short to medium term at a time when the Mugabe government is far from collapse.

The Zimbabwean case illustrates that there are some situations where military intervention in support of a humanitarian purpose is profoundly difficult. UK Prime Minister Tony Blair made a valiant effort in his International Community declaration (Chicago speech, 22 April 1999) to "identify the circumstances in which we should get militarily involved in other people's conflicts". He acknowledged the traditional role of the principle of non-intervention in maintaining international order, but made a major qualification with respect to acts of genocide and those occasions when "armed force is sometimes the only means for dealing with dictators" (Blair, 1999, p. 7). In this context he sited 'oppression' as a reason for intervention, e.g. when it "produces massive flows of refugees which unsettle neighbouring countries and threaten international peace and security" (Blair, 1999, p. 7). Interestingly, he also admitted that "national interests" would have to be invoked as a factor determining intervention, emphasizing that "not every wrong in the modern world could be righted... we would not be able to cope".

Whether or not Zimbabwe fits Blair's criteria for intervention is at best an academic exercise, if only because the constraints against any prospect of Western involvement would provoke immense hostile African reaction to such an enterprise. Restoration of 'benign imperialism' or otherwise (depending on one's perspective) is simply not an option, while 'national interest' is not directly at stake, as is the case with South Africa's involvement with Zimbabwe. Moreover, the strategic context is hardly appropriate for 'sensible and prudent' military operations designed to provoke, say, regime change. Indeed, the experience of Iraq and the prospect of long-term occupation may well have blunted Western appetite for intervention elsewhere and we should bear in mind that Zimbabwe does not figure on the radar screen of the so-called axis of evil. It is also worth noting that, if these constraints apply to Western governments, they apply even more strongly to South Africa.

A military coup seems improbable and, if one were to occur, could one be sure that a military regime would be sympathetic to the restoration of a legitimate government following 'free and fair' elections monitored by an appropriate external authority? Certainly any attempt to mount an internal cabinet or party coup would need the support of the army, while the success with which Mugabe has dealt with threats to his hold over ZANU–PF in the past does not encourage would-be pretenders to his throne. In the past South Africa has tried to promote talks between the MDC and the government with a view to establishing a government of national unity. These have been spectacularly unsuccessful. One remote and perhaps fanciful possibility is a secret Oslo-type peace process involving, for example, representatives of both government and opposition meeting under the auspices of a third neutral party—either a high-ranking UN representative or an individual politician from a country whose mediating role would be acceptable to both parties. It seems reasonable to conclude, however, that things would have to get a lot worse in Zimbabwe before such a prospect had any appeal for Mugabe.

This proposition might be seen as a variation on the one advanced by Richard Dowden in May 2005: "If we want Zimbabwe to survive there is no alternative: we have to talk to Mugabe" (Dowden, 2005). The hard question to answer in this context is: what about?

What can be said with certainty is that some resolution of the Zimbabwean crisis is crucial if South Africa is to confirm, indeed enhance, its status as a power of substance on the African continent. This outcome is essential if South Africa is to enjoy the support and respect of the international community as a 'good liberal citizen' of that community. There is much at stake: a possible permanent seat on the UN Security Council; equally, the credibility of NEPAD, in which South Africa has invested much political capital, as a vehicle for promoting good governance and decent economic and social progress.

It may be unfair to load South Africa with the burden of Zimbabwe's future, but no other power is available in the region to play that role.

Finally, the international community may simply have to wait for Mugabe's exit— a move which he has undertaken to make in 2008. His departure might just provoke a break in the stalemate on which both the international and the regional community could profitably capitalize.

At this stage the words of the International Crisis Group (2002) seem extraordinarily appropriate: "the US is waiting for South Africa; South Africa is waiting for the international community; everyone is waiting for everyone. SADC has demonstrated that no-one is willing to take the lead on Zimbabwe". A peculiarly African version of the 'Waiting for Godot' syndrome.

Acknowledgements

Some of the arguments addressed in this paper were discussed in a brief commentary, 'Zimbabwe: future imperfect?', *Journal of Conflict, Security & Development*, 5(3), pp. 363–370, 2005.

References

Adelman, M. (2004) Quiet diplomacy—the reason behind Mbeki's Zimbabwe policy, *Afrika Spectrum*, 39(2), pp. 249–272.

Blair, T. (1999) 'The Doctrine of the International Community', speech given to the Chicago World Affairs Council, Chicago, 22 April.

Dowden, R. (2005) We've got to talk to Mugabe, *The Times*, 16 May.

Evans, G. and Newnham, J. (1995) *Dictionary of International Relations*, p. 221 (London: Penguin).

Freeman, L. (2005) South Africa's Zimbabwe policy: 'unravelling contradictions', *Journal of Contemporary African Studies*, 23(2), pp. 148–170.

Geldenhuys, D. (2003) The Special Relationship between South Africa and Zimbabwe, Ad hoc publication No. 41, Institute for Strategic Studies, University of Pretoria, pp. 102–144.

IISS Strategic Survey (2004–05) *Zimbabwe: Mugabe's Impunity* (London: International Institute for Strategic Studies).

International Crisis Group (2002) All bark and no bite? The international response to Zimbabwe's crisis, *Africa Report 40*, p. 126 (Harare and Brussels: ICG).

Nel. P. and McGowan, P. (1999) *Power, Wealth and Global Order*, p. 320 (Cape Town: University of Cape Town).

du Plessis, A. (2004) State collapse and related phenomena: select theoretical perspectives, Institute for Strategic Studies, University of Pretoria, pp. 1–19.

Schoeman, M. and Alden, C. (2003) The hegemon that wasn't: South Africa's foreign policy towards Zimbabwe, *Strategic Review for Southern Africa*, XXV(1), pp. 1–28.

Untold Stories: The Commission for Africa and Zimbabwe

BEACON MBIBA
London School of Economics and Political Science, UK

The Commission for Africa: Process versus Outcome

In February 2004 the UK Prime Minister, Tony Blair, set up and launched the Commission for Africa (CFA) to take a fresh look at Africa's past and present and the international community's role in its development. Its authoritative report, *Our Common Interest* (CFA, 2005), has been widely applauded for its scope, simplicity, clarity, rigour, outreach and comprehensiveness—features that will make it a "valuable resource book for years to come".[1] Together with the Sachs Report on the Millennium Development Goals, the CFA report contributed in 2005 to the extraordinary interest in development generally and in Africa in particular. Yet, for some, the measure of its success will be in the implementation of its recommendations; to get buy-in of the dismissive USA, further actions from the ambivalent French, Germans and Japanese and, most significantly, for the UK itself to "put its money where its mouth is".

However, for many others, especially in Africa, the CFA was a failure before it started: because Africa did not need it.[2] Talbot (2005, p. 38) describes the CFA report as a document that makes the UK the "world leader in sanctimonious word mongering and hypocrisy". According to many in civil society and the NGO sector, and as presented by Clare Short at a School of Oriental and African Studies (SOAS) CFA meeting on 17 March 2005, the CFA had failed what was labelled the 'Wolfowitz Test'. The UK failed to mobilize Europe to veto the USA's nomination of Paul Wolfowitz as the new Director of the World Bank. This failure meant that the CFA ideals (as set out in Chapter 10 of its report) to open up World Bank, IMF and World Trade Organization (WTO) top posts for those from developing countries had not made any impact on the status quo.

To the dismay of those central to the CFA work, Western neoliberal commentary on the report has focused mainly on challenging the sensibility of recommendations on "doubling aid"[3] (Mistry, 2005) at the expense of many fundamental aspects of the work, such as those on debt cancellation, human development and capacity building, the role of the state, infrastructure and agriculture, South–South cooperation, and tackling corrupt practices of Western institutions (damaging to Africa), whether in Africa or outside it.[4] Such analysis of the report's content as well as monitoring of commitments and implementation is both welcome and important.[5] But for scholars of development studies and international relations, it is critical to reflect on the process of the CFA, where many stories remain untold since this partly explains failures witnessed relating to the product.

From the time the CFA was launched its reception was diverse, with questions ranging from the origins and desirability of the idea, political motivations behind its setting and ownership, to the selection of Commissioners.[6] The advisability of including Ethiopia's prime minister as Commissioner dogged the process all the way to the G8 Gleneagles Summit, a situation made worse by the poorly managed 2005 general elections in Ethiopia, at the end of which security forces gunned down 36 demonstrators in Addis Ababa. Under pressure, the UK announced an aid freeze on 15 June.[7] Clearly, the CFA could not be separated from the UK's bilateral relations with countries within and outside Africa. As the UK Secretary for International Development put it in a speech to African ambassadors on Africa Day 2005, the CFA was a political process and one that has shown that "politics works".

Thus, as a diplomatic and political process, a comprehensive analysis would need to be made of how the range of hostile and contradictory positions and actors were reconciled, coerced, mobilized or silenced in the CFA process and report. These include groups such as the radical pan-Africanists versus pessimistic neoliberals in the West, sceptical NGOs, the donation-fatigued British public and an African population suffering from acute 'consultitis'.[8] Given Zimbabwe's central position in British–African relations, in African geopolitics and in the contradictions in the development discourse—especially the global 'rights-based development agenda'— this paper will concentrate on this aspect within the range of issue: how and why Zimbabwe did or did not feature in the CFA process and report. If the CFA was about 'politics' at work and, given that regime change in Zimbabwe has been UK's top political priority in Southern Africa for almost a decade, how did this political process deal with Zimbabwe?

The point here is that, to be valuable, future commentary on the CFA should focus not only on the outcomes (the report and implementation of recommendations) but also continue to dig into the origins and process of this phenomenon.

Africa is a continent of diverse countries and stories; the CFA sought to capture all these—the good as well as the bad, the past and the present and from this to set priorities for an international agenda on which to build political coalitions to support sustainable development on the continent of Africa. Whether it be good stories or bad stories, Zimbabwe appeared to be conspicuous by its absence in the CFA story.

The first half of the paper describes the apparent exclusion of Zimbabwe from the CFA process and report and suggests explanatory factors, starting with the background of UK–Zimbabwe relations, relations of close friends who have fallen out really badly. The second half will provide a different 'grounded perspective' in which Zimbabwe features significantly in the unwritten text of the CFA process and report.

The Commission for Africa and 'Silence' on Zimbabwe: The Background

The CFA was not about Zimbabwe and, given the hostile relations between Zimbabwe and the UK since 1996/97, it may have been prudent not to let Zimbabwe dominate the CFA deliberations. For, as witnessed since 2000, no one would come out a winner in the process. In some of the public Zimbabwe–UK 'clashes', the UK appears to have come out politically more bruised. Recall the March 2000 'diplomatic bag' fiasco, during which the then UK Foreign Office minister Peter Hain described Zimbabwe as 'uncivilized',[9] the Johannesburg 2002 World Sustainable Summit on Development, at which the UK prime minister was 'ambushed' and 'humiliated' by leaders from Southern Africa, and the acrimonious Abuja summit (Commonwealth Heads of Government Meeting). No one has fully recovered from the Abuja debacle, including President Olusegun Obasanjo of Nigeria, who is seemingly now considered an 'enemy of the state' in Zimbabwe.[10] This was one of those key moments when the UK scored a 'short-term victory' but lost credibility and the warm support previously guaranteed from South African President Thabo Mbeki—described by US President George Bush as "our point man" in Africa on the Zimbabwe question. Making a connection between Zimbabwe, the Abuja Summit and the CFA, *The Independent* observed that:

> what looked like a trouble free act of high minded generosity to Africa by British Prime Minister Tony Blair has already run into difficulties. The British manufacture and control of the CFA may not help the PM to sell his findings in Africa. His earlier attempts to woo African leaders have also come unstuck. He fell out with Mbeki on Zimbabwe and the breach is now regarded as irretrievable. (*The Independent*, 2005)

More chillingly, it went on to conclude that "The fact that Blair has few allies on the Zimbabwe issue in Africa demonstrates a British diplomatic failure to understand how to win friends in Africa", adding that Blair's ally on Zimbabwe (Obasanjo) was ill-placed to sell the CFA, considering the poor governance in his own backyard.

For radical pan-Africanists, the CFA was (is) yet another 'colonial intrusion' based on Europeans' failure to understand Africa, leading to situations like that of Zimbabwe. On the other hand, neoliberal pessimists flagged the 'governance crisis' in

Zimbabwe as the very reason why the West should not bother with Africa. Thus, within this geopolitical context and as shown in Figure 1, Zimbabwe, an issue that has dominated media, political and diplomatic exchanges over the past decade received only marginal reference in the final report. Mentioning Zimbabwe would 'kill' the CFA process diplomatically. And, once mentioned, Zimbabwe's reaction would be unpredictable and most probably vitriolic. On 24 October 2004, in the middle of the night, Zimbabwe bundled out a South African trade union (COSATU) delegation,[11] sending to the world once again the message that even close friends would be treated viciously once they were perceived to be enemies of the ruling ZANU (PF). As described later, Murambatsvina in 2005 was yet another of these exhibits. Who would unnecessarily want to be on the receiving end of ZANU (PF) attention?

This paper has a three-stage hypothesis. First, although in diplomatic and political terms the Zimbabwe government was excluded from the CFA, it remained on the minds of those involved as well as of those commenting on its deliberations. The government of Zimbabwe was not in there but others were there who did the job of defending its interests to the extent that the balancing act was to make Zimbabwe become a disappearing discourse 'in the public domain'. Second, an analysis of key moments, actions of key actors and the technical process of the CFA reveals that, although there was political exclusion of Zimbabwe, Zimbabweans participated at the forefront of the CFA process; partly demonstrating their high technical and professional competence and global citizenship beyond Zimbabwe. As one European diplomat commented, "you just cannot do without Zimbabweans".[12] For example, they were leading and participating in the regional consultations. Third, the Zimbabwe government played its part on the African side. Just like those working on the CFA project, the Zimbabwe government appears to have succeeded in keeping

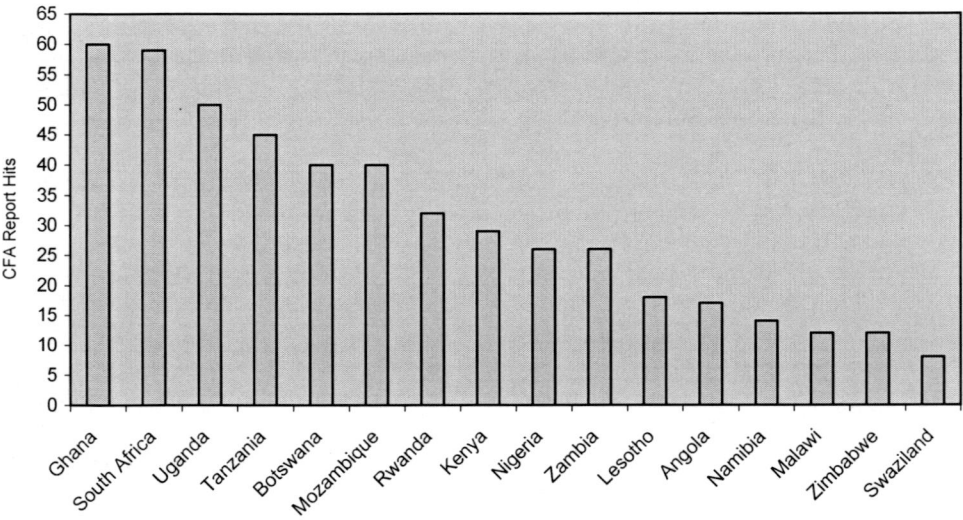

Figure 1. Number of times (approx.) country name appears in Commission for Africa report, 2005

silent on the CFA at least in public—but to have mobilized its allies as opportunities arose. In a way, the 'surprise' was not only how Zimbabwe failed to appear in the CFA process and report but rather how the Zimbabwe 'democratic movement' was invisible in the process. The CFA was a golden strategic opportunity through which the Zimbabwean 'democratic movement' could bring Zimbabwe to the centre of international development policy and politics. They let it slip through their fingers. They were not visible in the submissions, they were not there at the regional consultations in Africa, and, unlike their counterparts, for example from Ethiopia, they were not there in London at any of the meetings to press their case. Exploring why they failed to see and utilize this opportunity may reveal not only whom they represent but also give us pointers to the future of development and politics in Zimbabwe.

Skirting Zimbabwe: The Commission for Africa's Good and Bad Stories

The 'technocratic argument' is (was) that the Commission of Africa is (was) not about any particular country but about Africa. Consequently, the question of Zimbabwe and the Commission of Africa is irrelevant, out of context, mischievous or all these together. However, the question of Zimbabwe is relevant in a number of ways. The CFA methodology was to analyse things that work and those that don't in Africa—both in the present and in the past. Zimbabwe offers both these things. Africa's issues on good governance, collapsed, failed or fragile states, perceived electoral fraud, corruption, education and agricultural success stories, HIV/AIDS and response to it, natural resource conflict such as in the DRC—all at the core of the CFA idea—could not be debated adequately without reflecting on Zimbabwe. One may want to find out how Zimbabwe would fare on these issues—starting with the good stories.

Zimbabwe's success stories in agriculture before independence and in the smallholder sector after independence (Eicher, 2003; Gabre-Madhin and Haggblade, 2004), in education, health, the police and civil service generally before 2000–02 demand that Africans go back there to look for how things should work. Indeed, the CFA recommendations calling for reinvestment in the role of an effective state, rural infrastructure, higher education and agriculture constitute recognition of such evidence and endorse the then policy approach in Zimbabwe—without mentioning it by name. In most debates in the UK, Zimbabwe may now be described as a 'disappearing discourse'; it is no longer politically correct to mention it even in a positive light. A recent statement from the Association of University Teachers in London suggests that the Terrorism Bill will make it even more difficult, if not criminal, to debate Zimbabwe in UK universities.[13]

If Zimbabwe is not in the good stories, even historically, how about the bad stories? There were submissions to the CFA and letters to the press that used Zimbabwe's situation to illustrate points regarding Africa's development, especially on governance where Zimbabwe is taken as a byword for bad governance. Zimbabwe is presented as the most significant obstacle to or test case for the New Partnership for Africa's Development's (NEPAD) Africa Peer Review Mechanism (Verwey, 2004; Mistry, 2005; *Daily Mail*, 2005a) (just like Togo). It is also castigated for not taking serious action on corruption (like Kenya).[14]

Good governance on the part of Africa is at the core of the NEPAD programme, which is hugely endorsed by the CFA (see Chapter 4).[15] In contrast to Western media and neoliberal writings on governance in Africa,[16] the report is silent on Zimbabwe. A key observation during the CFA consultation process was that this 'silence' and 'skirting' was extensive. For example, at a BBC 4 Live Question Time, held at the School of Oriental and African Studies (SOAS), London on 25 May 2005 to discuss the CFA, Zimbabwe was never mentioned. This was in spite of questions and discussions on HIV and AIDS, corruption, polygamy and 'what should be done with leaders who stay for too long in power'. While South Africa, Botswana, Zambia, Kenya, Mozambique, Nigeria and Uganda came up as illustrations in the discussions of these issues, nobody dared include Zimbabwe. It appeared as if on every panellist's mind there were memories of previous debates (e.g. also at SOAS on 17 March 2005), when negative mention of Zimbabwe was received with vehement rebuttals from DRC, Ugandan and Sudanese activists in the audience. To avoid similar acrimonious ends to African debates, it appears an unwritten code has/had been established—not to mention Zimbabwe.

Diplomats, like some scholars, have (had) long realized the folly of raising the Zimbabwe question when there is an African audience. At a major European function, a senior American official remarked that he was "fed up with raising the Zimbabwe issue with Africans—the conversations are always bitter and fruitless".[17] When it comes to Africa generally and Zimbabwe in particular, the Americans are (were) taking a back seat; and are asking minimal questions and making few comments at public forums.

Fighting Zimbabwe's Corner

In their work the CFA Commissioners and the Secretariat had some 'behind closed doors' sessions. Whatever was discussed, if anything, regarding Zimbabwe in such sessions will thus remain 'behind closed doors'. But opportunities did arise on the fringes of the CFA process, from which we can glean a lot about the long shadow of Zimbabwe and what some at the core of the CFA process may have said behind these closed doors, i.e. defending Zimbabwe's interests.

Basically, in these public encounters, key African members of the Commission for Africa rallied in defence of the government in Zimbabwe, to the utter bewilderment of the Western media. Commissioner and President of Tanzania Benjamin Mkapa illustrated this when he asserted: "I don't see Zimbabwe as an illustration of bad governance, I don't buy it" and referred to economic problems in the country as "the cost of transformation...everything has a price". Rather than simply blame President Mugabe, the fault was equally on "the opposition parties, especially when they have decided to get into state house by hook or by crook as the main pillar of their policy" (Blair, 2005).

With determined consistency, President Mkapa defended Zimbabwe at every occasion during and after the CFA process if the need arose. He is likely to have taken a similar position behind closed doors. Commissioner and Prime Minister Meles Zenawi of Ethiopia has been touted as one among a 'new breed of African leaders' leading wisely. However, a review of the political process in Ethiopia reveals tensions that mirror those in Zimbabwe. Thus one can speculate that, given the 'storm clouds' gathering on the horizon of his own impoverished country,[18] Zenawi could also not raise or have allowed Zimbabwe to become an issue in the CFA process without bringing himself into the spotlight. Doing so would also raise a bilateral clash with other heads of state at the African Union (AU). And he is a shrewd operator aware of these dangers. After all, 'Bad Governance in Africa (Zimbabwe), is it their fault or ours?'[19]

With such Commissioners (heads of state in Africa) in the team, there is no way Zimbabwe would have featured negatively as an issue in the CFA process and reports. On the other hand, there was no way Blair would have cited Zimbabwe in a positive light. The outcome was what we got: see no Zimbabwe, hear no Zimbabwe, talk no Zimbabwe and write no Zimbabwe.

Zimbabwe: A 'Little White Island' Leading the Sceptics[20]

Scanning the consultative process, one is tempted to conclude that the Zimbabwe government excluded itself from the CFA process. At official level and through its ambassadors the government did not take part in the proceedings of the CFA, to a point where Zimbabwe's absence at diplomatic occasions was predictable if the UK was leading deliberations. Otherwise government representatives would make a brief appearance or take a back seat.

However, in some cases Zimbabwe was seen as a mobilizer of the sceptics. On 21 December 2004 there was a CFA 'informal' consultation exercise with African diplomats in Addis Ababa. As usual with these events, the chairman of the African diplomats (the Nigerian ambassador in this instance) was responsible for organizing the event. About two-thirds of the African ambassadors attended. The Nigerian chairman had problems setting up the event, not least because of problems with sceptics—most of whom stayed away—including Zimbabwe which was "mobilizing the sceptics".[21]

This familiar story of Zimbabwe's non-participation and the sceptics was evident in Rome at the end of March 2005. CFA Commissioner K. Y. Amoako had a meeting with Rome-based African ambassadors at the British Embassy to brief them on the CFA progress, key elements of the CFA report, its recommendations and to encourage debate on the CFA among their governments before the AU meeting on the eve of the G8 summit and the G8 itself. African countries represented were Cameroon, Gabon, Nigeria, Ghana, Mali, Burkina Faso, Senegal, Mauritania, Ethiopia, Tunisia, Eritrea, Sudan, Kenya, Zambia, Uganda, South Africa and Mozambique, with Zimbabwe absent as expected. Incidentally, those who attended appeared either poorly informed or sceptical, or both, about the CFA—a pity considering that, with the report out, the CFA process was almost complete.

Thus Zimbabwe was not the only sceptic. Francophone Africa had its own doubters—especially Central Africa and Cameroon. These raised questions on what added value the CFA would bring to development processes in Africa. Sceptics in North Africa and francophone Africa remained throughout, as they saw this as largely an 'English' and 'Commonwealth'-oriented initiative in which their interests were marginal. As observed at the Rome meeting referred to above, this was not helped by the fact that the CFA Secretariat had little French expertise and took time to notice the damage and to start producing literature in French as well. Once this realization was made, sceptics like Cameroon became strategic targets. For the UK, EU and USA, Cameroon has important economic and geopolitical significance as a link between Central and West Africa, and between the English and French speaking countries; it is a gateway to land-locked countries in the interior, on the route of the Chad pipeline, etc. Put President Biya into it and the strategic importance of Cameroon is easy to realize (unfortunately he could not be invited to the Gleneagles G8 'High Table').[22]

The scepticism may partly be of academic concern in the post-CFA era, but it had material implications for the CFA process and future implementation of the recommendations. With only weeks to the G8 summit, CFA commissioners and interlocutors were registering concern about the lack of enthusiasm for the CFA report from the francophone countries, particularly Senegal. The francophone Africa response remained lukewarm, partly because of fears throughout Africa and the AU that the CFA was trying to muscle out of the NEPAD initiative.[23]

Zimbabwe's regional partners (Uganda, Tanzania and Zambia) held national consultations on the CFA. Neighbours Botswana and South Africa had members on the Commission. Kenya, Zambia and South Africa hosted regional CFA regional consultations with civil society. Mozambique, Tanzania and South Africa received a visit from Chancellor Gordon Brown. So in Southern Africa, Zimbabwe was an 'island' not formally engaged with the CFA. But on the broader African scene it was not alone (see Figure 2). When left out of Commissioner Gordon Brown's itinerary, Swaziland complained, but, while Swaziland complained, Zimbabwe campaigned. It is not the first time nor the only way that Zimbabwe has appeared as a little white island in east and southern Africa. The term comes from a book describing white ruled Rhodesia of the 1970s.[24] A map of slums world-wide prepared by the UN HABITAT also shows Zimbabwe standing out as a little white island where there are no slums or squatters compared with its neighbours and the rest of the developing world (UN-Habitat, 2004, Map 5, p. 106). Being different is part of Zimbabwe!

Zimbabwe Very Much in the CFA Debates: The Scandinavian Concerns

In the composition of the CFA, in its consultations and outreach work, one would note the absence of Australia, the Dutch and the Scandinavians. The Latin Americans and Asians are also missing. Considering that South – South cooperation is an important aspect of alternative development partnerships, this needs to be taken as a significant hole in the work. But this is not surprising considering that the initial terms of reference of the Commission were about what the G8 could or should do to support Africa. It is this G8 definition that led to initial marginalization of the Dutch and the Scandinavians (they did not have a Commissioner in the CFA), despite the fact that these countries have some of the most enduring and effective partnerships with Africa and have already met the 0.7% GDP target for aid to Africa.

In their engagements with the CFA Scandinavians not only posed the question of why they were not represented at Commissioner level but also sought clarity on migration, gender and on Zimbabwe.[25] With regard to Zimbabwe, and making

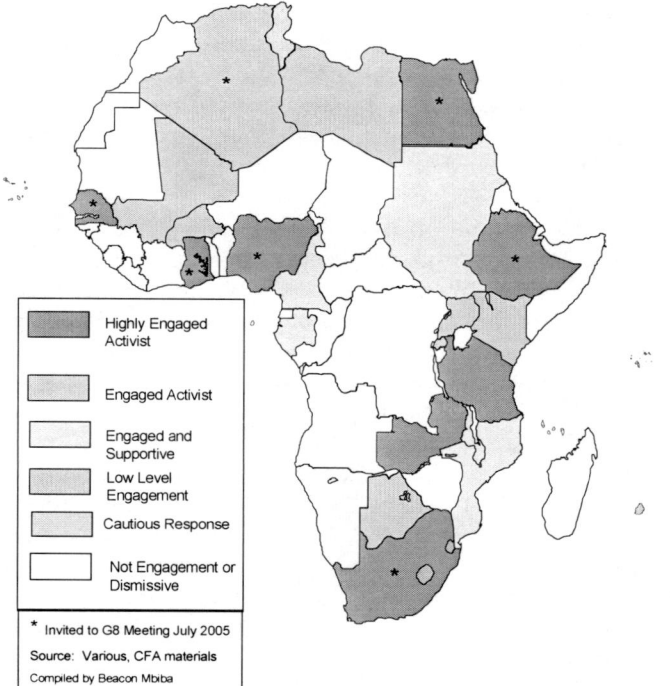

Figure 2. Zimbabwe as a 'little white island' leading the sceptics: summary of African attitudes to the CFA, January 2005

reference to borderline states (what in the UK are known as failed or fragile states), the question from the Swedes, for example, was how Zimbabwe affects EU – Africa relations and, in particular, how the UK – Zimbabwe relationship has an impact on the UK's dialogue and relations with other African countries. Thus, in terms of open debate, the Scandinavians were more than ready to 'skin the skunk' and not to gloss over the political implications for development and for UK – Zimbabwe bilateral relations in particular arising from the Zimbabwe question.

Zimbabwe Very Much in the CFA Debates: Regional Consultations and the Radical Critique

As described earlier, the CFA had a series of regional consultations with civil society; first, to solicit comments on the draft outline of issues identified by mid- to late 2004, second, to discuss key recommendations of the final report with a view to establishing how civil society groups would take forward some of the recommendations in the report.

At the December 2004 Lusaka Southern Africa regional consultation meeting it was the Zimbabwe issue that livened up the event on the second day. Thomas Deve attacked the neoliberal agenda behind the CFA and, in particular, the hypocrisy of the West on HIV and AIDS with regard to the suffering of Zimbabweans. He alleged that the big donors were withholding funding for Zimbabwe's HIV/AIDS programme simply because they did not agree with the government in power. In the end the victims ended up buying medications at exorbitant prices from middle men and dealers. He charged that, for as long as the CFA was not addressing such issues, it was of no use to Africans.

It was not only that he (and others) said these things, but how they said them—directly. Reflecting on this critique, a senior diplomat described it as a "Trade Unionist's speech that brought excitement in the whole event".[26] Delegates were left divided, some suggesting that Deve's kind of language was not compatible with the CFA. Others opined that, with such eloquent and informed cadres around Africa, the president of Zimbabwe did not need to worry—if he were to go there would be many that could equal him in presenting the Pan-Africanist critique of development. He thus should "just shut up and retire".

The significance of the exposure of the West's hypocrisy on African poverty, such as that made by Deve at the Lusaka CFA meeting, may be lost on some, but it was made clearer in early 2005 by Carol Bellamy of UNICEF. According to Bellamy, AIDS is killing a child every 15 minutes in Zimbabwe. Arguing for more cash to fight AIDS in the country she noted that "innocent children were suffering because donors opposed President Mugabe's regime ... the world must differentiate between politics and the people of Zimbabwe".[27] She also noted that global generosity, which rose with the Asian tsunami, had dried up for Zimbabwean children who are facing a deadly crisis every day of their lives. In comparative terms Zimbabwe had in 2004 received an equivalent of £2.10 per person from the Global Fund to Fight AIDS, TB and Malaria, compared with £34 elsewhere in the southern Africa region, leaving Zimbabwe 'an island of death'. Thus the language of a 'silent tsunami' in the CFA would be hypocritical if not applied to the plight of children in Zimbabwe. As it turned out, the Global Fund to Fight AIDS, TB and Malaria later released funds to Zimbabwe in mid-2005 (*The Herald*, 2005).

Zimbabwe Very Much in the CFA Debates: Regional Consultations and Representation

The contract to coordinate both the December 2004 (Lusaka) and June 2005 (Gauteng) southern Africa CFA regional consultations was given to the Southern Africa Poverty Research Network (SAPRN). Originally based in Harare, it now operates from Pretoria and is headed by Zimbabwean Sue Mbaya, whose team did a sterling job on both occasions. Thus Zimbabwe was at the core of the management of regional events in southern Africa. Churches were represented at the Lusaka meeting by pastors from Bulawayo. Professor Norman Nyazema, the South Africa-based Zimbabwean lecturer, pharmacist, media and telecoms investor, was there making passionate interventions on the social sector, HIV and AIDS. The summing up report had a large dose of his brain power as well.

Earlier, at a November 2004 International Institute for the Environment and Development (IIED)-organized Land Conference to feed into the CFA process, Zimbabwean Professor Sam Moyo and Organization for Social Science Research in East and Southern Africa (OSSREA) Chief Executive Officer Dr Alfred Nhema participated as experts, with Moyo's interventions leaving a mark on the deliberations.[28] At the G8/NEPAD Africa Dialogue on Africa's Comprehensive Agricultural Plan in Accra, Ghana in early May 2005, Zimbabweans based at SADC, the agricultural unions and intellectuals participated. Providing the conceptual round-up of the whole three-day event was none other than Professor Mandivamba Rukuni, Director of Kellog Southern Africa, Chairman of the Zimbabwe 1993/94 Land Tenure Commission, one time Dean of the Faculty of Agriculture at the University of Zimbabwe and now based in Pretoria. A similar pattern was repeated at the June 2005 CFA Regional Consultation meeting in Gauteng.

The message here is simple: Zimbabweans have become global citizens pursuing their professions at regional, continental and global levels. In doing so, Zimbabwe's experience, both good and bad, finds its way into the analysis of contemporary development events—even if the government of Zimbabwe may not be participating in these events itself. Thus, on reflection, Zimbabwe ended up very present in the Commission for Africa process.

But, surprisingly, Zimbabwean opponents of the ruling party in Zimbabwe (ZANU (PF)) were not visible at the major regional consultations. Many of these see themselves as civil society. Strategically, they could have mobilized to present their case at CFA events (with literature, demonstrations, speeches, etc.). This would have provided them with free media publicity, given the global interest in CFA activities. For example, in London, rather than stage solidarity marches or play drums at the Zimbabwe embassy, the Vigil group and its partners could have gone down to Trafalgar Square, where crowds gathered, and to the British Museum, where the report was launched. Similarly, on 25 May, they could have used the CFA/African ambassadors meeting to press for an African response on Zimbabwe favourable to their cause.

That nothing close to the above took place can be explained in several ways. First, the opposition to ZANU (PF) may now be so weak and in disarray that such strategic activity is beyond it. Second, there may just be "nothing left to struggle for, Zimbabwe is gone".[29] Third and most likely is that any such activities around the CFA would have put pressure on the UK prime minister, forcing him to put Zimbabwe on the CFA menu or, if not, making him be seen as indifferent to the Zimbabwe situation. The issue of deportation of Zimbabweans, as covered in the media around the time of the Gleneagles G8 Summit, illustrated just how embarrassing and contradictory the Zimbabwe issue can be for the UK leadership. To avoid such a scenario, and given the partnership between the UK government and many of the 'civil society' groups and opponents of ZANU (PF), is it likely that there was an understanding not to disturb the process?

Sir Bob Geldof Brings in 'Bob' and 'Kills' The Commission for Africa[30]

For over a year the CFA worked tirelessly to cultivate dialogue among global partners, skirting thorny and divisive issues like Zimbabwe. This appeared to work until the very last day, 11 March 2005, when the report was launched at the British

Museum. Here CFA Commissioner Bob Geldof killed the idea (and Blair endorsed this) when he called for President Yoweri Museveni of Uganda to stand down and called President Robert Mugabe of Zimbabwe a thug. Claiming that it was Africans who requested him to say it, he remarked:

> They have to get rid of corruption . . . The repatriation of stolen assets is [a] no brainer. The thugs, tired old men like Mugabe, took it out and now they are going to put it back and some of the banks have operated immorally, since they know they have been handling stolen cash.[31]

In an instant the public relations façade collapsed. The CFA process and report was crafted not to point fingers but to build partnerships. Its language was both academic and diplomatic, persuasive and conciliatory. By using the F word and name calling Bob Geldof destroyed it in a stroke. Mugabe may be an old man, but tired he appears not. Money was indeed looted from Africa. But Mugabe has repeatedly asked detractors to "show us the loot . . . and give it to the poor if you see where it is". So in this respect the proposal to repatriate stolen funds is not new for Mugabe. Mugabe supports it and has challenged Britain to go ahead and implement it. One does not need a CFA report for that.

But there are real fundamental questions that arose from Geldof's public statements against the leaders of Zimbabwe and Uganda. When it comes to looting of funds, activists allege that there are millions of late Nigerian president Sani Abacha's money in the UK taken from Nigeria's public funds, as well as millions of former Kenyan president Daniel Arap Moi's money taken from Kenya. Why not deal with these well publicized and obvious cases? The hatred (some) people may have for President Mugabe appears to blind them to obvious facts. They use Mugabe as a cover for their failures. Referring to the purported looting by her president, one Zimbabwean scholar retorted:

> Zimbabweans are lucky. Whatever Mugabe has looted, he has invested in *Gracelands*.[32] We can all see it and it has contributed to the real estate of Harare . . . you can benefit from that value if you want. Its not like money stashed away in Switzerland.[33]

When it comes to corruption, tiny Lesotho has done a lot to expose the fact that corruption at the Lesotho Highlands Water Project was a partnership between local officers and international construction companies and banks. But, despite the evidence against large corporations regarding corruption on this project (as well as around plunder in the DRC), the USA, Britain and Europe have generally taken a lukewarm response to calls for action against these companies. "There is weak evidence", is the official chorus response. Publicly to demonize Uganda and Zimbabwe when all these issues are still outstanding exposes the hypocrisy of those who do so. Hence the CFA process and approach—not to name names.

Geldof's CFA report launch reference to corruption gave succour to Pan-Africanists who consider the city of London to be a major player in the systematic looting of Africa. This is a phenomenon which Tony Blair should tackle head on in London if his concerns for Africa are serious and genuine. Ugandan Tajudeen Abdul-Raheem captures this kind of critique:

> For a report that took the bold step of acknowledging that there was nothing African about corruption and admits that it is systemic and has both African and non-African actors and perpetrators, it was very ironic that its activities were held at the British Museum—a place that has been a major beneficiary of looted historical and aesthetic assets from all over the world especially Africa. Tony Blair could have shown some genuine remorse and willingness to really change things for the better by handing over some of these stolen treasures as a symbolic gesture that business will not continue 'as usual'... The Commission for Africa's report will get more buy-in if Britain leads by example instead of lecturing the rest of the world on being good or fair towards Africa. It can race fast to meeting its own Millennium Development Goal target of 0.7% of GDP as a contribution to global aid. At present it is hovering around 0.4%.[34]

Incidentally, at this time Italy was in the process of returning to Ethiopia the 1700-year-old stone Obelisk, looted 70 years ago.[35] In an article entitled 'Africa demands UK to practice own summons' Esther Nakkazi pushed the same sceptical view prevailing among Africans.[36] Similarly, writing on Britain's role on corruption, Action Aid (2005) noted that British Banks are holding US$1.3 billion that has been looted from Nigeria by the Abacha family and that the UK has not cooperated with Nigerian efforts to recover the looted wealth. It demanded action on this.

The public comments also brought public scrutiny of those key to the CFA. The Ghanaian activist Yao Graham lashed out at the UK prime minister, stating "Tony Blair, the main salesman for the report embodies the political double standards that have undermined earlier progress on the report's proposals".[37] Meanwhile, on the same day, 12 March 2005, *The Daily Mail* attacked the prime minister, presenting a banner headline that portrayed him as 'The Great Deceiver'. It went on in bold:

> Exactly two years ago, Mr Blair took us to war on a lie. The more we learn about it the more we realize we can never trust the honesty or judgement of this dangerous plausible con-man... adept at selling a false prospectus... his capacity for deception and falsehood. (*The Daily Mail*, 2005b)

The *Daily Mail* language of falsehoods on this occasion rings similar to that of Professor Jonathan Moyo, Mugabe's former minister of publicity and information. Publicly calling Tony Blair a liar, as the *Daily Mail* was doing, is exactly what the president of Zimbabwe had been saying over the years, calling him *B-liar* and not Blair. The *Daily Mail* portrayal was not lost on Africans; if the British people no longer trust their leader and call him a 'deceiver', why should the Africans?[38] The link between the CFA and the Iraq war was again brought up—if the CFA was not a colonial project, then it was a way to draw attention away from the Iraq war. Corporate Watch followed up with a scathing adverse report on the CFA suggesting that big corporations that create poverty and havoc in Africa were behind the neoliberal solutions in the CFA report and the G8 agenda.[39]

For this paper the point is not about whether these positions were valid or not but to underline that these were debates the CFA had been at pains to exclude from the process but which, in one stroke, were brought centre stage. Commissioner Bob Geldof did the sceptics a big favour they had not bargained for. In Uganda statements and public demonstrations against Bob Geldof were staged. "Who is Bob Geldof anyway?' they chanted.

Mrs Tibaijuka Brings the Commission for Africa to Harare

In a way one could argue that the Zimbabwe government did not oppose the Commission for Africa. Opportunities arose at various global and regional forums where the president of Zimbabwe could have turned his vitriol on the UK prime minister and the CFA project. Instead he chose not to do so. In fact, other than around the general elections of early 2005, when the ruling party in Zimbabwe adopted a 'Bury Blair' campaign slogan, the period of the CFA process was characterized by a general lull in 'fireworks' in Zimbabwe – UK relations, with the Zimbabwe government appearing to make 'reconciliatory' statements, especially after the elections.

An indirect Zimbabwe government view of the CFA can be gleaned from a June 2005 report carried in the Harare *Herald* newspaper (considered a pro-government publication) on the occasion of the Africa Economic Summit, Cape Town, at which the Commission for Africa was a major agenda item.[40] The paper introduced the issue thus:

> This year could mark a turning point for Africa as combined forces of the G8 and the Commission for Africa (CFA) focus the world's attention on forging partnerships and mobilizing resources to improve the continent's plight. Africa's transformation is expected to dominate deliberations at the G-8 meeting scheduled for July in Scotland, while the CFA has already come up with a report to guide the process.

This favourable opening statement was followed by more positive quotations from the CFA report. In addition to this positive endorsement of the CFA's significance another point needs to be emphasized. The *Herald* (and by implication the Zimbabwe government) chose not only to be factual and positive but also to be respectful of the CFA in its article. This is important considering the cynicism in Africa *vis à vis* the report and the fact that the NEPAD Secretariat, the African Union and many others have referred derogatorily to the CFA as 'The Blair Commission for Africa'.[41] On this occasion Harare chose not to follow suit. If it was part of its 'guerrilla strategy to lull the enemy', then they did it well.

On the side lines of a regional civil society meeting held at Gauteng in South Africa in early 2005, the issue of how Zimbabwe viewed the CFA was discussed separately with a Zimbabwean leader of MWENGO, a regional NGO based in Zimbabwe and then with a senior public servant also from Zimbabwe.[42] Surprisingly, both held similar views, namely that, as far as government officials, professionals, NGOs and technocrats were concerned, they would have welcomed opportunities to discuss the CFA at national level as had been the case in neighbouring countries. They viewed the CFA as a development debate first and as politics second—a view that seems to be confirmed by how the CFA was treated in the *Herald* report of June 2005.

True to their guerrilla credentials, the Zimbabweans waited for their moment to attack. The occasion was when Mrs Anna K. Tibaijuka went to Harare (as Special Envoy of the UN Secretary General) tasked to investigate and report on the humanitarian impacts of and response to Operation Murambatsvina.[43] Initially the government of Zimbabwe appeared to welcome this mission but it became hostile when the UK prime minister was seen as making predetermined conclusions about the mission, encouraging the Special Envoy to come up with a 'good report' that he (the prime minister) would take to the UN Security Council (GoZ, 2005, p. 8, *The Herald*, 26 July 2005). It is at this point that Harare brought up Mrs Tibaijuka's role as Commissioner on the CFA.[44] The allegation was that, given this role, she was now carrying an agenda to implement the ideas of her CFA boss. It was unfortunate that Blair made those remarks for Mrs Tibaijuka is in fact an independent thinker, an informed open-minded revolutionary who will stand for what she deems good for Africans—within the Commission for Africa and elsewhere. She does not deserve some of the abuse she got around the Operation Murambatsvina investigation and report.

Even with Mrs Tibaijuka 'bringing' the CFA to Harare, one can also observe that nothing specific was targeted in the report itself. Rather, it was the ideological framework under which it was instituted and the motivation behind it that were targeted and contested.

Conclusion

In both historical and present day terms Zimbabwe represents a clash of ideological and political cultures that needs resolving if development is to take place. Further, and very significantly, Zimbabwe 'holds the answers' to how Africa will or should develop; what is happening there is a fundamental clash of political and ideological cultures whose resolution is at the crux of development. Events in Zimbabwe continue to reverberate throughout the African continent and beyond; between 2000 and 2004 it was the 'fast-track' land reform and more recently, from early 2005, it is Operation Murambatsvina. These are controversial but still need our scholarly analysis, not mere condemnation. Consequently, scholars who shy away from Zimbabwe are not serious and only do themselves a disservice in doing so.

Although the CFA was silent on Zimbabwe, others were not and it is important to analyse these other perceptions on possible linkages and how such perceptions affected the outcomes of the CFA and how this may affect implementation of the recommendations in the future. This paper has attempted to explore the diplomatic and political dynamics that may explain why Zimbabwe appears to have been marginalized in the CFA process and report, relative to its geopolitical importance and the global attention it has received in the media over the past decade. However, rather than total exclusion, this paper shows that Zimbabwe ended up part of the CFA process in ways not obvious if one simply reads the report. It has shown why and how those at the core of the Commission collectively, though for different reasons, found it prudent to exclude Zimbabwe in public discourse on the CFA.

In large measure, this reflects the general position of Zimbabwe as a 'disappearing discourse' within the UK's and the West's dialogue with African leaders. Zimbabwe did feature significantly as a 'leader' of the sceptics of the CFA Commission. The CFA was a UK exercise to restructure global geopolitics of 'development' and Zimbabwe's exclusion, or exclusion in the debate, has to be understood from that political perspective.

Acknowledgements

The author would like to thank all those respondents whose views are cited in the paper and all colleagues at The Commission for Africa (both in London and in Africa) for their comradeship when the author was Research, Outreach and Policy Analyst for the Commission for Africa London, 2004–05. The views expressed in this paper remain those of the author and do not in any way represent those of The Commission for Africa. Visit http://www.commissionforafrica.org.

Notes

1. President of the International Fund for Agricultural Development (IFAD), Rome, 1 April 2005.
2. *The Guardian*, 12 December 2004, p. 8; 'Tajudeen firm grip on Africa? A Pan Africanist view', *The Nation* (Kampala), 7 October 2004; 'How Europe tricks Africa', *The Nation* (Nairobi), 11 March 2005; and J. Cornish 'Blair the colonial governor? Southern Africa Review', *The Sunday Mirror* (Harare), 10 July 2005.
3. See also Bob Baulch, 'Commission for Africa report response', Institute of Development Studies (2005), University of Sussex.
4. 'The Blair report unveiled', *Africa Confidential*, 4 March 2005.
5. One African-based initiative is led by The Most Rvd. Archbishop Njongonkulu W. H. Ndungane, Anglican Archbishop of Cape Town, who is mobilizing to set up a monitoring network '*The African Monitor*' to be up and running by early 2006.
6. It emerged that the idea was the brainchild of Bob Geldof that was cultivated and nurtured by Prime Minister Tony Blair over a full year of fancy diplomatic and political footwork at a cost no less than £6 million to the British taxpayer.
7. See 'UK halts aid over Ethiopia deaths', 15 June 2005, at http://news.bbc.co.uk/africa/. The public will not know if this announcement was followed through.
8. 'Consultitis' is a term describing an over-researched and over-consulted community. See Chuke-Emeka Chikezie, 'The Commission for Africa: who is framing who?', at http://www.bond.org.uk/networker/april04/opinion.
9. 'Zimbabwe: UK "arrogant" over diplomatic row', at http://news.bbc.co.uk/1/hi/world/africa/673787.stm and other related articles in the media.
10. Zimbabwe Parliamentary Debates, 3 November 2004.
11. See *ibid.* on how delegates of the Congress of South African Trade Unions (COSATU) were bundled out of a hotel and dumped at the Beit Bridge border post out of Zimbabwe, despite a High Court Order instructing the executives to leave them alone.
12. Comments made on the sidelines of the G8/NEPAD summit on the Implementation of the Comprehensive Africa Agriculture Development Plan (CAADP), Accra, 5–6 May 2005.
13. 'The Terrorism Bill and academic freedom', Association of University Teachers, October 2005, available at: http://www.aut.org.uk/media/pdf/5/9/terrorbill_parlbriefing.pdf, accessed 30 October 2005.
14. Various submissions to CFA, including one by Mike Cook, 9 February 2005, dealing with land rights.
15. All CFA regional consultations with civil society in 2004 called for the CFA to embrace NEPAD and not to marginalize it.
16. See, for example, Plaut (2004) and Mistry (2005).

17. Further details not provided to maintain anonymity for security reasons.
18. Consider the post-May 2005 elections accusations of fraud and the fatal shooting of 22 protesters in Addis Ababa. The world remained silent. Why silent for Addis Ababa and very vocal for Harare?
19. Title for an IDS seminar run by Mick Moore (IDS) and Simon Taylor (Global Witness) at Northumberland Lodge, 23 February 2005.
20. Idea of 'a little white island' comes from Parker (1972).
21. Notes from a discussion with a West African diplomat, Addis Ababa, 12 March 2005.
22. For the UK getting Cameroon on side via the CFA process would also have helped in other areas, not least the Olympic Games 2012 bid.
23. Cornish (2005), 'Blair the colonial governor?'.
24. It ironic that, save for the colour of the people, Zimbabwe now looks like a 'little white island', a term chosen to describe 1970s Rhodesia. See Parker (1972).
25. The Germans also appeared miffed at having been left out of the CFA.
26. Senior diplomat, Lusaka.
27. 'Cash call to fight AIDS in Zimbabwe', *Metro* (London), 18 March 2005, p. 2.
28. Conference on 'Land in Africa: Market Asset or Secure Livelihood?', Church House, London, 8–9 November 2004, organized jointly by the International Institute for Environment and Development and The Royal Africa Society, London.
29. View from former civil society activists, London.
30. 'Bob' is President Mugabe's nickname, well used all over southern Africa and shared with many. Although arising from 'Robert', it is also a common nickname given by farm labourers to their heavy-handed white employers.
31. *The Guardian*, 12 March 2005, p. 13.
32. 'Gracelands' is the Zimbabwe public's name for the expensive presidential mansion under construction in the up-market Borrowdale area of Harare and derives from the First Lady's first name, Grace.
33. Zimbabwean female scholar, London, March 2005.
34. See 'Prophet Blair has no audience in Africa! A Pan Africanist view', *The New Vision* (Kampala), 17 March 2005.
35. BBC News, 19 April 2005, at http://bbc.news.co.uk/Africa/
36. *The Monitor* (Kampala), 17 March 2005, p. 16.
37. Yao Graham, *The Guardian*, 12 March 2005, p. 22.
38. In Nairobi Chege Mbitiru called the CFA "Blair's 'big lie'". See 'Africa could gain from Blair's "big lie"', *The Nation*, 9 May 2005.
39. See report at http://www.corporatewatch.org.uk.
40. Victoria Ruzvidzo, '2005 expected to mark turning point for Africa', *The Herald* (Harare) reporting from Cape Town, at http://www.zimbabweherald.com/, accessed 3 June 2005.
41. *The Guardian*, 12 October 2004, p. 8.
42. For security reasons, information that may lead to the identification of the public servant cannot be included here.
43. For details, see the report at http://www.UN-HABITAT.org
44. 'Tibaijuka furthers Blair's interest', Editorial, *The Herald* (Harare), 26 July 2005.

References

Action Aid (2005) *African Commission for Britain*, report released 23 February 2005, at http://www.actionaid.org.
Blair, D. (2005) Blair's African ally supports Mugabe, *The Daily Telegraph*, 18 February 2005, at http://www.telegraph.co.uk/news/.
Commission for Africa (2005) *Our Common Interest: Report of The Commission for Africa* (London: Commission for Africa/Penguin), available online at: http://commissionforafrica.org
Cornish, J. (2005) Blair the colonial governor?, *Southern Africa Review, The Sunday Mirror, Harare*, 10 July 2005.
The Daily Mail (2005a) Recolonise Africa, Saturday essay by Andrew Roberts, 8 January 2005, pp. 20–21.

The Daily Mail (2005b) The great deceiver, 12 March, pp. 16–18.

Eicher, C. (2003) Flashback: fifty years of donor aid to African agriculture, paper presented at the Conference on Successes in African Agriculture, INWent, IFPRI, NEPAD, CTA, Pretoria, 1–3 December.

Gabre-Madhin, E. Z. and Haggblade, S. (2004) Successes in African agriculture: results of an expert survey, *World Development*, 32(5), pp. 745–766.

Government of Zimbabwe (GoW) (2005) *Response by Government of Zimbabwe to the Report by the UN Special Envoy on operation Murambatsvina/Restore Order* (Harare: Republic of Zimbabwe) August.

The Herald (Harare) (2005) Zim Global Fund Seal US$10.3 million agreement, *The Herald, Harare*, 9 April 2005.

Institute of Development Studies (2005) 'The Implications of a Major Increase in Aid to Less Developed Countries': a one-day seminar organised by The Institute of Development Studies, University of Sussex, 21 March 2005, The Victoria Thistle Hotel, London (see http://www.ids.ac.uk).

Mistry, P. S. (2005) Commentary: reasons for sub-Saharan Africa's development deficit that the Commission for Africa did not consider, *African Affairs*, 104(417), pp. 665–678.

Parker, J. (1972) *Rhodesia: Little White Island* (London: Pitman).

Plaut, M. (2004) Blair and Africa: the Africa Commission, *Review of African Political Economy*, 31(102), pp. 704–711.

Talbot, A. (2005) The Commission for Africa report: sanctimonious word-mongering and hypocrisy, *African Renaissance*, 2(3), pp. 34–39.

The Independent (2005) Can the Tony and Bob show really do any good in Africa?, 5 October 2004, at http://www.News.independent.co.uk

UN-HABITAT (2004) *The State of the World's Cities, 2004/2005* (London: Earthscan and Nairobi: UN-HABITAT).

Verwey, L. (2004) *NEPAD and Civil Society Participation in the APRM*, IDASA Occasional Papers, available at: http://www.idasa.org.za

The HIV Epidemic in Zimbabwe—The Penalty of Silence

SUNANDA RAY AND FARAI MADZIMBAMUTO

Introduction

The denial of fundamental human rights in countries like Zimbabwe is closely linked with the reasons why the HIV epidemic has raged there for the past 15 or so years. The epidemic thrives on secrecy, stigma, gender inequity, economic disempowerment, poor accountability and monopolies of knowledge. Many of the people who died in the 1990s and later were infected with HIV during the period 1985–90 while accurate information on the existence of HIV and how to protect oneself from it was actively suppressed by politicians and the medical profession. Although the rates of new infections seem to be slowing, young people are still getting infected every day and the disintegration of public health services over the past five years has made the lives of families living with AIDS much worse. The attitude of governments, policy makers and decision makers towards protection of human rights is reflected in their approach to tackling the HIV epidemic. The tension between individual rights to privacy and confidentiality versus public health approaches to protecting the health of communities is played out more in favour of powerful elites than of ordinary people.

Living with HIV is not just a rights issue for those who test positive. There are concerns for the families who live with them, look after them and care for their children during illness and after death. Rights to safety, shelter, health, education and so on also apply to families living with HIV and AIDS and who carry the consequences of family members dying in early life. The costs to the country are often underestimated. In Zimbabwe and other countries of southern Africa there has been an enormous loss on all levels of valued citizens who still had much to contribute: authors, musicians, teachers, farmers, factory workers, health workers, politicians, social workers, community workers, and many more—the people who make up the social fabric of a country. We are losing our creative voices, our collective stories and memories, our history as well as generations of economically active citizens, and with them the training, skills, wisdom and intelligence that were invested in them. We also have to consider the rights of all our children to grow up in environments of security, of freedom from fear and anxiety, of confidence that they will not be left destitute and homeless. There is a suppressed national grief, which has not been confronted or comforted, for the 3000 people in Zimbabwe alone who die each week from AIDS, for all those who have died before, for the families left to cope without their loved ones in a situation made worse by a sense of powerlessness to change the course of this epidemic.

In its Declaration of Commitment on HIV/AIDS adopted in June 2001 the UN General Assembly acknowledged the connection between HIV/AIDS and human rights:

> The full realization of human rights and fundamental freedoms for all is an essential element in a global response to the HIV/AIDS pandemic, including in the areas of prevention, care, support and treatment, and that it reduces vulnerability to HIV/AIDS and prevents stigma and related discrimination against people living with or at risk of HIV/AIDS.

At every level there has been poor leadership in responding to the HIV epidemic, especially with a human rights approach to HIV. Lack of political will is a major constraint. From the beginning of the epidemic in Zimbabwe politicians consistently refused to acknowledge publicly either the severity of the HIV epidemic or the existence of people living with HIV in their midst. Those who watched the unfolding of events in East Africa and warned of a similar catastrophe in southern Africa were accused of being alarmist and unpatriotic. Patriarchal attitudes on the part of doctors meant that vital information related to risk of HIV or use of condoms for prevention was censured. When treatment became available within limited public resources, it was first absorbed by politicians who assumed entitlement by their positions and by the part they played in the liberation struggle: six ministers received ARV treatment through the AIDS Levy (Masunda, 2001). There was no cry of foul from the medical leadership indicating they shared that perception of entitlement. The leadership needed in other sectors of society did not emerge. Church leaders have not shown by example the compassion deserved by those of their congregations who were struggling with the stigma of living with HIV. Business leaders were not concerned about the loss of labour from their workplaces. Their attitude was that there were plenty more men queuing for jobs at the factory gates, willing to replace those who became sick. This changed only when it became clear that managers were also dying and were expensive to replace. (This was the response SR received when approaching factory managers to implement HIV education for their workers during the 1992–95 period.)

History of HIV in Zimbabwe

Zimbabwe was one of the earliest countries to start screening blood donors for HIV when the test became commercially available in 1985. One reason for this was an excellent volunteer-based national blood donation and transfusion service (NBTS). The NBTS was also involved in selling blood products to Europe for foreign exchange and wanted to protect its market by assuring the safety of its commodity (for a description of purchase by Europe of plasma from Africa, see Garfield, 1994]). The data collected by the NBTS on screening blood donors, on prevention of transmission of HIV through blood donation and on the ethical approach towards informing donors of their results put the NBTS at the forefront of research on HIV in Africa. What this meant was that we knew from 1985 that we had a public health disaster looming.

In Zimbabwe the decision was made that all clinical diagnoses of AIDS had to be accompanied by a positive HIV test, and for this result to be given to patients. There was a lot of confusion over different reasons for doing HIV tests. One reason was for purposes of screening blood; here the results would not be given to donors but were sufficient to discard units of blood. Another was anonymous HIV testing for surveillance purposes to monitor the size of the problem and rise in prevalence. The third reason was for diagnosis of patients who were presenting with typical symptoms of the disease so that they could ideally take action to prevent passing on the infection to partners. The media at this time reflects this confusion but also the authoritarian stance taken by leaders of the medical profession and Ministry of Health (MOH).

An article in the *Herald* newspaper at the end of December 1987 quoted a statement from a senior Ministry of Health spokesperson that 250 000 people in Zimbabwe had the AIDS virus, but did not explain how this figure was arrived at (*The Herald*, 1987). At that time the country's population was close to nine million. Published information from that period shows that 2% of blood donors were HIV positive in 1987 (Emmanuel *et al.*, 1988). Specimens from 401 patients attending one rural hospital found 3.2% to be HIV positive (Mertens *et al.*, 1989). Patients presenting with sexually transmitted infections (STIs) in two clinic sites outside Harare in 1987 were 6% HIV positive (UNAIDS, 2004). In Karoi district 15% of patients presenting in 1986–89 with *herpes zoster* were found to be HIV positive, a figure the researchers suggested indicated that 12.5% of the local population was positive (Dehne *et al.*, 1992). Although the evidence was mounting of a serious problem, in that year the 300 cases of AIDS initially notified by the MOH to the World Health Organisation (WHO) was downsized to 119 because of uncertainty about the accuracy of the HIV test.

Following the openness of that first announcement, there was a dramatic condemnation of doctors who were giving patients positive HIV results: It is quite evident from reports reaching us that some of these doctors come up with such diagnoses to cover up their professional shortcomings. They feel baffled in attempts to diagnose conditions which their more experienced colleagues could easily diagnose correctly and manage with excellent results. As a result of the irresponsible pronouncement from a small section of our doctors, some patients' confidentiality has been compromised. Some people who may or will never develop Aids [sic] are now stigmatized while possibly many who are carrying the virus are moving about completely free and continuing to engage in high risk Aids promoting behaviour. (Dr Daniel Makuto, Secretary for Health, in *The Herald*, 1988a)

The article ended with the statement that "any doctor engaging in such practices should expect to meet the wrath of the courts, with no sympathy from the Ministry of Health, should a patient decide to take legal action against the doctor".

The story came out in the paper on a Saturday morning. We remember it well, because we went shopping that day and had friends come up to us saying, in effect, you doctors, you have been lying to us about this disease, trying to frighten us.

Four days later the *Herald* headline read, 'Positive Aids results may prove false' on a story that described the complications of population-based screening tests that may give false positives (*The Herald*, 1988b). An earlier story quoting the Harare City Medical Officer of Health also stated: "Blood test for Aids not conclusive, says city MOH". He went on to say: "our present impression is that this test, done indiscriminately, is more dangerous than the infection itself as it has led to suicides, ostracization and the loss of jobs".

The result of these statements by senior health officials and with publicity in the print media, was to give the public the impression that the HIV test was unreliable and not to be believed, but also that doctors who gave these results were being unprofessional and also not to be believed. Most doctors kept their heads below the parapet, and the majority of people continued in their denial that they were at risk of becoming infected. The finer points of the difference between testing as a screening instrument in asymptomatic people and testing to aid a clinical diagnosis were not spelled out to the public. Many of the patients who were being tested already had symptoms of HIV-related illness, as defined by the WHO, such as *herpes zoster* (shingles), persistent enlarged lymph glands, chronic diarrhoea or weight loss (see Appendix 1). Some already had AIDS and were dying. The response was not to show true medical leadership by recognizing the public health risk to the nation, by making sure that doctors were trained in making accurate clinical diagnoses of HIV and AIDS and educating and informing their patients on the reality of this emerging epidemic. Instead doctors who were addressing this illness in their patients were chastised through the media and warned against getting involved. Those who tried to warn about the lessons from East Africa, which had already gone through this, were accused of being alarmist. Others were threatened.

In stark contrast, health authorities in Uganda took the decision to use a modified clinical case definition developed by the WHO to diagnose AIDS that did not rely on laboratory testing (Widy-Wirski *et al.*, 1988) because of their limited resources in the post-war days of the mid-1980s. Patients already sick with combinations of indicator symptoms that showed immunosuppression with no other cause could be informed that they had a strong chance of having AIDS.

AIDS was first diagnosed in Uganda as the clinical entity of 'Slim' in 1982 in trading villages on the borders of Tanzania and Lake Victoria. As in most countries, it was initially regarded with suspicion, fear and discrimination. Yoweri Museveni and the National Resistance Movement came to power in 1986 following a devastating civil war. They received aid from Cuba as part of the reconstruction, including training of their army. Cuba had at that time a strict policy of testing, quarantine and education of people with HIV and sent more than half of a group of Ugandan soldiers back home when they tested positive for HIV (Kalinaki, 2002; UNAIDS, n.d.]. Museveni recognized the risk to the army, what that meant for his power base, and declared openly that AIDS was threatening to become a disaster and called for international help to fight the epidemic. At the same time people diagnosed with AIDS and their families got together in a support group that became known as The AIDS Support Organization (TASO) (Kaleeba and Ray, 1991) with the support of the president. The AIDS Control Programme was launched in 1987 and the Uganda AIDS Commission a year later. A key part of the success of the Uganda experience was the partnership between government, research bodies and non-governmental organizations that went right to district level, as well as the openness of key individuals in speaking of their HIV status. Philly Lutaaya, a well loved pop star in Uganda, toured schools and communities on a mission to show everyone that he was the human face of AIDS before he died in 1989 (Kaleeba and Ray, 1991).

Zimbabwe also sent teachers, doctors and others to Cuba for training who were similarly tested and sent back if found to be HIV positive. These people received very little support or counselling about their status, and experienced the end of their dreams of receiving professional training, resulting in some committing suicide. The Zimbabwean government could have taken similar measures to Uganda at that time but chose to suppress not only the information about the reality of HIV in communities, but also those who wanted to give patients the choice to learn about their illness. Confidentiality became paramount—no one should be told—and some medical leaders expressed reservations about non-medical professionals (such as social workers) being involved in counselling since they may not have observed the same strict confidentiality. At one meeting of university academics held in a hotel to discuss hypothetical cases of AIDS, the waiters were asked to leave the room in case they witnessed what was being discussed. At the same meeting, given the scenario that 50% of infants born to HIV positive mothers were likely also to be positive, there was agreement among many of the doctors present that the women should not be told their status since there was a 50% chance of the babies being *negative*. The paternalistic attitude of many doctors, that they know what the public needs to know and what it should not for its own good, has persisted, with the result that people have not had the information they needed to make decisions for themselves and their families.

Thus the message was clearly sent out that this infection was so bad, such a vile thing, that it should not be mentioned. This is the basis of the stigma that persists to this day. Those who carry the stigma of HIV and AIDS are labelled shameful, as having done something bad, which must not be spoken of. This has similar origins to the stigma of leprosy, where afflicted people in biblical times had to ring a bell to warn others to stay away from them, to smear their faces with ashes so they would be known. In some ways HIV is worse since this is an infection that is carried through the most intimate of ways, through sex and blood contact, and, until recently, ended with the premature death of young people. The silence around the epidemic was perpetuated throughout society, with managers anxious about their promotion and training chances, while factory workers and domestic workers worried about their job security. Everyone was so apprehensive about the direct impact of disclosure of status on themselves that they usually did not get tested to confirm their worst fears, nor did they focus on how to stop HIV reaching more and more people. The power of the elite ensured that many domestic workers did get sacked while the bosses protected their jobs. The culture of 'I don't want to know, so no one would want to know' was such that insurance companies who made a negative test a requirement for high insurance premium holders did not arrange counselling when they rejected applications on health grounds. There were several suicides as a result of this brutal way of receiving a test result, but again the concept of support and advice at the point of giving results was a long time coming.

Health education messages that came out at this time all over Africa enhanced this sense of badness. The message 'AIDS KILLS' was predominant, with images of terror and monsters. Associations were clearly drawn with sex with prostitutes, so posters showed pictures of shady-looking women in mini skirts in alleyways as carriers of infection, as bad women. For many women, to be HIV positive became synonymous with being accused of being a prostitute. The ordinariness of getting infected was overlooked, that in high prevalence situations, anyone having unprotected sex was at risk, even with a regular partner, if their status was unknown. The taboos of discussing sex and death were very entrenched. The duality of standards that accepted multiple partners for men but condemned women for having more than one partner made discussion about individual risk behaviour very difficult, especially for women, who would hide their past and present experiences. Many men made poor risk assessments with their partners, assuming young girls were 'fresh' (virginal) and married women were 'clean', at the same time as blaming women generically as 'carriers' of disease (Ray *et al.*, 1998). Many married women, indignant that their virtue should be questioned, felt angry that their men were not acting responsibly, taking care of them and their children, and making good decisions for the family, as their construction of manhood determined. So the discourse was set at distrust but with bitterness and silence, with partners circling around each other not knowing what each had done, at the same time as carrying out the most intimate of physical contact with each other—without protection.

There was a dislocation between the reality of the numbers of people with AIDS the Ministry of Health was putting out ('out there') and the internalization of risk by individuals that comes from being given advice on a one-to-one basis ('real to me'). The reluctance to discuss with people that they had HIV began to change in 1989 as civil society organizations took a more prominent role in setting up support groups. A strategic move by the Society of Women and AIDS in Africa (SWAA) made Sally Mugabe, the former First Lady of Zimbabwe, its patron at its inaugural conference in Harare (although her husband did not speak openly about AIDS in Zimbabwe until several years later). The Family AIDS Counselling Trust in Mutare, the AIDS Counselling Trust in Harare and Matabeleland AIDS Council in Bulawayo started seeing clients slowly but depended on referrals from clinicians who avoided testing their patients. No one was allowed to give a clinical diagnosis of HIV without a positive test result. The Women and AIDS Support Network had its first conference in 1989 following the SWAA meeting, where the epidemiology of HIV prevalence was presented, showing how women were younger and more vulnerable than their male partners (Willmore and Ray, 1989). These were small islands of support in an environment that actively discouraged people from knowing their status. People were warned to 'Be careful' without the fundamental principle of behaviour change being addressed: individuals have to feel at risk, but also they need to feel in control of the actions that are necessary to deal with the risk, and to be supported in a social environment to change their behaviour.

By now the first data on HIV prevalence from surveillance of key indicator groups was emerging. The testing was anonymous and unlinked, so none of the people testing positive this way were given their HIV results. Individuals could only get tested at this time if they went to a doctor who was willing to test them. Because of the link with STIs, and the common route of transmission, patients attending public clinics for STIs were monitored for HIV. In 1987 median HIV prevalence among patients attending STD clinics was 6% from two testing sites outside Harare, while in Harare it was already 52% in 1990. By 1995 median HIV prevalence from seven testing sites was 65%, and 71% in Harare. Among women attending STD clinics in 1996 HIV prevalence was 53%.

Pregnant women attending for antenatal care (ANC) already had blood specimens taken for syphilis testing, and now had unlinked samples of blood tested for HIV also: 10% of pregnant women in Harare, Bulawayo and Chitungwiza were HIV positive in 1989, 16% in 1990 and 20% in 1997. In areas such as large-scale commercial farms, growth points, border towns and mines, HIV prevalence among ANC attendees was much higher, around 35% from 1997. Most countries with predominantly heterosexual HIV transmission monitor their prevalence through antenatal clinic surveillance. UNAIDS has shown that prevalence from pregnant women can be extrapolated to the general population of reproductive age (15–49), although prevalence in men has tended to be lower than in women in recent times. This is mainly because of women's increased biological vulnerability to HIV infection but also because men tend to have more sexual partners than women and therefore the potential to pass the infection to more women. Figure 1 shows the trend of HIV in pregnant women in Africa from 1990 to 2002, emphasizing the continued increase in prevalence in Southern African countries while it declined in Eastern Africa.

Epidemiology of HIV in Zimbabwe and Demographic Impact

Twenty years since we were first able to test for HIV in Zimbabwe, it is still one of the worst affected countries in the world. The UNAIDS estimate for the end of 2003 was 24.5% of adults aged 15–49 years, 1.8 million adults and children living with HIV, of whom 120 000 are children under 14 years, 980 000 orphans under the age of 18 (an increase of 150 000 since 2001) and 170 000 deaths in 2003.

A recent UNAIDS press release (October 2005) indicated that the percentage of those infected between the ages of 15 and 49 fell from 24.6% in 2002 to 21.3% in 2004. The decline is attributed to a reduction in reported number of sexual partners and an increase in condom use with non-regular partners. The fall from 35% in 2000 to 24.6% was not lauded as the result of success in HIV prevention programmes, rather the reduction in prevalence was caused by correction of previously flawed estimates. UNAIDS defends the reliability of the new statistics saying they are based on a variety of studies by different organizations that have reached similar estimates. Community-based studies such as that by the BRTI team in Manicaland confirm that HIV prevalence is in this range: 19% in men and 28% in women in 1998–2000; infection rates were highest in small towns (27% in men, 46% in women) but were also high in tea and forestry estates, roadside settlements and villages (15%–18% in

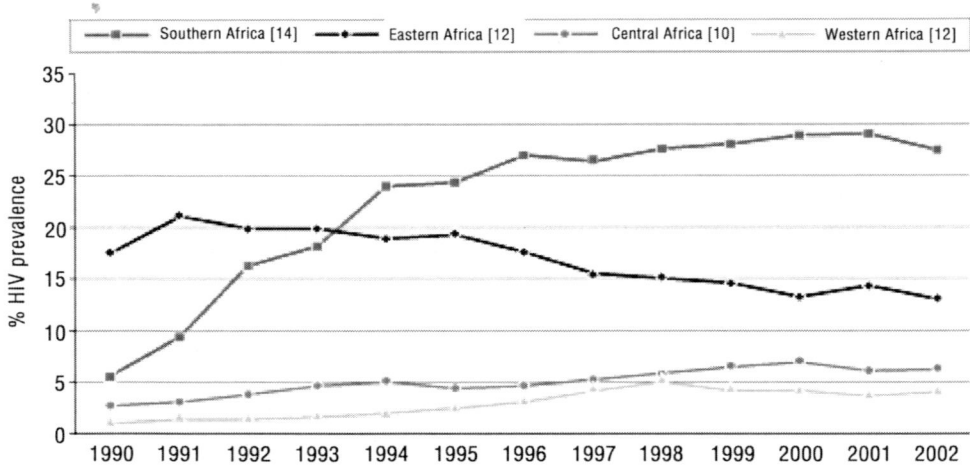

Figure 1. Median HIV prevalence (%) in antenatal clinics in urban areas, by sub-region, in
sub-Saharan Africa 1990–2002. *Source*: Adapted from WHO AFRO 2003 Report

men, 22%–28% in women) (Nyamukapa and Gregson, 2005). UNAIDS warns
against complacency since the figures are still high. Indeed, some 3000 Zimbabweans
still die each week of AIDS-related illnesses and the prevalence is not declining at a
similar rate to that seen in Uganda over a similar time period.

Figure 2 demonstrates the higher prevalence of AIDS in young women over men,
particularly pronounced in Zambia, South Africa and Zimbabwe. In the earlier stages
of the epidemic, more men than women were infected and at an older age, leading to
higher mortality among men and more families left fatherless. The current situation is
of more women living with HIV and at a younger age. Research in Zimbabwe has
shown that children left without their mother struggle more than those whose fathers
have died because of the allocation of resources within families (Nyamukapa and
Gregson, 2005). A strong case can be made for women therefore receiving targeted
access to treatment. The best entry point for this is through antenatal care, where
there is an emphasis on prevention of infection in the 75% of women still HIV
negative, as well as on providing much greater resources towards supporting HIV
positive women to stay healthy, for their own sakes as well as those of their children.
In other treatment schemes, such as through workplace programmes, men have often
received access that is denied to their partners, and in more community-based
schemes limited resources have ensured that men get first access because of being
heads of household. So the entitlement culture preferentially supports gender
inequity. The current collapse of health services, especially in the public sector, will
clearly not facilitate reaching pregnant women with HIV programmes.

The 1980s in southern Africa saw declines in infant and maternal mortality, rates
of illness and death from infections like tuberculosis, measles and diarrhoeal
diseases, very much a product of integrated and better resourced health services. As a
result of AIDS, life expectancy at birth in many southern African countries has
dropped dramatically, partly thanks to deaths in children under five years but also
because of deaths in many adults in their 20s and 30s. Figure 3 shows how the decline
started in Zimbabwe and Zambia around 1990, with the eight-year advance

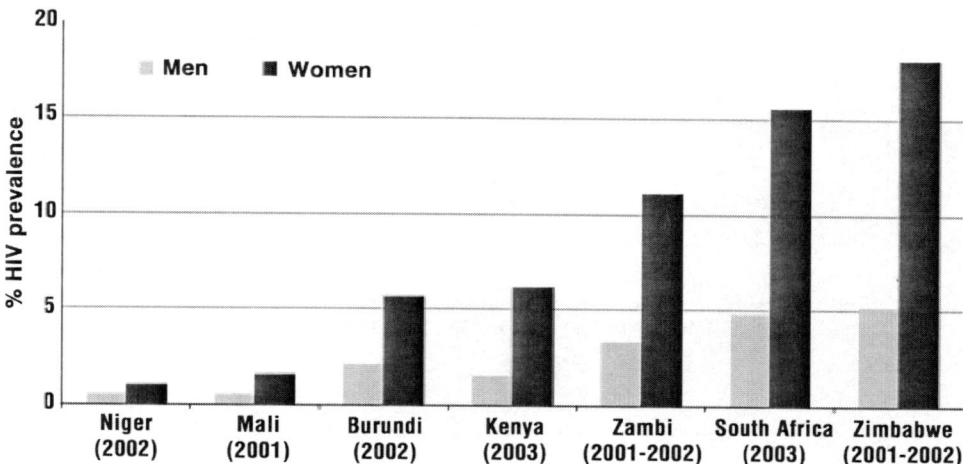

Figure 2. HIV prevalence among 15–24 year olds in selected sub-Saharan African countries, 2001–03. *Source*: UNAIDS (2004)

Zimbabwe made in the 1980s over Zambia disappearing by 2000. Botswana, South Africa and Swaziland follow after a lag of five years. By the year 2002 life expectancy at birth in Zimbabwe had fallen to 37.9 years from 60 years in 1985–90, according to a World Health Report of 2004. UNAIDS predicts that in the worst-affected countries of eastern and southern Africa up to 60% of today's 15-year-olds will not reach their 60th birthday.

The demographic impact of these early deaths is demonstrated in Figure 4, using South Africa as an example. The principles can be applied to most countries in Southern Africa allowing for time lags—Zimbabwe would already be showing greater demographic impact in the year 2000. Age–sex pyramids display the percentage or actual amount of a population in bands of gender and age. The population graphic for rich countries is bell shaped in that there is a low birth rate, but in stable situations nearly all these children live into adulthood and die when they are in their 70s and 80s. Developing countries show a more pyramid shape, with a wide base reflecting higher current birth rates and a younger population, with higher death rates affecting each bar so that an apex is reached in ages 60s and 70s with a much smaller proportion of adults surviving to old age. The year 2000 approximates this pyramid in South Africa, with some small indications of deaths from AIDS. In the 2025 projection, however, distortions in all the age bands can be seen as deaths in the under-fives mean that fewer children grow into adolescence and young adulthood; then big gaps appear in the 35 + age bands, with more deaths in women than men as the epidemic matures. The striking feature of this pyramid is of the dependency ratio: the young people at the base of the pyramid and the older people at the top are relying on wealth created by smaller and smaller proportions of middle aged adults. Some of these adults will be sick and relying on care from their aging family members and their children. Children are initially looked after by their grandparents, and then become the carers and heads of household for their sick parents and their elderly grandparents.

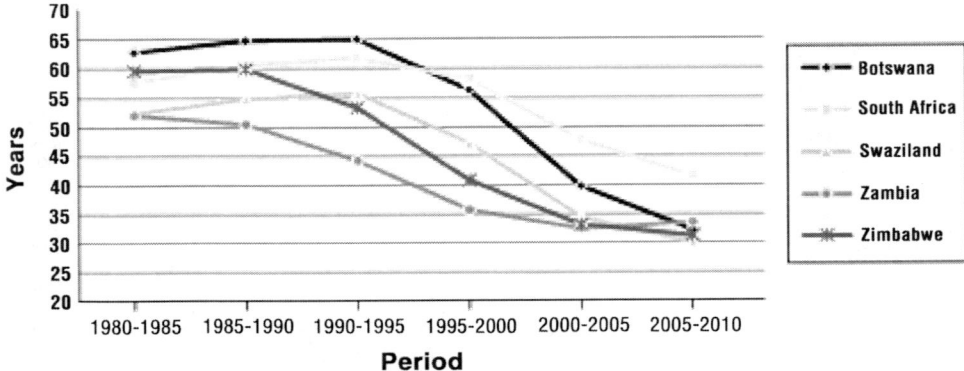

Figure 3. Life expectancy at birth in selected most-affected countries. *Source*: UN Population Division, World Population Prospects: the 2002 Revision

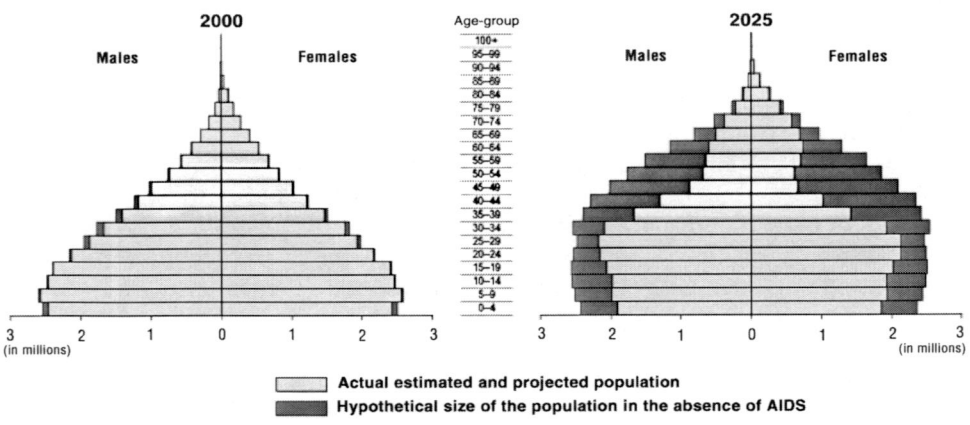

Figure 4. Population size with and without AIDS, South Africa 2000 and 2025. *Note*: Red bars represent the hypothetical size of the population in the absence of AIDS. Yellow bars represent the actual estimated and projected population. *Source*: UN Population Division

Social Environment Predisposing to HIV Transmission

Poverty makes people vulnerable to becoming infected with HIV at the same time as exacerbating the impact of HIV on communities. To some extent HIV initially became widespread because of development: good roads and transport systems that enabled people to move from country to country, from urban to rural areas. The first groups of people to be identified with HIV (mainly as blood donors) were in the army, police, or were school teachers, mainly men who were separated from their families during work and had other sexual partners during their travels. A UNAIDS survey undertaken in 1999 showed that 55% of the Zimbabwean army was HIV positive (UNAIDS, 1999), while the UNDP's *Zimbabwe Human Development Report* in 2003 indicated that three-quarters of soldiers died of AIDS within a year of leaving the army (UNDP, 1999). As the epidemic became established, more people in rural areas became infected, especially women, who did not initially have reliable information on the existence of HIV, and then had less ability or resources to prevent it. Health services in particular that provided advice, prevention and treatment for sexually transmitted infections, were less developed and less accessible to rural communities, with the exception of some faith-based hospitals based in more deprived areas. The high level of new and untreated STIs, together with late reporting for treatment because of stigma or cost of treatment, is closely associated with propagation of the HIV epidemic.

The influence of unequal gender relationships is found throughout the story of HIV in southern African countries. The main risk that young women face is their dependence on men for economic survival but also for the social status that comes with being 'a wife'. Sexual relationships are often formed as a buffer to socio-economic insecurity. Women more often work in the informal sector, in seasonal and insecure employment. They are more likely to have poor and insecure housing tenure, especially if they are in informal relationships as girlfriends or mistresses of married men who pay their rent. Early sexual debut and early cessation of schooling are indicators of risk in young women. They tend to form relationships with men 5–10 years older than themselves who are prospective marriage partners, whereas young men tend to have relationships with women of a similar age or slightly younger. Within the age range 19–28 years men with jobs are more likely to be HIV positive than those unemployed, probably because they have more disposable income to spend in beerhalls and on payment for sex or casual partners. They usually have more partners concurrently and use condoms inconsistently but in casual relationships rather than marriage (Gregson *et al.*, 2002). Frequent use of alcohol is linked with payment for sex, inconsistent condom use and acquisition of STIs.

The features listed in Table 1 make households and communities more likely to be severely affected by HIV-related morbidity and mortality in terms of decreased income, increased or diverted expenditure, stress, and ability to function (Loewenson and Whiteside, 1998; Woelk, 1997; Loewenson and Whiteside, 1996).

The economic crisis in Zimbabwe, as well as the collapse of the health service, has worsened the impact of poverty on the HIV epidemic. Childhood and maternal mortality are soaring as infectious diseases go untreated and immune systems are undermined by poor nutrition. Loss of livelihoods means loss of means to pay for basic medications such as antibiotics or pain relief. Other southern Africa countries are also struggling with desperate food shortages and the impact of HIV on their communities. However, there is a distinction between neglect and intentional infliction of poverty and violence. In Zimbabwe people have been purposefully deprived of food aid, had clinics closed down, been thrown off commercial farms where they worked as farm workers, been beaten and threatened, all for political reasons. Rape is also used to intimidate and humiliate, such as in the use of political violence by the youth militia during the elections, where women were violated in front of their families on the pretext that they were opposition supporters (Soros, 2004).

Violence and Social Disruption

The silence from the medical profession has again been very loud during the recent mass eviction campaign '*Murambatsvina*' in which 700 000 people lost their homes

Table 1. HIV related illness, mortality and dependency

- depletes available labour and reduces skills and experience
- diverts productive labour to caring activities and reduces incomes from production
- reduces remittances (urban to rural; formal to informal)
- reduces rural food and crop production and depletes cattle ownership
- causes changes in food production and consumption per capita
- increases costs of caring and social support
- increases costs of employee benefits, medical aid and insured benefits
- depletes assets and savings
- increases demand for health care resources in the public, private and home-based sectors beyond those available
- reduces market demand as a result of reduced purchasing power in the community
- depletes human resources in the health and social sectors
- reduces resources available to deal with other health problems
- weakens or overburdens social protection and community mutual support
- can reduce investment in child health, education and well-being, especially in orphans, leading to long-term effects in the next generation
- can create despondency, stress and fatalism

and livelihoods. The violent and arbitrary way people were displaced and made homeless was frightening to everyone. Those living in 'shacks' were not the only victims. The health implications were so severe that not to protest seemed a dereliction of duty: no shelter in the middle of winter, most people's only livelihood lost, resulting in no food, people with chronic illnesses separated from their medication and source of health care. A UN investigation reported on the negative effect of the evictions on thousands of people and families living with HIV, including orphans and vulnerable children, and child-headed households, who were denied access to safe water, sanitation, nutrition and basic health care, including HIV services, through the displacements. Some of the civil society groups looking after HIV positive people tried to trace their displaced clients. Over 79 500 people living with HIV, who were part of treatment or home-care programmes, were displaced (Kapp, 2005). The implications involved mortality, poor drug compliance leading to resistance, deteriorating health which would make it impossible for people to look after their children and loss of morale. Despite protests from medical associations outside Zimbabwe about the impact of these evictions on the health of the people, there has been no public statement from the leadership of the medical profession within Zimbabwe speaking on behalf of patients.

One of the consequences of institutionalized political violence in Zimbabwe has been fear within the health system. Patients are afraid to access the system and health workers are afraid to treat. At the peak of the farm invasions and brutality, and also during the elections, victims of violence sought treatment away from where they had been attacked, and doctors preferred to transfer patients to the central hospital rather than treat them locally. A recent example is of a ZANU (PF) ex-combatant who was refused treatment by a local hospital after he had been assaulted by Leo Mugabe (a ZANU (PF) MP), a nephew of President Robert Mugabe (Dongozi, 2005). The ethical duty of the health professionals to treat with impartiality is thereby lost by the profession as a whole.

Lack of SADC Collaboration

Countries of the Southern Africa Development Community (SADC) (Angola, Botswana, Democratic Republic of Congo, Lesotho, Malawi, Mauritius, Mozambique, Namibia, South Africa, Swaziland, Tanzania, Zambia, Zimbabwe) carry the burden of AIDS in Africa but have not worked together sufficiently or with urgency to address the epidemic. The added strain of food shortages, weakened health infrastructure through poor investment and migration of health workers, as well as spiralling costs of importing drugs and equipment, has decimated their capacity to respond. The instability in Zimbabwe has had implications for the whole region. In the past, Zimbabwe produced agricultural surpluses that could be used to offset shortages in neighbouring countries. The first 20 years of independence saw major advances in primary care development and training of health workers that provided models for other countries in the region, as well as postgraduate research and training opportunities at the University of Zimbabwe medical school. Zimbabwe was one of the first countries to develop legislation against discrimination of people with HIV in the workplace for the private sector through tripartite negotiations between the trade unions, government and business sectors. This piece of work catalyzed the development of the SADC Code of Conduct on HIV in workplaces. Many of these collaborations in the SADC region have fallen by the wayside with the worsening position of Zimbabwe in the region. In addition, legislation like this needs championing since fear of disclosure prevents most workers from accessing benefits. People living with HIV are often unfamiliar with their rights and may not be able to challenge their employers if they lose their employment when their HIV status becomes known; they may therefore also lose their benefits.

Regional collaboration on the manufacture of anti-retroviral (ARV) therapies would go a long way to addressing the need for treatment in the region. Apart from South Africa, none of the SADC countries has the capacity to manufacture drugs from raw materials. In the past two years the private sector in Zimbabwe has imported formulations for processing treatment but this is very dependent on availability of foreign exchange. Here Cuba provides another example. Even with its low HIV prevalence rate (0.1% of adults), Cuba began manufacturing generic versions of six different (ARV) drugs in 2001 because it was prevented from importing drugs by the US trade embargo. There are now 1500–2000 people on ARV treatment, with a mortality rate that has fallen to 7% of AIDS cases. Because of its success in providing treatment for its own population, Cuba is now looking to export generic drugs at low prices to other developing countries, especially in Africa (Avert, 2005). In the face of adversity, if the political will exists to find solutions, there can be benefits for a wider recipient population.

Zimbabweans with HIV in the UK

The violence, and economic and social collapse in Zimbabwe have sent people out of the country like a cloud into neighbouring countries and further. Many are HIV positive and may not have access to support, care or treatment where they have gone. They are faced with the same problems they faced in Zimbabwe: stigma, fear of disclosure, children orphaned, the cost of death and of funerals. In addition, their families are faced with the costs of sending their bodies home if they die abroad, sometimes to the detriment of their children who need that money for their education.

During 2004 59% of the 7275 new diagnoses of HIV in the UK were hetero-sexually acquired, with the majority (70%) of these in women. Of these heterosexual diagnoses, 73 % (3129) were acquired through exposure in Africa, mainly among those born in and who had migrated from Africa, but including some who had travelled there. Zimbabwe accounts for 38% of the African exposure. The majority of children (82% of the 112) with HIV acquired through parent-to-child trans-mission were born to women infected in Africa (Health Protection Agency, 2005). Women are more likely to be picked up if they have asymptomatic HIV if they are pregnant and attend antenatal care in Britain. The Department of Health introduced guidelines in 1999 for all pregnant women to be tested for HIV as a routine part of antenatal care. The proportion of HIV positive women being diagnosed before delivery has increased. In 2003 about 90% of all HIV infected women giving birth in England were diagnosed before delivery, providing opportunities for prevention of transmission to infants through treatment, method of delivery and avoidance of breastfeeding. Antenatal HIV testing is carried out as an opt-out system, where all women are tested unless they specifically refuse to be tested, rather than as an opt-in where they can choose to get tested or not. The concentration of counselling is then on those who are identified as positive. The opportunity that is lost here is for one-to-one counselling for those who test negative but are nevertheless at high risk of infection. In Zimbabwe, 5% – 10% of women become HIV positive during the 1 – 2 years of pregnancy and breastfeeding. Zimbabwean women may be exposed to the same risks from their partners in Britain and need to know how to protect themselves, for instance by using condoms.

New migrants from Africa to Britain are anxious about the legality of their status, and reluctant to present themselves to any authorities, including health services, unless they have to. Most refuse to be tested for HIV for several reasons, remain unaware of their status and present late when they are already sick with AIDS. If they are asylum seekers they may be fearful that they may have their applications rejected if they are known to be HIV positive. In addition, NHS charges publicized in the media for non-residents deter asylum seekers from seeking any health care. HIV carries the same heavy burden of stigma among migrants as it does 'back home' and creates the same major barrier to effective interventions. Women have more access to information than men through their contact with reproductive health services, while male new migrants continue to have unprotected sex, particularly if they do not recognize the risks within their relationships in Britain (they may feel they have left AIDS behind in Africa). The end result is that their health and that of others is put in jeopardy.

The National Health Service in Britain recognizes that it is better to make education, testing and treatment accessible for people with HIV. Treatment with ARVs makes it 60% less likely that HIV will be transmitted if unprotected sex occurs. If early detection and treatment of HIV-related illness prevented one case of onward transmission, it would save the NHS between £500 000 and £1 000 000. At an average cost of £7000 per year, providing anti-retroviral therapy is more cost-effective than treating repeated opportunistic infections, especially tuberculosis, which has major health implications for the wider public health. In addition, the personal costs carried by families are huge for new migrants. It is still very important for Zimbabweans to be buried in Zimbabwe, so families make considerable efforts to take the bodies of the deceased back home, with major financial implications. Similarly, children who are orphaned are transported home, sometimes to lifestyles they are totally unfamiliar with and families they hardly know.

It is problematic to relate these figures to Zimbabwe because the collapse of 'ordinary' health care means that most people living with HIV are not provided with any kind of supportive health services. Many opportunistic infections go undiagnosed and untreated, people are sent home to die in increasingly difficult circumstances. The more fortunate are able to tap into a home-based care programme run by churches or NGOs who receive donor funding. The successes of the government TB programme in the 1980s have been eroded by the loss of skilled staff, laboratory shortages, transport costs, and fuel shortages that prevent outreach, especially in rural areas. Within Zimbabwe activists have drawn considerable attention to provision of ARVs: only 12 000 people are receiving ARVs out of the 270 000 estimated to need them. At least half of these receive their treatment through private means and from the private sector. Many in the diaspora are sending funds home to support purchase of treatment for family members and to support family members financially who have been left devastated by deaths from AIDS.

Many health workers who left Zimbabwe to work in Britain are following a long-standing tradition of migration from poor areas to rich in search of the means to better themselves and their families. Whereas this used to be from the rural to the urban areas, globalization now means travelling to other countries to send remittances home, to pay school fees, to buy land, bricks, fertilizer, seed and pesticides. As things have become worse in Zimbabwe, these remittances are increasingly being used to buy food and healthcare. Those who are surviving often depend on support from outside. These health workers are gaining new insights, skills and training that will be useful when they return home. They have been exposed to a different way of management of HIV and AIDS, of information governance and confidentiality, of health promotion, of professionalism that should not stigmatize regardless of personal belief. The lessons learnt of good and bad practice in Britain can be applied both in working for their diaspora contemporaries and in what they take back with them.

Health workers are often quite conservative. In developing countries they often see themselves as the chosen ones, deserving of status and influence because of their training. They are invested in by their families to support other family members to climb the ladder. This becomes their preoccupation rather than solving the evils of the world, or feeling some sense of justice for their patients. From outside this environment they will have witnessed the importance of healthcare as a human right that all endeavour to achieve for the common good. They have had to understand the meaning of international solidarity, the impact of international activism with various organizations (Action Aid, Oxfam, Médecins Sans Frontières (MSF), and so on] campaigning on behalf of people in the world who do not have access to treatment for AIDS, in collaboration with developing country activists like those from the Treatment Action Campaign in South Africa. The key lesson that Zimbabwe will benefit from is one that even so-called democratic countries still have to fight hard for. This is that all citizens have to be engaged in making governments and institutions accountable for their activities. These institutions have to work in partnership with civil society organizations that have the right to challenge them to act democratically on behalf of people's best interests. This is often regarded as threatening and destabilizing on the part of those with power, but is an essential feature of a mutually constructive society.

The Role of Activism

There has been an expansion in activism nationally and globally as a result of access to anti-retroviral treatment. The World Trade Organization (WTO), patent law, generic medicines, the stamping ground for a small band of dedicated campaigners from the 1970s, are now common currency for HIV activists. A major instrument in making knowledge sharing powerful has been access to email and the internet, allowing thousands to find information and stories about others' experiences: how to access treatment, how much generics cost in one country versus another, how to manage side-effects, what courses are being run where. This knowledge is no longer the preserve of doctors and academics to share as they choose, rather they can be challenged on what they can contribute. This was a major lesson learnt from the gay community in the USA in the 1980s when it made doctors and politicians respond to its concerns. The internet facilitates debate in areas many have never had access to before. On a Southern Africa HIV/AIDS information dissemination service (SAfAIDS) email listserve, we ran an interview with Tarisai, about choosing to have a baby despite her HIV positive status in Zimbabwe (Communication Initiative, 2002). We had replies from all over the world, both agreeing and disagreeing with her position, but many saying they had never understood before the reality of a mother making these choices, which was brought home so vividly by this posting. The story was reprinted in several newsletters for those who did not have access to electronic media. People go into internet cafes in small towns and growth points to get access to information on HIV, as well as through school and college libraries.

On the other hand, the medical profession is still struggling to see its role in providing information for patients. During 2002 people working in home-based care programmes expressed a need for professional support in addressing the pain suffered by patients dying at home with AIDS, who are looked after principally by relatives and volunteers with no health training. The Anaesthetic Association had pioneered chronic pain management in Zimbabwe and was directly responsible for the setting up of the hospice movement in the country in the 1970s for management of people dying from cancer. In this arrangement trained nurses were authorized to continue providing drugs like codeine and morphine for patients after they had had the original prescription from the consultant. Home-care managers were requesting help with protocols that would extend the principles of terminal care used by the hospice movement to the use of stronger pain relief for people dying from AIDS. This was an opportunity for doctors to make a difference to the terminal care of thousands of people. The Anaesthetic Association discussed the issue at length. It was felt to be beyond the resources and capacity of the association to go beyond their current workload and campaign for different regimes of drug availability, regulation and prescribing. Even developing a set of guidelines that could be used to develop policies on pain management at home-based care level was seen as insurmountable, as was the suggestion of a booklet for patients on self-management of pain. It was seen as the role of NGOs to provide information for families living with AIDS, not the responsibility of doctors to provide leadership in developing programmes for home-based care.

In Zimbabwe activists for treatment need much more solidarity from their friends abroad. Not only do they have to campaign for more treatment to be made available for the size of the problem, they also have to draw attention to the impact of food shortages and poor health care facilities on their health. They have to challenge the government to respond to their needs in the middle of a major crisis and the Global Fund to look for alternative means of putting money into the treatment campaign besides going through the government. They have to fight tokenism on the part of senior health officials, such as the CEO of the tertiary referral hospital in Harare (population 1–2 million), who said in *The Standard* (Harare, 13 November 2005): "As of now the Opportunistic Infections Clinic at Parirenyatwa has a register of up to 250 infants and 300 plus adults who are accessing ARVs. Those on the register are getting the drugs." Donors who funded many of the previously successful programmes, such as the essential drugs management schemes and the national TB programme have pulled out of Zimbabwe because of the lack of accountability and poor governance. Activists within Zimbabwe have condemned the refusal of international donors to continue funding government programmes on health, since Zimbabwe only receives $4 (average annual donor spending per HIV infected person) compared with $74 in the rest of southern Africa. According to UNICEF Executive Director Carol Bellamy, speaking in Johannesburg:

> The world must differentiate between the politics and the people of Zimbabwe. Every day children in Zimbabwe are dying of HIV/AIDS, every day children are becoming infected, orphaned, and forced to leave school to care for sick parents. The global generosity towards tsunami victims was inspiring, but it has dried up for Zimbabwean children who are facing a deadly crisis every day of their lives. (UNICEF, 2005)

However, it is the government of Zimbabwe and its leadership who are responsible for the health of its people, not international donors. In fact, the health service in Zimbabwe was able to develop in the 1980s mainly because of donor funding, but dependency on this over the long term is not sustainable. Donor money will follow when there are adequate systems in place to guarantee that it is used for those in greatest need rather than based on political entitlement. It is the government that should be held accountable for the failure of the AIDS response from the start of the epidemic. Ironically the government instead manipulates the situation so that the donors are blamed from within the country rather than the country itself. Mugabe's government is seen as being belligerent towards the West, whereas other governments in the region have cooperated with international donors. Despite the continuing economic crisis, some activists feel there is no point in fighting the government since it controls the resources (Timberg, 2005). In fact, donors have continued to fund research and treatment programmes that are run by the university and by NGO partnerships such as MSF that provide ARVs for small projects.

In South Africa the Treatment Action Campaign (TAC) took a legal protest route by challenging the government on access to treatment based on the right to health as enshrined in the constitution. It went so far as to accuse the Minister of Health of culpable homicide for negligently causing the deaths of people who had died of AIDS without treatment (TAC, 2003). This action had the effect of raising debate around the right to health and the right to treatment, but also challenged the government to justify how it set its priorities in health expenditure, what a country can or cannot afford in providing health care for all. It squarely set the responsibility for provision of health care with the government and not with the international community.

South–South collaboration on training HIV activists finds a fine model in the TAC in South Africa. Advocacy and activism are crucial means of reasserting pride and self-worth for families living with HIV and AIDS by campaigning for the right to access treatment and care. TAC runs treatment literacy courses for groups of positive people all over southern Africa, so that people living with HIV know how to manage their illnesses as well as how to get the best information from their health workers. Their campaign on tackling stigma by encouraging the wearing of T-shirts proclaiming HIV positivity whether the wearer was positive or not, showing that we are all living with and affected by HIV, made major inroads into taking away some of the badness associated with being HIV positive.

Conclusions

The population effects of HIV and AIDS will be felt for the next 50 years or more. The implications for social reconstruction have not been put on the agenda yet. UNAIDS has clearly stated that "unless the AIDS response is dramatically strengthened by 2025, 38 African countries will have populations which will be 14% smaller than predicted in the absence of AIDS. In the seven countries where prevalence exceeds 20%, the population is projected to be more than one-third smaller due to the epidemic" (UNAIDS, 2004). Within these predictions of demographic impact we have also to consider the impact of the loss of tranches of people with knowledge, skills, experience and potential that cannot be easily replaced. At every level the consequences of the loss of young people means destruction of communities, families, occupations, culture and history. The agriculture sector is already reeling from the loss of labour in rural areas of southern Africa, even as climate and environmental changes are making this worse.

Zimbabwe shares many of the reasons for carrying an HIV burden with the rest of the region. The secrecy and betrayal of human rights, as well as failing public health systems are common to many countries. What is different in the current phase in Zimbabwe is the intentional infliction of violence and deprivation on its people. Governments are strong either because they impose their will on people or because they work in partnership with civil society and institutions in their countries. Only the second approach truly guarantees the well-being of all constituents. The civil society response has to be to strengthen internal and external relationships crucial to this partnership. SADC has a major role to play in this by enabling the frameworks developed for human rights that have already been signed up to by member countries.

Lessons from the failure to manage the HIV epidemic need to be assimilated with urgency. In this health professionals continue to bear a great responsibility to provide professional leadership but also to bring all the key players together and recognize the role of greater society in addressing its problems. In this they should work together with other medical associations in the region to uphold the principles of just and equitable access to healthcare, to advocate on behalf of their patients, and to establish an authority independent from governments so that they are part of the civil society fabric that holds governments accountable for how they provide for the well being of their citizens.

Note

Sunanda Ray and Farai Madzimbamuto are founder-members of the Zimbabwe Association of Doctors for Human Rights (ZADHR).

References

Avert (2005) www.avert.org/aidstarget.htm

Communication Initiative (2002) Tarisai's story—interview with Dr Sunanda Ray, at www.comminit.com/Commentary/sld-4989.html

Dehne, K. L., Dhlakama, D. G., Richter, C., Mawadza, M., McClean, D. and Huss, R. (1992) Herpes zoster as an indicator of HIV infection in Africa, *Tropical Doctor*, 22(2), pp. 68–70.

Dongozi, F. (2005) Mugabe's reign of terror, *The Zimbabwe Standard*, 6 November.

Emmanuel, J. C., Bassett, M. T., Smith, H. J. and Jacobs, J. A. (1988) Pooling of sera for human immunodeficiency virus (HIV) testing: an economical method for use in developing countries, *Journal of Clinical Pathology*; 41(5), pp. 582–585.

Garfield, S. (1994) *The End of Innocence—Britain in the time of AIDS*, pp. 66–69 (London: Faber and Faber).

Gregson, S., Nyamukapa, C. A., Garnett, G. P., Mason, P. R., Zhuwau, T., Carael, M., Chandiwana, S. K. and Anderson, R. M. (2002) Sexual mixing patterns and sex-differentials in teenage exposure to HIV infection in rural Zimbabwe, *The Lancet*, 359, pp. 1896–1903.

Health Protection Agency (2005) *SOPHID Survey 2004 UK* (London: Health Protection Agency).

The Herald (1987) 250 000 have AIDS virus in Zimbabwe, 31 December, p. 5.

The Herald (1988a) Doctor slams AIDS scaremongers, 13 February, p. 1.

The Herald (1988b) Positive AIDS results may prove false, 17 February, p. 4.

Kaleeba, N. and Ray, S. (1991) *We Miss You All, Noerine Kaleeba: AIDS in the Family* (Harare: Women & AIDS Support Network). Second edition (2002) available from SAfAIDS, at www.safaids.org.zw

Kalinaki, D. (2002) We are sick and suffering; we want you to accept us, *New Internationalist*, 346, June.

Kapp, C. (2005) Operation 'Restore Order' wreaks havoc in Zimbabwe, *The Lancet*, 366, pp. 1151–1152.

Loewenson, R. (1998) *Economic Impact of AIDS in Zimbabwe*, TARSC monograph, Harare, at www.tarsc.org

Loewenson, R. and Whiteside, A. (1996) Social and economic issues and HIV/AIDS in Southern Africa, paper commissioned by SAfAIDS, Harare, available at: www.safaids.org.zw

Masunda, D. (2001) Six ministers HIV-positive, *Financial Gazette*, 22–28 November, pp. 1, 43.

Mertens, T., Tondorf, G., Siebolds, M., Kruppenbacher, J. P., Shrestha, S. M., Mauff, G., Gurtler, L. and Eggers, H. J. (1989) Epidemiology of HIV and hepatitis B virus (HBV) in selected African and Asian populations, *Infection*, 17(1), pp. 4–7.

Nyamukapa, C. and Gregson, S. (2005) Extended families' and women's roles in safeguarding orphans' education in AIDS-afflicted rural Zimbabwe, *Social Science and Medicine*, 60(10), pp. 2155–2167.

Ray, S., Latif, A., Machekano, R. and Katzenstein, D. (1998) Sexual behaviour and risk assessment of HIV seroconvertors among urban male factory workers in Zimbabwe, *Social Science and Medecine*, 47(10), pp. 1431–1443.

Soros, E. (2004) *The HIV/AIDS catastrophe in Zimbabwe*, at www.worldpress.org

TAC (2003) Civil disobedience campaign, 20 March, at www.tac.org.za/newsletter/2003/ns20_03_2003.htm

Timberg, C. (2005) In rural Zimbabwe AIDS still means death, *Washington Post*, 20 April.

UNAIDS (2004) Engaging uniformed services in the fight against HIV/AIDS. Zimbabwe alarm over HIV prevalence in armed forces (www.uniformservices.unaids.org), accessed 24.6.2004.

UNAIDS (n.d.) Engaging uniformed services in the fight against HIV/AIDS, Uganda country overview, at www.uniformservices.unaids.org

UNAIDS/WHO (2004) *Epidemiological Fact Sheet*, 2004 update (Geneva: UNAIDS/WHO).

UNDP (2003) *Redirecting our Response to HIV/AIDS: The War for Survival, Zimbabwe Human Development Report* (UNDP).

UNICEF (2005) http://www.unicef.org/infobycountry/zimbabwe_25622.html

Widy-Wirski, R., Berkley, S., Downing, R., Okware, S., Recine, U., Mugerwa, R., Lwegaba, A. and Sempala, S. (1988) Evaluation of the WHO clinical case definition for AIDS in Uganda, *Journal of the American Medical Association*, 260, pp. 3286–3289.

Willmore, B. and Ray, S. (1989) *AIDS—An Issue for Every Woman*, proceedings of a conference held in Harare, 23–24 November 1989 (Harare: Women and AIDS Support Network).

Woelk, G. (1997) Assessment of the health context of the AIDS epidemic in Zimbabwe, paper prepared for the National AIDS Co-ordination Programme, Harare, October.

Appendix I

1. WHO Case Definition for AIDS Surveillance (Formerly Bangui/WHO/Clinical)

WHO clinical case definition for AIDS in an adult or adolescents (>12 years of age) when diagnostic resources are limited. For the purposes of AIDS surveillance an adult or adolescent (>12 years of age) is considered to have AIDS if at least two of the following major signs are present in combination with at least one of the minor signs listed below, and if these signs are not known to be related to a condition unrelated to HIV infection.

Major signs (2 or more):

- Weight loss of at least 10% of body weight
- Chronic diarrhoea for >1 month
- Prolonged fever for >1 month (intermittent or constant)

Minor signs (1 or more):

- Persistent cough for >1 month
- Generalized pruritic dermatitis
- History of *herpes zoster*
- *Oropharyngeal candidiasis*
- Chronic progressive or disseminated herpes virus infection
- Generalized lymphadenopathy.

The presence of either generalized Kaposi sarcoma or cryptococcal meningitis is sufficient for the diagnosis of AIDS for surveillance purposes.

The Rule of Law in Zimbabwe

ROBERT MARTIN
Professor of Law, Emeritus, University of Western Ontario, Canada

Introduction

Why does or should the rule of law matter? The rule of law is *the* essential element in constitutional government (Nwabueze, 1973, p. 2). Most of the states in the world have constitutions, but only a minority has a *constitutional* system of government (Loewenstein, 1963, p. 149). Constitutional government is, by its nature, limited government. The rule of law demands that every organ of the state act within the terms of the limitations imposed upon it by the law and by the constitution. The rule of law thus seeks to ensure that the state will not behave in an arbitrary, corrupt, or oppressive fashion (International Commission of Jurists, 1988, p. 144). The rule of law is largely a procedural notion; it does not address substantive questions. If the constitution and the law of a particular state are unjust and oppressive, the rule of law will not limit the injustice or oppression. A strange aspect of the legal system of apartheid South Africa was that the organs of the state tended to observe the rule of law (International Commission of Jurists, 1988). If the rule of law creates the possibility of limiting corrupt and oppressive behaviour by officials of the state, its desirability in contemporary Africa seems self-evident (Slinn, 1991). This simple conclusion may suggest why the Commonwealth Heads of Government issued the Harare Declaration in 1991. The Declaration states that the "fundamental political values of the Commonwealth" include: "democracy, democratic processes and institutions which reflect national circumstances, the rule of law and the independence of the judiciary, just and honest government" (*The Commonwealth Yearbook*, 1999, p. 38).

It is likely that, in the latter part of the 20th century, no one wrote as strongly in favour of the rule of law as the English historian E. P. Thompson (Thompson, 1975). He argued that the rule of law could impose "real control" on "arbitrary power" and was, thus, an "unqualified human good" (1975, p. 261).

Writing in 1985, I attempted to assess the applicability of Thompson's ideas in the African context and asserted that:

> the rule of law, when made concrete through working institutions, can be a most serviceable bulwark against anti-democratic forces which can be held at bay until the concrete conditions are realized within which people can create democracy for themselves. This may not sound very significant in the polite confines of academic discourse, but it would be a substantial boon to journalists who would otherwise disappear, to urban adolescents who are randomly arrested and tortured, and to helpless peasants who must submit to the depredations, great and small, of soldiers and agricultural extension officers. The rule of law is a shield behind which ordinary people can fight against bureaucracy (Martin, 1985, p. 136).

Zimbabwe is a beautiful and magnificent country, but one which is, today, largely in ruins. This essay explores the vicissitudes of the rule of law in that unhappy country. The body of the essay is divided into four parts as follows: 1890 to 1923; 1923 to 1965; 1965 to 1980; and 1980 to today.

1890 to 1923

1890 is significant because it was in that year that Europeans first entered the territory that is now Zimbabwe. It must not be thought, however, that Zimbabwe's history begins with the arrival of Europeans (Keatley, 1968, pp. 60 – 74).

The overwhelming majority of the people of Zimbabwe is African. The African population is made up of two significant groups—the Shona, who constitute 80% of that population, and the Ndebele, who make up the remaining 20%. The Shona people lived in the eastern and southern parts of the country. A Shona kingdom ruled over much of the south. At the centre of the Shona kingdom was a great stone city built on a plain just south of the present-day Masvingo. This city was called Zimbabwe. It flourished in the 12th century, during the reign of King Monomatapa.

My first visit to the Zimbabwe site was in 1972. It was then described as the 'Zimbabwe ruins'. The settlers in Rhodesia were not prepared to accept that Africans could have conceived and constructed a marvel like Zimbabwe. Consequently, fantastic explanations for the city's origin were commonplace. Since independence, the obvious fact that Zimbabwe was built by the Shona has been accepted and the site has been renamed 'Great Zimbabwe'.

Artefacts unearthed at Zimbabwe show that its people were trading with places as far away as India and China. The most significant artefacts unearthed at Zimbabwe were unique carved soapstone birds. The Zimbabwe bird appears today on the national flag. A Zimbabwe bird decorates the peak of Rhodes House in Oxford.

The Ndebele are an Nguni-speaking people who arrived in Zimbabwe during the vast expansion of the Zulu empire which took place in the early years of the 19th century. The Ndebele have lived in the southwestern part of the country since then. The leader of the Ndebele in 1890 was King Lobengula, a son of the great Zulu general, Mzilikazi.

On 26 June 1890 a gang of freebooters called the Pioneer Column entered the territory that is now Zimbabwe (Martin and Johnson, 1981, p. 35). This group, led by Leander Starr Jameson, was acting for the British South Africa Company. The Company had been incorporated by royal Charter and was operated by Cecil Rhodes, then the prime minister of the Cape Colony. The invasion and conquest by a British chartered company was sufficient in law to vest title to the land in the Crown and to deprive the African occupants of that land of their rights in it.[1] Some sense of the scope of the rule of law in colonial Africa can be gleaned from the fact that a British court was prepared to hold that an act of piracy could create a valid title to land.[2]

Settlers flooded into what was now described as 'Rhodesia'. These settlers were, generally, bluff and coarse buccaneers drawn by rumours of gold and land. It has been asserted that the Company had been granted a Charter in order to:

> avoid the scandal and disorder to which a scramble for the natural resources of the country would lead unless the white immigrants were placed under effective control.[3]

A capital was established and named Salisbury after the then British prime minister, Robert Cecil, Marquess of Salisbury. The British union flag flew over Salisbury, but the country was governed by the British South Africa Company. The Company was kept afloat by Rhodes' personal fortune and the vast wealth of DeBeers (Keatley, 1968, p. 165). Dr Jameson had the title 'Administrator' and, in that capacity, supervised a sort of government, a system seldom troubled by legal or constitutional niceties. Keatley put it well:

> In due course Southern Rhodesia was to build up an orthodox Civil Service, but it is small wonder that the men who turned up at the beginning to try their hand as administrators in the unorthodox empire of Dr Jameson tended to be soldiers of fortune, or plain human misfits. (1968, p. 173)

As a sort of check and balance, there was a British Resident Commissioner in Salisbury.

The Africans who lived in 'Southern Rhodesia' were not prepared to acquiesce quietly in the seizure of their land. The Ndebele people resisted the initial incursion by the Pioneer Column. This resistance was crushed and, as a result, the Ndebele kingdom was destroyed. In 1896 a major revolt against settler domination broke out. This event was unique in that the Ndebele and the Shona joined together to oppose the settlers. The revolt, known as the *Chimurenga*, was defeated, primarily because of the vastly superior military technology of the Europeans (Ranger, 1967). It is helpful to quote Hilaire Belloc's brilliant piece of doggerel which neatly summed up the history of European colonialism in Africa:

> Whatever happens, we have got
> the Maxim gun, and they have not.

With African resistance effectively crushed, it began to become clear that an alternative to rule by the Company was necessary. Southern Rhodesia could not depend forever on Cecil Rhodes' personal fortune. The settlers were not happy with being governed by the Company's board of directors in London (Buell, 1965, p. 207).

The obvious alternative was to become a British colony. This idea did not appeal to the settlers, since becoming a British colony would have meant that the power of the settlers would have been superseded by that of the Governor, who might well have had unacceptable ideas about protecting the 'natives' and their interests. In 1922 there was a referendum in which the settlers decided that they preferred 'responsible government' to colonial status. The settlers also agreed to buy their freedom from the Company for £2 million (Keatley, 1968, pp. 206–207). In 1923 Southern Rhodesia became a British colony, but an unusual one. Real power lay with the settler prime minister, rather than with the governor.

After 1923 Southern Rhodesia was formally a British colony. Scrupulous observance of the rule of law was not a hallmark of British colonial administration in Africa (McAuslan, 1974, pp. 5–10; Seidman, 1969, p. 47). Judicial decisions twisted principles in order to uphold colonial authority and deny redress to the colonized.[4]

1923 to 1965

While Southern Rhodesia was a colony, it was definitely a colony not like the others (deSmith, 1964, pp. 42–43). Southern Rhodesia enjoyed something very close to dominion status. 'Dominion' is a deeply imprecise notion. The word referred to a country which was a member of the then 'British' Commonwealth and which was not a fully sovereign, independent state, but nonetheless enjoyed self-government and a substantial degree of autonomy (deSmith, 1964, pp. 1–18). Many of the remaining fetters on the autonomy of the Dominions were removed by the Statute of Westminster of 1931. The Dominions all had European governments and, in 1923, included Australia, Canada, the Irish Free State, Newfoundland, New Zealand and the Union of South Africa.

Doris Lessing is, in my view, the greatest living writer not to have received the Nobel Prize. She was born in Persia in 1919 and was taken to Southern Rhodesia by her family in 1925. She remained in southern Africa until she moved to the UK in 1949. If one wishes to catch the flavour of colonial Southern Rhodesia, it is essential to read Doris Lessing. Her novels *The Grass is Singing* (1950), *Winter in July* (1966), and *The Sun Between Their Feet* (1973) are set in Southern Rhodesia, as are her collections of stories *This Was the Old Chief's Country* (1951) and *Nine African Stories* (1963). Her magnificent novel sequence, *Children of Violence* (1952–1964) is set in Southern Rhodesia and South Africa. She has also published two collections of essays about her homeland: *Going Home* (1957) is a scathing criticism of settler society and politics; *African Laughter: Four Visits to Zimbabwe* (1992) is a misleading, albeit optimistic, book about blacks and whites working together in harmony to build their new, shared country.

In 1930 the Rhodesian legislature enacted the Land Apportionment Act . This is, undoubtedly, the most significant statute ever enacted in the country. The 1930 Act affects and even defines politics and economics today. The practical effect of the Act was to divide the land of Southern Rhodesia equally between the European minority and the African majority.

By the end of the Second World War, colonialism, in the eyes of both the colonizers and the colonized, had lost whatever legitimacy it might have possessed. The various European colonial powers were confronted with a stark choice—either get out, or fight. The British made the right choice. India gained its independence on 15 August 1947. Once India was independent, the liquidation of the rest of the British Empire was inevitable. France made the wrong choice. It decided to stay on in Indo-China, thereby unleashing a war that would last for 30 years. Primarily because of the large numbers of settlers—*pieds noirs*—in Algeria, France decided to try to hang on. An especially nasty war was the result (Horne, 1987).

The British began their withdrawal from Africa in 1957 when the Gold Coast became independent as Ghana. From Ghana in 1957 to Swaziland in 1968, Britain steadily liquidated its African empire. The only serious problems occurred in Britain's two settler colonies—Kenya and Southern Rhodesia.

Predictably enough, the whites in Southern Rhodesia began to move in the opposite direction. There was a postwar surge in "settler confidence" (Keatley, 1968, p. 214). This manifested itself in a push for federation, meaning a union of Southern Rhodesia, Northern Rhodesia and Nyasaland, all governed by whites from Southern Rhodesia. The settlers in Kenya had long favoured East African federation, seeing it as a means by which Tanganyika and Uganda might be brought under their control (Dilley, 1966).

In 1953 the UK Parliament created the Central African Federation. This new state was led by a white from Southern Rhodesia as prime minister. Salisbury was, thus, the capital of both the Central African Federation and of Southern Rhodesia, and the seat of two white governments. As African nationalism brought independence to one colony after another, white politics in Southern Rhodesia became more intransigent. In 1962 a militant settler party, the Rhodesian Front, was formed. African nationalism had been growing and organizing itself in Southern Rhodesia. Africans were not prepared to accept their subordinate status forever. The African National Congress (ANC) of Rhodesia, largely under Ndebele leadership, had been formed in 1934. By 1961 the ANC had become ZAPU, the Zimbabwe African People's Union.

Events in other parts of Africa were to have a substantial effect on Southern Rhodesia. While Britain and France liquidated their African empires, Portugal decided to try to hold on to its. Portugal was the poorest and most backward country in western Europe. Its three African colonies—Angola, Guinea-Bissau, and Mozambique—gave it a certain standing in the world. Armed struggle against colonialism broke out in the three colonies in the 1960s (Minter, 1972). In 1952 an armed revolt against settler rule erupted in Kenya (Barnett and Njama, 1966; Itote, 1967). Harold Macmillan gave his famous 'wind of change' speech in Cape Town on

3 February 1960. Very clearly, the leaders of South Africa decided the wind of change would stop at the Zambezi. Angola, Mozambique, Southern Rhodesia and South-West Africa would provide a buffer zone to keep African nationalism at bay. Thus was Rhodesia drawn into a broader southern African conflict.

The tide of history was not running in a direction favourable to the interests of European settlers in Africa. In Kenya the settlers asked the British government to send troops to assist them. In 1953 a substantial British force arrived in Kenya. As soon as the first British soldier set foot on Kenyan soil, the power of the settlers was broken. African nationalists in Kenya could now disregard the settlers and deal directly with the British government. As a result, on 12 December 1963, Kenya became independent, with an African government.

A Kenyan strategy began to commend itself to African nationalists in Southern Rhodesia. Their belief was that, if they could create sufficient disorder in Rhodesia, the settler government might call for the assistance of British troops and, when those troops arrived, they could disregard the settlers. As a consequence, rioting and violence broke out in the African townships in 1960. This outbreak was suppressed with vigour, indeed so drastically that liberally-minded Rhodesians claimed the country had become a "police state" (Keatley, 1968, p. 325). This was achieved through two statutes—the Preventive Detention Act and the Law and Order (Maintenance) Act. In 1963 Britain wound up the Central African Federation. In the same year Nyasaland became independent as Malawi, and in 1964 Northern Rhodesia became independent as Zambia.

The most reactionary white politicians in Southern Rhodesia came together in 1962 to form the Rhodesian Front. Ian Smith became leader of the Rhodesian Front, which won all the white seats in the Southern Rhodesian election of 1965. Independence—which meant a settler state—had been the issue in a white referendum held in 1964. The vote was overwhelmingly in favour of independence. A strong indication that Britain would not send troops to Southern Rhodesia in the event of a Unilateral Declaration of Independence (UDI) (Hall, 1969, pp. 101–103) seemed to clear the way for UDI. Buoyed by the knowledge that UK Prime Minister Harold Wilson would not take action, Smith issued his UDI on 11 November 1965.

1965 to 1980

Almost from the moment of its birth, the rebel state of Southern Rhodesia was an international pariah. The only state to accord it recognition was the Republic of South Africa. The response from the UK was muted. No action was taken against Ian Smith and his colleagues, who were, technically, probably engaged in treason. On 16 November 1965 the UK Parliament enacted the Southern Rhodesia Act, 1965. This Act declared that Southern Rhodesia remained part of Her Majesty's dominions. In 1969 the Judicial Committee of the Privy Council decided that no legal recognition could be given to the rebel regime or any of its acts.[5]

With the *deus ex machina* of British intervention rendered unlikely, it became obvious to African nationalists that they would have to liberate themselves from settler rule. A major development had occurred in July 1963. A group called the Zimbabwe African National Union (ZANU) broke away from ZAPU to form a new party. The significant differences between ZAPU and ZANU lay in their leadership.

The leadership of ZAPU was older, somewhat moderate and primarily Ndebele, while the leadership of ZANU was younger, more militant and primarily Shona. In 1974 Robert Gabriel Mugabe became the leader of ZANU. ZAPU and ZANU each had its own army—ZAPU's was called the Zimbabwe People's Revolutionary Army (ZIPRA) and ZANU's was called the Zimbabwe African National Liberation Army (ZANLA). In the late 1960s both armies launched guerrilla war against Smith (Caute, 1983). This liberation struggle was referred to as the Second *Chimurenga* in order to connect it to the First *Chimurenga*, the Shona/Ndebele revolt of 1896–97. *Chimurenga* is a Shona word which means 'revolution'.

The ZAPU leadership had good ties with Kenneth Kaunda, the President of Zambia. As a result, ZIPRA was able to establish bases in Zambia. From these bases, ZIPRA soldiers crossed the Zambezi into Rhodesia. ZIPRA's first encounters with the Rhodesian Army were not successful and many of its soldiers were killed. In 1970 Southern Rhodesia changed its name to Rhodesia and turned itself into a republic. The level of the fighting intensified into the 1970s, although the Rhodesian Army, under the operational control of Lt Gen. Peter Walls, usually got the upper hand. ZIPRA soldiers, often operating in the Kariba Valley, were neither well trained nor well equipped. ZANLA tended to operate largely in northeastern Rhodesia.

A major change occurred in 1975. By 1974 Portugal was fighting three wars in Africa. The strain of supplying and equipping a large conscript army became unbearable. There were two coups in Portugal in 1974. The leaders of the second coup decided that the time to liquidate Portugal's African empire had come. In 1975 Mozambique became independent under a Frelimo (Mozambique Liberation Front) government. This event led to a major transformation of the struggle in Zimbabwe. Mugabe and Samora Machel, President of Mozambique, began to become allies. As a result, ZANLA was permitted to operate from bases in western Mozambique. ZANLA had adopted a Maoist approach to guerrilla warfare and, after 1976, more and more of its guerrillas flowed across the Mozambique border into Rhodesia. The war was going badly for Smith and his armed forces. Smith began to search desperately for an 'internal settlement' which would exclude ZAPU and ZANU. In 1979 the whites in Rhodesia were asked by the Smith government to approve a new constitution. As a result, a country called Zimbabwe–Rhodesia, headed by an African Prime Minister, Abel Muzorewa, came into being. In 1976 there had been a rapprochement between ZAPU and ZANU, which led to a new grouping called the Patriotic Front. Smith realized the war could no longer be continued. British Prime Minister Margaret Thatcher convened a conference which opened at Lancaster House in London in September 1979. There were three parties at the conference:

- the Muzorewa–Smith delegation;
- the Patriotic Front;
- the UK delegation.

The Patriotic Front did not like the terms proposed for the government of an independent Zimbabwe. There were two points which Mugabe especially disliked. First, Zimbabwe was to have a parliament consisting of a Senate and a House of Assembly. There would be 100 seats in the House of Assembly and 20 of these seats were to be reserved for whites. Second, there was to be an ironclad constitutional guarantee of property rights. President Machel put tremendous pressure on Mugabe to sign the agreement (Christie, 1988, p. 109).

The agreement was signed on 21 December. There was a ceasefire; Zimbabwe – Rhodesia became the colony of Southern Rhodesia; a British governor, Christopher Soames, was sent out; and settler rule was at an end.

1980 to the Present

To understand events in Zimbabwe in the period immediately after independence, it is necessary to grasp the overall geopolitical situation in southern Africa. This period was largely defined by the increasingly desperate attempts of the government of South Africa to maintain apartheid right up to the bitter end.

South Africa appeared to have lost its buffer zone. Angola, Mozambique and Zimbabwe were all independent states with African governments. The wind of change was now at South Africa's borders. In a last-ditch attempt to defend apartheid, the government of South Africa adopted a desperate strategy. The Republic of South Africa began to wage war on its neighbours (Hanlon, 1986).

The seeds of this assault by South Africa had been sown by the government of Rhodesia. Ken Flower was a police officer with experience in Kenya in the 1950s. He became head of the Central Intelligence Organization (CIO), which operated out of Prime Minister Ian Smith's office. It was apparent that an independent Mozambique under a Frelimo government posed a serious threat to Rhodesia. The CIO determined on a course of destabilizing Mozambique. To this end, it established an anti-Frelimo group called Renamo (Mozambique National Resistance—MNR). Once Zimbabwe was independent with an African government that was friendly towards the government of Mozambique, there was no reason to continue to support Renamo. After 1980 South Africa took over financing and supporting Renamo. Renamo, which devastated much of rural Mozambique, was noted for its extreme brutality (Magaia, 1988).

The depredations of the MNR's armed bandits (*bandidos armadas*) had an unexpected effect on Zimbabwe. Like many other African countries, Zimbabwe is landlocked. After independence, its main link to the rest of the world was through the Mozambican port of Beira. Harare was linked to Beira by the 'Beira Corridor', which was made up of a road, a line of rail, and an oil pipeline. The MNR attacked the Corridor regularly. By 1989 half of Zimbabwe's army was deployed along the Corridor in an attempt to protect it against Renamo attacks.

After it had decided to withdraw from Africa, Portugal had no difficulty deciding what to do in Mozambique. Frelimo was the only significant nationalist organization and, in 1975, Portugal handed over power to Frelimo.

The situation in Angola was less clear; indeed, it was totally unclear. There were three liberation movements: The People's Movement for the Liberation of Angola (MPLA), the National Union for the Total Independence of Angola (UNITA), and the Angolan National Liberation Front (FNLA). The Portuguese did not know what to do and simply bugged out. Civil war amongst the three parties noted broke out. The MPLA had a generally Marxist – Leninist political orientation and strong ties to the USSR. South Africa did not want to see the MPLA become the government of Angola and in 1975 it made a major strategic error, one which led directly to the end of apartheid. The South African Defence Force (SADF) invaded Angola from bases in the Caprivi Strip in order to forestall an MPLA government. The Cuban army intervened to support the MPLA and, as a result, war between the Cubans and the SADF ensued. This culminated in 1988 in a major battle in southeastern Angola near a town called Cuito Cuanavale.

The battle raged throughout most of 1988. Cuito Cuanavale can be seen as southern Africa's Dien Bien Phu and as a historical turning point on the order of Gettysburg, Midway and Stalingrad. The SADF was badly defeated. Cuito Cuanavale was a major set-piece battle with tanks, artillery and aircraft being used by both sides. The SADF lost many of its modern aircraft—Mirages and Mystères. Because of an international arms embargo, the SADF was not able to replace these losses. My surmise is that, stripped of much of their airpower, the senior officers of the SADF advised the government that apartheid could no longer be maintained. Thus, Cuito Cuanavale meant the end of apartheid. In February 1990, Nelson Mandela was released from prison and apartheid was over (Mungazi, 1988).

It was at the beginning of this dramatic and volatile period that Robert Mugabe began his work to establish an independent Zimbabwe. The immediate tasks confronting Mugabe and ZANU – PF in early 1980 were to make the ceasefire work and to prepare for the election. The election was held in March 1980 and was a triumph for Mugabe. ZANU – PF won 57 of the 80 African seats in the House of Assembly, thereby gaining a clear majority of the 100 seats in the House. The governor installed Mugabe as prime minister of Zimbabwe. The prime minister went on radio and television to address the nation. His theme was reconciliation. He announced that there would be two white ministers in his government. General Walls was asked to be the Commander of the new Zimbabwe National Army, which was to be formed by merging ZIPRA, ZANLA and the Rhodesian Army (Martin and Johnson, 1981, pp. 330 – 331). This did have certain legal consequences. Zimbabwe's air force was a museum of the British aircraft industry. While the Zimbabwe Air Force did have jet fighters, these were ancient—Hawker Hunters, Gloucester Meteors and deHaviland Vampires. In 1983 several of these aircraft were destroyed on the ground. Suspicion immediately focussed on white officers in the Air Force and several white officers were detained.[6]

A ceremony was held at Rufaro Stadium in Salisbury on 18 April 1980 to formally recognize the independence of the Republic of Zimbabwe. The Constitution of Zimbabwe was not ideal. There was to be a ceremonial president as head of state. The prime minister was head of government. Twenty per cent of the seats in the House of Assembly had been allocated to just over 4% of the population. This was, unfortunately, too reminiscent of voting arrangements in Southern Rhodesia. The constitution stipulated further that the provision creating the 20 seats for whites in the House of Assembly could not be amended for seven years. The property rights guarantee looked to many like an attempt to put the Land Apportionment Act of 1930 on a permanent basis. The key features of this guarantee were:

- as a principle, property could not be acquired compulsorily by the state;
- anyone whose property the state wished to acquire was guaranteed access to the High Court, where the state would be required to justify the acquisition;

- if the state did acquire property, the former owner had a right to compensation, not just 'fair', 'adequate', or 'reasonable' compensation, but 'full' compensation;
- when compensation was to be paid, the former owner was entitled to receive the compensation in a currency of his choice.

Many Zimbabweans saw the property guarantee as a challenge. For the first decade after independence land was the primary political issue in Zimbabwe. As a practical matter, the property rights guarantee could not be amended for 10 years after independence (Hatchard, 1991a, p. 79).

In the early years after independence, the rule of law was generally observed and Zimbabwe was governed in accordance with its constitution. The white seats in the House of Assembly and the property guarantee were regularly and aggressively criticized. A certain amount of decolonization did take place. In 1982 the capital, Salisbury, was renamed Harare; at the same time Fort Victoria was renamed Masvingo.

White farmers were urged to sell their land on what was called a 'willing-buyer-willing-seller' basis. Farmers who sold their land were compensated by the state. In 1987 it became practically possible to make substantial changes to the constitution. The 20 white seats in the house of Assembly were abolished by the Sixth Amendment to the Constitution. The Seventh Amendment to the Constitution created an executive president. The first president of Zimbabwe had been the Rev. Canaan Banana. He stepped aside to allow Robert Mugabe to move into the new, enhanced presidency.

Mugabe's treatment of his predecessor was, in my opinion, shoddy, callous and graceless. The available evidence suggests that Banana was bisexual. His sexual dalliances with male employees at State House became something of a national scandal. He was charged with committing sodomy and unnatural acts and placed on trial. The ex-president was found guilty in 1999 and sentenced to one year in prison. He died on 10 November 2003 (Meldrum, 2003). A more humane man than Mugabe might have intervened to spare Banana the humiliation and indignity to which he was subjected. It is difficult to avoid asking whether the fact that Banana was Ndebele had anything to do with the way he was treated. In August 1987 I visited State House in Harare to have tea with President Banana, who was a gracious, charming and thoroughly delightful host.

While the rule of law was generally observed during the 1980s, the various constitutional amendments which were adopted definitely paved the way for what was to come. One commentator observed that "overall the eleven constitutional amendments have led to a strengthening of presidential power and a consequent weakening of the safeguards thereon" (Hatchard, 1991a, p. 101).

The commitment to the rule of law was tested by two judicial decisions in the late 1980s. The Supreme Court of Zimbabwe found that corporal punishment was "inhuman and degrading" and abolished it.[7] The response of the legislature was to overrule the decisions by amending the constitution to permit the inflicting of corporal punishment on juveniles (Hatchard, 1991b).

What follows may be difficult to grasp in the light of recent events, but in 1990 the Supreme Court of Zimbabwe delivered a judgement which is remarkable for the depth and the strength of its commitment to maintaining the rule of law.[8]

Ian Smith was the prime minister of Southern Rhodesia who issued UDI in 1965. After the ceasefire in the war, Smith was not murdered, he was not imprisoned, his property was not confiscated, and he was not forced to leave the country. In fact, he remained at liberty, continued to enjoy his considerable wealth, and was elected to parliament in 1980 and 1985. In 1986 Smith travelled to the UK and gave a television interview in which he asserted that African rule was ruining Zimbabwe. The House of Assembly reprimanded Smith for making these remarks.

In 1987 Smith went to South Africa and spoke out in favour of apartheid. This time, the House of Assembly suspended Smith and stopped his pay and allowances. The Supreme Court subsequently held that the Speaker of the House, Edwin Mutasa, had acted unlawfully and quashed the orders suspending Smith and stopping his pay.

Since this became an issue later, it may be helpful to look at the composition of the court which ruled in Smith's favour. The court consisted of Chief Justice Dumbutshena (Martin, 1987), the first African to be Chief Justice; Justice Gubbay, a white Zimbabwean; Justice McNally, an Irishman; Justice Korsah, a black Ghanaian; and Justice Manyarara, a black Zimbabwean.

The Mugabe government's first major assault on the rule of law took place in 1983. In that year, Mugabe unleashed the *gukurahundi* against the Ndebele people. *Gukurahundi* is a Shona word denoting the seasonal rains that wash away the detritus of the previous year's crops. It signifies purging and purification (Power, 2003). Mugabe's Fifth Brigade, trained in the Democratic People's Republic of Korea (North Korea), rampaged through Ndebele country, murdering, raping, pillaging and burning. Twenty-five thousand Ndebele may have died.

But the land question would not go away. In 2000 Mugabe began a major assault on white Zimbabweans. This destroyed the rule of law, the economy, and just about everything else in Zimbabwe. The situation had got so bad by 2003 that Doris Lessing felt obliged to speak out. She noted that, just before independence in 1980, President Nyerere of Tanzania and President Machel of Mozambique had both spoken to Mugabe. They said, "You have the jewel of Africa in your hands...Now look after it". Lessing continued: "Twenty-three years later, the 'jewel' is ruined, dishonoured, disgraced" (Lessing 2003).

Just about every word uttered by Mugabe, the government and ZANU during the process of the seizure of European-owned farms was a lie. The goons carrying out the seizures were regularly described as 'war veterans'. In the mid-1980s the people who had actually fought during the liberation struggle were called 'ex-combatants'. Many ex-combatants were given warm thanks and gratuities of a few hundred Zim dollars, but most were forgotten. It should be recalled that there was a ceasefire in December 1979. Based on my viewing of television news coverage of the farm seizures, I can only surmise that, if any one of the so-called 'war veterans' had actually fought during the liberation struggle, he must have been three years old at the time. The seizure of the farms was often called the 'third *Chimurenga*'. It was a gross calumny of the brave patriots who fought in the 1890s and 1970s to suggest a connection between them and the drunken, racist thugs who carried out ethnic cleansing from 2000 to 2002. The official justification for the farm seizures went roughly as follows: 'They stole our land and we are simply taking back what is rightfully ours'. This, too, was a lie.

Nearly two-thirds of these farmers had bought their farms after independence and thus held titles issued not by Ian Smith or the British colonial regime but by the Mugabe government. (Power, 2003).

The year 2000 was a turning point in the history of Zimbabwe because it was in that year that the seizures of the white-owned, or perhaps more accurately, 'commercial' farms began and the country was launched on its descent into barbarism and anarchy. Why should this have happened in 2000? I cannot give a precise answer to that question, but some informed speculation may be helpful. There seem to have been three factors. The first is South Africa's aggression against its neighbours during the death throes of apartheid. The brutality with which South Africa's surrogates had ravaged the region was hardly calculated to promote amicable and productive relations between blacks and whites anywhere in southern Africa. Second, of course, was the land question in Zimbabwe. The fact that, 20 years after independence, Europeans still owned large and lucrative farms was a standing provocation to many Zimbabweans. The third factor is political. Robert Mugabe's party, ZANU (PF), had been in power since independence and its power seemed to be beyond challenge. In 2000 President Mugabe had put forward proposals for constitutional change. The proposed changes would have entrenched and expanded the president's powers. The proposals were defeated, largely because of the efforts of Morgan Tsvangarai, a trade union leader. One result of this exercise was the formation of an opposition political party, the Movement for Democratic Change (MDC), led by Tsvangarai (Meldrum, 2000). Mugabe was deeply upset by these political setbacks and tended to see Tsvangarai as both an ally and a puppet of the whites. It is, I believe, the confluence of the three factors noted which explains why the farm seizures began when they did.

On 15 February 2000 the Mugabe government lost a referendum on its package of constitutional changes. On 16 February the so-called war veterans began occupying commercial farms (International Bar Association, 2001). The number of farm seizures increased in March 2000. On 17 March the High Court ordered that the seizures stop and that the police remove illegal occupiers from farms. These orders were disregarded. On 16 April President Mugabe ordered the police not to enforce orders of the High Court. Verbal attacks were made on the judges, especially the judges who were white. In November 2000 a gang of 200 so-called war veterans attacked the Supreme Court in central Harare. These thugs jumped on tables and shouted: "Kill the judges".

The Zimbabwe government neither prosecuted any of these goons nor condemned their behaviour. The leader of these so-called war veterans was a physician named Chenjerai Hunzvi. Hunzvi gave himself the *nom de guerre* 'Hitler'. Hunzvi's choice of sobriquet was carefully calculated to cause as much humiliation as possible for white Zimbabweans. During the Second World War many Rhodesians had fought in the British armed forces. The best known of these Rhodesians was probably Marshal of the Royal Air Force Sir Arthur Travers Harris. Commonly known as 'Bomber Harris', he was Air Officer Commanding-in-Chief RAF Bomber Command. Ian Smith was a fighter pilot in the RAF. Photographs of Smith show a badly scarred face, the result of a Spitfire crash.

It will be tedious to continue to call Hunzvi's thugs who seized the farms the 'so-called war veterans'. Since most of these goons were young, and since they were led by a man who called himself 'Hitler', it may make sense to call them the 'Hitler Youth'.

Verbal attacks on the judges continued and intensified. In December 2000 President Mugabe described the judges as guardians of the "white racist commercial farmers". In January 2001 Mugabe publicly accused Chief Justice Anthony Gubbay of aiding and abetting racism. I know Tony Gubbay and respect and admire him. Any accusation that he might have been a racist is both grotesque and laughable. It is worth remembering that Mugabe himself had appointed Gubbay Chief Justice of Zimbabwe. In March 2001 Chief Justice Gubbay resigned. The International Bar Association delegation to Zimbabwe concluded that he was 'forced' from office.

I met Anthony Gubbay in 1997 at the School of Law, Trinity College, Dublin at the first African Workshop on Constitutional Government. This gathering was a one-week seminar for the Chief Justices of Commonwealth African states. Gubbay established warm and productive relations with his African fellow judges. He seemed to be especially friendly with the Chief Justices of two of Zimbabwe's neighbours— Richard Banda of Malawi and Matthews Ngulube of Zambia. The Workshop became an annual fixture and Gubbay was in regular attendance. He arrived at the 2001 Workshop in August of that year, only a few months after his ordeal at the hands of Mugabe, Hunzvi, and the Hitler Youth. It was touching to observe the genuine warmth and sympathy with which the African judges welcomed him.

The final event of the 2001 Workshop was a dinner at the King's Inns in Dublin, the headquarters of the Irish bar. At the end of the dinner two African judges made speeches about Gubbay. Each criticized Mugabe for having attacked and subverted the rule of law, praised Gubbay for his courage and integrity, and called on him to return to Zimbabwe in order to continue his work for his country. When the speeches concluded, all the African judges stood to applaud Gubbay. Many were in tears. This was a magnificent moment, one which I shall treasure as a highlight of my legal career.

Conclusion

The seizure of farms by the Hitler Youth destroyed the rule of law in Zimbabwe. What the Hitler Youth did is, in my view, best described as a drunken orgy of murder, rape and destruction. Did it accomplish anything worthwhile or of value to Zimbabwe?

Southern Africa is an arid region. Indeed, two of the countries in the region— Botswana and Namibia—are largely desert. Water is scarce and essential. It is worth reflecting on the coat of arms of the Republic of Botswana. The national motto is *Pula*, the seTswana word for rain. The national currency is called the Pula.

There are no naturally occurring lakes in Zimbabwe. The two largest—Lake Kariba and Lake Kyle—were created by damming rivers. The commercial farms in Zimbabwe were highly productive. The main reason for this productivity was the fact that these farms were heavily capitalized, being equipped with a great deal of farm machinery and, most important, irrigation systems.

When the Hitler Youth seized these farms, its thugs destroyed all the farm machinery, including the irrigation systems. So the Hitler Youth took highly productive farms and turned them into barren plots of land bereft of any agricultural value. Looked at in this light, the unleashing of the Hitler Youth can only be seen as the act of a madman and a traitor. A rational programme of land reform would have been highly desirable and might have been a great benefit to Zimbabwe. The so-called 'third *Chimurenga*' was land *destruction*, not land *reform*.

Acknowledgements

In June 2005 an earlier version of this essay was delivered as a public lecture at the School of Law, Trinity College Dublin. The author wishes to thank Barbara Martin, Frances Lethbridge and Marianne Welch for their generous and capable assistance.

Notes

1. Re Southern Rhodesia, [1919] AC 211 (J.C.).
2. *Ibid.*
3. [1919] AC at 217.
4. R. v. The Earl of Crewe; ex parte Sekgome [1910] 2 K.B. 576 (C.A.} and Wallace-Johnson v. R. [1940] A.C. 231 (J.C.).
5. Madzimbamuto v. Lardner-Burke [1969] 1 A.C. 645 (J.C.).
6. Austin and another v. Chairman of Detainees' Review Tribunal and another [1988] L.R.C. (Const.) 532.
7. Ncube v. S. [1988] L.R.C. (Const.) 442 and A Juvenile v. S. [1989] L.R.C. (Const.) 774.
8. Smith v. Mutasa [1990] LRC (Const) 87.

References

Barnett, D. L. and Njama, K. (1966) *Mau Mau from Within* (New York: Monthly Review Press).
Buell, R. L. (1965) *The Native Problem in Africa*, Vol. 1 (London: Cassell).
Caute, D. (1983) *Under the Skin: The Death of White Rhodesia* (Evanston, IL: Northwestern University Press).
Christie, I. (1988) *Machel of Mozambique* (Harare: Zimbabwe Publishing House).
The Commonwealth Yearbook (1999) (London: Hanson Cooke).
deSmith, S. A. (1964) *The New Commonwealth and its Constitutions* (London: Stevens and Sons).
Dilley, M. R. (1966) *British Policy in Kenya Colony* (London: Cassell).
Hall, R. (1969) *The High Price of Principles: Kaunda and the White South* (London: Penguin).
Hanlon, J. (1986) *Beggar Your Neighbours: Apartheid Power in Southern Africa* (Bloomington, IN: Indiana University Press).
Hatchard, J. (1991a) The Constitution of Zimbabwe: towards a model for Africa?, *Journal of African Law*, 35(1–2), pp. 79–91.
Hatchard, J. (1991b) The fall and rise of the cane in Zimbabwe, *Journal of African Law*, 35(1–2), pp. 198–204.
Horne, A. (1987) *A Savage War of Peace: Algeria 1954–1962* (London: Papermac).
International Bar Association (2001) *Report of Zimbabwe Mission, 2001* (London: IBA).
International Commission of Jurists (1988) *South Africa: Human Rights and the Rule of Law* (London: Pinter).
Itote, W. (1967) *Mau Mau General* (Nairobi: East African Publishing House).
Keatley, P. (1968) *The Politics of Partnership* (London: Penguin).
Lessing, D. (2003) The jewel of Africa, *The New York Review of Books*, 10 April.
Loewenstein, K. (1963) Reflections on the value of constitutions in our revolutionary age, in D. E. Apter and H. Eckstein (Eds), *Comparative Politics* (New York: Free Press).

Magaia, L. (1988) *Dumba Nengue: Run for Your Life* (Trenton, NJ: Africa World Press).

Martin, D. and Johnson, P. (1981) *The Struggle for Zimbabwe* (London: Faber).

Martin, R. (1985) Rethinking 'law and development', *Journal of Modern African Studies*, 23(1), pp. 133–137.

Martin, R. (1987) Zimbabwe's Chief Justice: a witness to changing times, *The Lawyers Weekly*, 11 September.

McAuslan, J. P. W. B. (1974) Prolegomenon to the Rule of Law in East Africa, reprinted in R. Martin, *Personal Freedom and the Law in Tanzania* (Nairobi: Oxford University Press).

Meldrum, A. (2000) Worker's hero and thorn in side of Mugabe, *The Guardian*, 27 April.

Meldrum, A. (2003) Canaan Banana, president jailed in sex scandal, dies, *The Guardian*, 11 November.

Minter, W. (1972) *Portuguese Africa and the West* (London: Penguin).

Mungazi, D. A. (1988) *The Last Defenders of the Laager: Ian D. Smith and F. W. de Klerk* (Westport, CT: Praeger).

Nwabueze, B. O. (1973) *Constitutionalism in the Emergent States* (London: Hurst).

Power, S. (2003) How to kill a country, *Atlantic Monthly*, December 2003.

Ranger, T. O. (1967) *Revolt in Southern Rhodesia* (London: Heinemann).

Seidman, R. (1969) The reception of English law in Africa revisited, *Eastern Africa Law Review*, 2(1), pp. 47–85.

Slinn, P. (1991) A fresh start for Africa? New African constitutional perspectives for the 1990s, *Journal of African Law*, 35(1–2), pp. 1–7.

Thompson, E. P. (1975) *Whigs and Hunters: The Origin of the Black Act* (London: Allen Lane).

Burnt Toast and Manhood: Gendered Imaginings of the Nation in 1990s Popular Fiction

RANKA PRIMORAC
New York University in London, UK

Introduction

In 1993, in her influential sociology of Zimbabwean writing, Flora Veit-Wild asserted that black and white Zimbabwean literary traditions stemmed from "completely different social and political background[s]" (Veit-Wild, 1993, p. 6) and could therefore not be studied alongside each other. In 2005, in contrast, Kizito Muchemwa examined a selection of texts belonging to both traditions and stated: "although emerging from traditions that differ in style, [these texts] address the same historical experience" (Muchemwa, 2005, p. 202).

This essay is in alignment with Muchemwa's view, on which it wishes to elaborate and expand. Zimbabwean texts of all kinds have always been united by a *national* space-time of origin, despite colonial regimes' attempts to carve up this space along racial lines. It is arguable that Zimbabwe's "unique but multiple historical experience as a nation" (Chennells, 1993, p. 127) is complexly inscribed in texts belonging to *both* traditions. Furthermore, the work of scholars such as Kaarsholm (1991) and Chiwome (1998) on the war novel, Harris (2005) and Muponde (2005) on representations of childhood and Wylie (2005) on poetry and landscape, shows how recurring textual figures can converge and interweave, helping to create cross-racial repertoires of culturally endorsed meanings. In studying how such cultural codifications are modified and contested over time, scholars should avoid focusing solely on what Drew Shaw, in this collection, calls "towers on the literary landscape". I have argued elsewhere (Primorac, 2005) for the need to pay attention to the non-canonical and popular Zimbabwean texts of all kinds. This essay focuses on the constructions of masculinity and the nation in two such texts, one written by a white and the other by a black male Zimbabwean writer, both published in 1995: Roland K. Hill's *Burnt Toast on Sundays* and Vitalis Nyawaranda's *The Swinging Graduate*.

Imagining the nation has always gone hand in hand with "the inscription of specific symbolic roles for male and female historical actors" (Boehmer, 2005, p. 5), and it is arguable that Zimbabwean African nationalisms have never been anything other than patriarchal (see, for example, Kaler, 1998; Sylvester, 1999; Ansell, 2001; Campbell, 2003). This reading of novels by Hill and Nyawaranda is performed against the background of the most recent official Zimbabwean nationalist narrative—the 'patriotic history' that came into being at the last turn of the century, accompanied by the violent land redistribution officially known as 'The Third *Chimurenga*' (uprising).

'Patriotic history' is built around the assertion of fixity and continuity of historical claims and identities (see Ranger, 2004). It establishes an unbroken link between the goals and methods of all phases of Zimbabwe's anti-colonial resistance, and locates the origin of authentic African agency in 'traditionally' understood rural spaces and values—which are, in turn, grounded in certain normative understandings of femininity and masculinity. An *Introduction to Shona Culture* explains that, in rural Shona societies, "the complementarity between the sexes is encouraged, [and] mores that govern it are laid down and transmitted to children at the earliest possible age" (Mutswairo *et al.*, 1996, p. 52). In arguing against the calls for a new constitution in Zimbabwe recently, Robert Mugabe has said: "In our own societies in Africa, when a man turns into a woman or a woman into a man, we say 'aah, there is something wrong, he or she is abnormal'" (Mugabe, 2005, p. 9). Members of the opposition, Mugabe was implying, had, in proposing constitutional amendments, transgressed against the normatively patriotic—that is, male—identities. Paradoxically, this fixing of gendered roles and fixation on rural spaces links Mugabe's 'patriotic history' with its arch enemy—Iain Smith's version of Rhodesian (settler colonial) nationalist narrative, against which it purports to still be battling. Rooted in discourses of the Empire, Rhodesian settler myths also locate the origin of the nation in an archetypal maleness, which comes into being far from the city spaces—through the conquering of the untamed bush (on this, see Chennells, 1982). This parallel should not come as a surprise: as John Day (1975) has pointed out, African and settler nationalist discourses have been locked in a relationship of mutual echoing and reproduction since the 1960s.

The mid-1990s—the time of publication of Hill's and Nyawaranda's novels—were a time of transition in Zimbabwean politics and culture. The official insistence on the rhetoric of socialism and 'reconciliation' between the races was over, but the full-scale, officially endorsed renewal of racial animosities was as yet half a decade away. In 1995 Robert Mugabe stunned the nation by marrying his former secretary, with whom, it was revealed, he already had two children. While some commentators pointed out that the rise in the regime's corruption seemed to coincide with the president's opulent Christian wedding, others noted that the reaffirmation of the ageing president's virility increased his 'representativeness' in a society that had always placed a high premium on family life (see Chan, 2003, p. 99). 1995 was also the year of parliamentary elections. Joshua Nkomo was still alive, the Movement for Democratic Change (MDC)—the only opposition party that has posed Mugabe's ZANU (PF) a serious threat—had not yet been formed, and Mugabe received another full parliamentary mandate. But rumours of corruption were rife, the problem of HIV/AIDS was emerging into the foreground of the national consciousness, and the pre-election campaigning contained some scathing verbal attacks on the country's white community (Chan, 2003, p. 102).

In the field of literature the first generation of Zimbabwe's post-independence giants—Dambudzo Marechera, Stanley Nyamfukudza, Shimmer Chinodya, Chenjerai Hove and Tsitsi Dangarembga—had already started to interrogate a wide range of officially endorsed social constructs. But their texts thematized mostly the pre-independence era, and internationally acclaimed works by Alexander Kanengoni and Yvonne Vera, which combined stylistic experimentation with a scathing political critique of the post-independence period, had not yet appeared (on this, see Primorac, 2006). Hill's *Burnt Toast on Sundays* and Nyawaranda's *The Swinging Graduate* are unknown outside Zimbabwe and they have not attained canonical status inside the country: they belong to the masses of locally published popular and 'light' reading with which Zimbabwe's bookshops were flooded at the time. Such texts have, thus far, escaped critical attention almost completely. And yet they, too, are part of an era in which cultural products of all kinds contributed to the creation of a public sphere "where critical thinking, thought experiments, satire, dreams and utopias" (Kaarsholm, 2005, p. 22) were still to a large extent possible. It is precisely as 'thought experiments' regarding the interface of masculinity and the nation that this essay aims to read Hill's and Nyawaranda's works. On one level both these texts extol the 'traditional' family as the seedbed of the independent nation; in this sense they are harbingers of the cultural logic that is now asserting itself as dominant inside Zimbabwe. On another level, however, I will seek to show how they deconstruct this logic from the inside, giving the lie to the current 'patriotic' claim of absolute continuity of nationalist cultural traditions. Finally, it will be seen that the two texts echo and mirror each other in ways that might seem uncanny to those who would still insist on the complete apartness of black and white cultural forms. In destabilizing the notion of two racially separate cultural spheres, they undermine the key tenet of the current nationalist mythology in Zimbabwe.

Both *Burnt Toast on Sundays* and *The Swinging Graduate* tell stories about young Zimbabwean men in search of partners. Both appear to be set in the 1980s: characters in *Burnt Toast on Sundays* refer to seeing the Tom Cruise film *Top Gun*, whereas *The Swinging Graduate* is peppered with references to the policy of reconciliation and the recent arrival of independence. Their respective heroes, white rancher Tom and black university graduate Taurai, are physically attractive, middle-class young men who share the same basic problem: each is beseiged by local girls who wish to marry them—partly because of their obvious charm, handsomeness and wit, and partly because of the financial security they represent. Both Tom and Taurai reject the local girls and turn to partners who are from England; for both, this brings about unforeseen complications as the Englishwomen they have chosen do not fit in with the customs of the Zimbabwean countryside. In the end, both characters enter adulthood and are able to look with more understanding at the youthful phase of their respective lives.

In generic terms Hill's text falls within the tradition of 'settler-conservationist' popular writing, stemming from the colonial settler novel (as described in Chennells) and continued after independence by writes such as David Lemon (1983; 1998; n.d.), Emily C. Dibb (1981; 1989) and Keith Meadows (1996), all of whom produced narratives concerned with the preservation of Zimbabwean wildlife. On the other hand, the back cover of Nyawaranda's novel informs readers that he "already has to his credit ten published Shona novels and plays", and *The Swinging Graduate* can certainly be related to the oral literature-influenced didacticism of the Shona novelistic tradition, intent on both entertaining readers and edifying them in questions of morality (as explained by Chiwome, 1998). Both of these texts, however, strain the boundaries of such narrowly defined generic affiliation. By questioning the obviousness of categories to do with gender and nation, they also problematize the received notions of genre.

Burnt Toast and Manhood

The burnt toast from the title of Hill's comic novel refers to the hero's inability to perform the 'female' (that is to say, 'civilized' and 'domestic') action of cooking, and signifies his state of post-colonial bachelorhood. The opening chapter describes in detail his struggles with the kitchen utensils while making breakfast on a Sunday morning, but also specifies that he has no such problems on other days of the week, when his (black) maid Judith is on duty: "The awesomeness of Sundays without any domestic staff suddenly struck him. He would have to cook his own breakfast" (Hill, 1995, p. 3). (By way of anticipation and parallel it should be said that Nyarawanda's novel, too, is filled with references to food and cooking, none of it performed by the hero Taurai; it is all done for him at various stages of the novel by his different girlfriends.)

Hill's Tom Burnham is sole heir to a large piece of land—a cattle ranch near Gwanda in Matabeleland. Although prone to disasters in the kitchen, he is extremely proficient in the outdoors survival skills that have for generations been emphasized by settler literature as a mark of accomplished settler male identities: shooting, improvising solutions in the bush when charged by wild animals, cattle-dipping and the like. "There are a lot of dangerous wild animals about", Tom tells a prospective girlfriend, "but at the same time you have to remember that the most dangerous African wild animal is a man with a gun" (p. 136). He is also possessed of a farcical sense of humour, and a single, white, male best friend, with whom he has lived through innumerable outdoor escapades. In all this he resembles the protagonists of generations of earlier settler novels, including, for example, the hero of Cosbie Garstin's *The Sunshine Settlers*, originally published in 1918 (Garstin, 1971). In texts such as these (as Chennells has shown), white male identities are constituted through a series of oppositions: to white men from Europe/Britain, to white women, and to African natives.

Together with his physical toughness and resourcefulness in the wild, the chief signifier of the 'Africanness' of Tom's identity is his body: the novel constantly emphasizes the attraction of his green eyes, and, in an early chapter, he cannot hide "the swanky leanness and sinewy health of [his] twenty-four-year-old naked body" in the mirror (p. 2). His British brother-in-law Seldon, who appears in the last chapter, possesses precisely the opposite qualities: when Tom has to slaughter an ox for dinner, Seldon "faint[s] clean away", looks green and talks in a shaky, high-pitched voice (pp. 337–338).

When it comes to white women, the novel makes it clear that Tom is not eligible to big-city girls, because their habits are incompatible with life in the bush (see pp. 48–67). He is, however, immensely attractive to all the single girls in the neighbourhood. He tests potential marriage candidates by having them fry eggs for him in his kitchen; this novel, too, subscribes to the concept of 'complementariness' of male and female identities by insisting throughout on a strict division between male and female kinds of activity. During an outdoor picnic on the ranch, for example, the men "offered a round of drinks" while "the ladies followed by organizing plates of food" (p. 245). In an earlier chapter, a wife advises her husband to ask Tom for a loan by talking "some men's talk first; you know, about fishing and golf and ankles [sic] and the usual silly things men talk about when ladies aren't around" (p. 184). Tom's early encounters with women are described in terms of the stereotypical trope of the 'battle of the sexes'. On the other hand, when he starts courting Janet, the future Mrs. Burnham, she needs to be constantly protected and rescued from the dangers and mishaps involved in various outdoor activities and pursuits—until she finally learns that this kind of a life is to be her lot if she decides to marry Tom and live on the ranch.

In matters of sexuality Hill's novel looks back to a bygone era and insists on describing the process of courtship as completely asexual. Its young characters' entertainment in rural Matabeleland consists of a series of dances in formal evening wear; when Tom and Janet go to Victoria Falls, their relatives insist that they should be chaperoned and sleep in single bedrooms—and they conform without objecting. In keeping with this is the fact that the novel never envisages the possibility of Tom's future wife being non-white, despite being set in the countryside around Gwanda. When Tom runs out of marriage prospects in Zimbabwe, he in effect creates a new settler out of Janet, who is forced to undergo a transformation of identity in order to fulfil the requirements for the role of his wife. Clearly, no amount of egg-frying skills could ever make Tom contemplate a partnership with a non-white Zimbabwean woman—for instance the travel agency employee who sells him the plane ticket to London, and whose femininity is completely disregarded by the text.

The fact that Tom and Janet's key contribution to the Zimbabwean nation will be related to the preservation of its wildlife is also in keeping with settler texts and ideologies of the past. Tom's ranch is a safe haven for the endangered species of black rhino, and it is mishaps and dangers connected to one of the animals Tom keeps on his ranch that Janet must learn to survive and accept, if she is to internalize the values of her adopted home. Tom insists that the animal is not his property: "'It's not mine. It belongs to the nation'" (p. 261). In the novel's final chapter, which describes Tom and Janet's wedding, readers learn that the animals have reproduced—and when the wedding ceremony is attended by a 900-pound baby rhino, Janet shows her newfound stamina by not panicking as it plucks at her bouquet. The symbolism of the scene is unmistakable: the future of Zimbabwean wildlife is guaranteed by the existence of men like Tom Burnham. And so it would seem that, by extending and recreating the key tropes linked to the colonial concept of white colonial masculinity, Hill's novel is engaged in reproducing the national ideals of the past, and is, indeed, rejecting the possibility of a 'reconciled', racially integrated nation. But this is not entirely the case.

Although it cannot quite bring itself to transgress against the colonially produced interdiction against cross-racial intermarriage, *Burnt Toast on Sundays* is well aware that the nation to which it refers is not a colonial one. "'This is modern Zimbabwe'", says Tom in an early chapter (p. 14), and it is true that the white characters on whom the novel centres are accompanied by black ones, whom the text refers to in a non-racist manner. Chapter 8, for example, describes how Tom's friend Jimmy is proud to be promoted by his black boss Mr Chivonga, while Chapter 4 shows Tom responding to a call for the preservation of national wildlife resources issued by "Doctor Samuel Ndlovu of the Department of National Parks and Wildlife" (p. 71). Tom speaks Ndebele and listens to Afro-jazz; more importantly, the novel makes a point of not representing the white community it describes as an all-powerful national elite. It refers to it, instead, as "the small white community of Gwanda" (p. 86), thus placing the importance of its own romance-inflected narrative accurately on the scale of national-level events. Finally, the grotesquely farcical quality of one of the novel's sub-plots (to do with Mrs Hardgreeves, the future mother-in-law of Tom's friend Jimmy) lends the entire narrative a dream-like, emphatically conventional flavour, reminiscent of Ray Cooney's farces, which were often on the programme of Harare's Reps theatre at the time. This explodes any kind of realist-style verisimilitude *Burnt Toast on Sundays* may otherwise have appeared to aspire to. Although Hill's novel does not denounce or discredit the settler nationalist myths of the past, it may be said to undermine and modify them in a benevolent and self-knowing manner. In this, it resembles the work of Lemon and Dibb from the first two decades of independence. In the mid-1990s it may have seemed both possible and likely that hard-core 'Rhodesian' sentiments were gradually becoming a thing of the past.

Beds, Women and Graduates

In a tell-tale coincidence, both *Burnt Toast on Sundays* and *The Swinging Graduate* begin with descriptions of their heroes in bed, first thing in the morning. But while, in keeping with *Burnt Toast*'s general air of chastity, Hill's Tom Burnham wakes up alone on his ranch on a woman-less Sunday morning, readers of Vitalis Nyawaranda's *The Swinging Graduate* first encounter its hero, Tendai Gore, as seen through the eyes of a female lover: "She found him lying on the bed with his face up" (Nyawaranda, 1995, p. 3). The 'swinging' of the novel's title refers to Taurai's progress through the beds of several girlfriends, all of whom wish to make him their husband. White men pose no threat to Taurai, and *Burnt Toast on Sundays* tells us why. But *The Swinging Graduate* resembles Hill's novel in referring to male–female relationship in terms of male 'conquest'. From the point of view of female characters, on the other hand, Taurai is, like Tom, a desirable marital 'catch'. This, however, is not because he possesses a large area of commercially viable land. In fact, in an early chapter of the novel Taurai refers to the fact that land ownership is a part of the nation's unfinished business—something that *Burnt Toast on Sundays* remains conspicuously silent about. "'Land is entrusted to [peasants] by the state, in fact, by the headman, who in turn has land entrusted to him by a chief. It is the chief who is ultimately answerable to the state. The pastureland is owned communally. At least this was the order of things before Independence. A new order may emerge now that we have gained our independence'" (p. 47). Taurai's desirability as a husband stems from the fact that he is a university graduate and has a government teaching job: he can therefore lend financial security to the black Zimbabwean woman he marries— once he has finished paying the *lobola* or bride-price to her family, and provided financial help to his own parents and siblings.

This points to another difference between Tom and Taurai: both have inherited strong links to the countryside from their elders. But for Taurai, unlike for Tom, this means financial obligations rather than privileges—and Taurai's obligations include a debt to the nation:

> Funny that not so long ago, they, as students, had taken part in a demonstration of solidarity in which they pledged their unstinting support for the government's efforts to bring light to all corners of the country, particularly the remotest areas that had hitherto been neglected by the colonial regime. (p. 5)

While a key aspect of Tom's masculine identity resides in the qualities and actions of his body, in Taurai's case it is his intellect—which has been developed by the state through university education—and he is now obliged to pay off the debt in the neglected and problematic rural segments of the national space. And so, while Tom has had enough of obligation-free Sundays, Taurai longs for more of them, and he longs to fill them with the kind of sexual escapades unthinkable in the world of Hill's novel.

Taurai is pursued by two women: Spiwe, a street-smart fellow graduate who inhabits city spaces and is therefore linked with moral decay and corruption, and Joyce, the innocent and chaste childhood sweetheart whom his family has long expected him to marry. Nyawaranda's novel has inherited the city/country binary foregrounded in colonial-era novels in indigenous languages (on this, see Veit-Wild, 1993), which is also underscored by the currently official preference for the 'African authenticity' of Zimbabwe's rural areas. The rural/urban spatial opposition appears to be upheld at the end of Nyawaranda's novel, where, after much 'swinging', Taurai returns to his family's rural home, leaving behind both the city and Spiwe, and their corrupt and dangerous ways:

> He remembered the games they used to play on the sandy banks of Nyahove river, and the secret village loves that were inevitably followed by marriages. He longed for those village dances under the brightly moonlit nights of the winter months in the village. They would dance all night away in wild abandon to the throbbing rhythms of the African drums. (p. 176)

But the novel also complicates and undermines the clear-cut city/country dualism by introducing Taurai's third lover, who links both spaces with the world outside Zimbabwe: the English girl Louise, whom he meets while teaching in the countryside and whom he ends up living with in Harare.

Louise resembles Hill's Janet in that she, too, learns to become Zimbabwean: in her case, this means learning a local language (Shona) and endorsing the official government policies of Marxism and socialism. But, while Tom is able to answer negatively when his friend Cliff asks him whether he has "got a girl into trouble" (Hill, 1995, p. 9), Taurai (whose friend Leo encourages his city-bred promiscuity) does make Louise pregnant—and this is where *The Swinging Graduate* most seriously diverges from both the anachronism of Hill's moral stance and the purity of the present-day official view of the Zimbabwean countryside. For, when at the novel's end Taurai decides to return to the village, he also decides to take his son Tatenda with him—even though this son is mixed race, and his mother has been rejected by Taurai's traditionally minded family. Despite all this, Taurai plans to integrate the boy into village life, and insists on minimizing the racial difference between them: "Although he had not met the boy, he could imagine him looking very much like him, the father, save for the skin colour and hair, perhaps" (p. 176). In addition, Taurai will be returning to the countryside alone: his promiscuity has caused him to be abandoned by *all* of his lovers (Spiwe, Joyce and Louise), and this compromises his 'traditionalist' view that "In African culture, a man was free to move wherever he wanted and with whomever he chose, at whatever hour suited him" (Nyawaranda, 1995, p. 104). Ultimately in *The Swinging Graduate* neither normative masculinity nor the rural spaces can, in themselves, function as the source of stable identities, harmonious domesticity or national fulfilment.

Several ironies contained in the text of *The Swinging Graduate* contribute towards complicating the currently official image of an idyllic, rural-based nation. First, the fact that Taurai—a pillar of the independent nation—turns out to have spent the war of liberation in Iain Smith's army, and this, rather than merely the Shona 'tradition', is what causes his family to reject Louise: their son's involvement with white people has caused them enough complications (at the hands of the nationalist guerrillas) already:

> You know very well that we have just come out of a bloody war with these Boers. How can you bring us the very snake whose head we were struggling to smash only yesterday? Will they not say we've been collaborators all along? Do you still remember how the boys nearly killed us when they discovered you had joined Smith's army? For these reasons, we say your wife-to-be is unwelcome in this homestead (p. 78).

A white daughter-in-law is as unwelcome in Taurai's home milieu as a black one would presumably have been in Tom's. But unlike *Burnt Toast on Sundays*, the *Swinging Graduate* allows for the possibility of cross-racial affection and compatibility: Taurai and Louise are united by both class and education, and Taurai cannot agree with the views expressed by his mother.

Second, the implication of the government at the heart of urban corruption: Spiwe, Taurai's former lover from the university and the embodiment of city-based temptation, is revealed to be working for Zimbabwe's secret service and sleeping with her newly rich bosses, who drive Mercedes cars and threaten Taurai with violence. Finally, the fact that, in the novel, university students (the would-be bringers of light to the neglected countryside) turn out to be instrumental in both spreading the HIV/AIDS infection in the city and in preventing information about it from being made public (p. 107; for a history of the official silence about the AIDS pandemic, see the article by Sunanda Ray and Farai Madzimbamuto in this issue). All this goes a long way towards undoing both the neatness of the city/country opposition and the alignment of the countryside with nationally desirable masculinities. In this respect *The Swinging Graduate* resembles the late works of Marechera (1980), Mungoshi (1997) and Chinodya (1998). In the 2000s official discourses underwent a hardening with regard to the types of gendered identities that were considered properly 'patriotic'. But if Zimbabwean popular fiction is anything to go by, just over a decade ago this cultural slide seemed neither likely nor inevitable.

References

Ansell, N. (2001) "Because it's our culture!" (Re)negotiating the meaning of *Lobola* in Southern African secondary schools, *Journal of Southern African Studies*, 27(4), pp. 697–716.

Boehmer, E. (2005) *Stories of Women: Gender and Narrative in the Postcolonial Nation* (Manchester: Manchester University Press).

Campbell, H. (2003) *Reclaiming Zimbabwe: The Exhaustion of the Patriarchal Model of Liberation* (Cape Town: David Phillips and Trenton, NJ: Africa World Press).

Chan, S. (2003) *Robert Mugabe: A Life of Power and Violence* (Ann Arbor, MI: University of Michigan Press).

Chennells, A. J. (1993) Marxist and Pan-Africanist literary theories and a sociology of Zimbabwean literature, *Zambezia*, 20(2), pp. 109–129.

Chennells, A. J. (1982) Settler myths and the Southern Rhodesian novel, PhD thesis, University of Zimbabwe.

Chinodya, S. (1998) *Can We Talk and Other Stories* (Harare: Baobab Books).

Chiwome, E. M. (1998) The interface of orality and literacy in the Zimbabwean novel, *Research in African Literatures*, 29(2), pp. 1–22.

Day, J. (1975) The creation of political myths: African nationalism in Southern Rhodesia, *Journal of Southern African Studies*, 2(1), pp. 52–65.

Dibb, C. E. (1981) *Ivory, Apes and Peacocks* (Bulawayo: Books of Zimbabwe).

Dibb, C. E. (1989) *The Conundrum Trees* (Harare: Modus Publications).

Garstin, C. (1971) *The Sunshine Settlers* (Bulawayo: Books of Rhodesia).

Harris, A. (2005) Writing home: inscriptions of whiteness/descriptions of belonging in white Zimbabwean memoir/autobiography, in R. Muponde and R. Primorac (Eds), *Versions of Zimbabwe: New Approaches to Literature and Culture*, pp. 103–117 (Harare: Weaver Press).

Hill, R. K. (1995) *Burnt Toast on Sundays* (Harare: HarperCollins).

Kaarsholm, P. (1991) From decadence to authenticity and beyond: fantasies and mythologies of war in Rhodesia and Zimbabwe, 1965–1985, in P. Kaarsholm (Ed.), *Cultural Struggle and Development in Southern Africa*, pp. 33–60 (Harare: Baobab Books).

Kaarsholm, P. (2005) Coming to terms with violence: literature and the development of a public sphere in Zimbabwe, in R. Muponde and R. Primorac (Eds), *Versions of Zimbabwe: New Approaches to Literature and Culture*, pp. 3–23 (Harare: Weaver Press).

Kaler, A. (1998) A threat to the nation and a threat to the men: the banning of depo-provera in Zimbabwe, 1981, *Journal of Southern African Studies*, 24(2), pp. 347–376.

Lemon, D. (1983) *Ivory Madness* (Harare: College Press).

Lemon, D. (1998) *Killer Cat* (Harare: College Press Publishers).

Lemon, D. (n.d.) *Hobo Rows Kariba* (Harare: African Publishing Group).

Marechera, D. (1980) *Black Sunlight* (Oxford: Heinemann).

Meadows, K. (1996) *Sand in the Wind* (Bulawayo: Thorntree Press).

Muchemwa, K. (2005) Some thoughts on history, memory and writing in Zimbabwe, in R. Muponde and R. Primorac (Eds), *Versions of Zimbabwe: New Approaches to Literature and Culture*, pp. 195–202 (Harare: Weaver Press).

Mugabe, R. (2005) We won't go back to the Commonwealth, *New African*, 441, pp. 6–12.

Mungoshi, C. (1997) *Walking Still* (Harare: Baobab Books).

Muponde, R. (2005) Children of resistance: childhood, history and the production of nationhood in two Zimbabwean novels, in R. Muponde and R. Primorac, *Versions of Zimbabwe: New Approaches to Literature and Culture*, pp. 119–130 (Harare: Weaver Press).

Mutswairo, S., Chiwome, E., Nhira, E. M., Masarire, A. and Furusa, M. (1996) *Introduction to Shona Culture* (Harare: Juta Zimbabwe).

Nyawaranda, V. (1995) *The Swinging Graduate* (Harare: Juta Zimbabwe).

Primorac, R. (2005) The eye of the nation: reading ideology and genre in a Zimbabwean thriller, in R. Muponde and R. Primorac (Eds), *Versions of Zimbabwe: New Approaches to Literature and Culture*, pp. 161–176 (Harare: Weaver Press).

Primorac, R. (2006) *The Place of Tears: The Novel and Politics in Modern Zimbabwe* (London: I. B. Tauris, forthcoming).

Ranger, T. (2004) Nationalist historiography, patriotic history and the history of the nation: the struggle over the past in Zimbabwe, *Journal of Southern African Studies*, 30(2), pp. 215–234.

Sylvester, C. (1999) Women in rural producer groups and the diverse politics of truth in Zimbabwe, in M. H. Marchand and J. L. Parpart (Eds), *Feminism/Postmodernism/Development*, pp. 182–203 (London: Routledge).

Veit-Wild, F. (1993) *Teachers, Preachers, Non-Believers: A Social History of Zimbabwean Literature* (Harare: Baobab Books).

Wylie, D. (2005) 'Mound has mountains': poetry and ecology in eastern Zimbabwe, in R. Muponde and R. Primorac, *Versions of Zimbabwe: New Approaches to Literature and Culture*, pp. 147–160 (Harare: Weaver Books).

The Struggle for Land in the Shona Novel: Allegory, Seizure and Betrayal

MAURICE TAONEZVI VAMBE

Institute for Curriculum and Learning Development, University of South Africa

Introduction

Since 2000 there has been intensification in the use of language describing land in Zimbabwe in terms that suggest that people have a common way of understanding and relating to this land. This language of 'oneness' between Africans and the land attempts to forestall debate about different perceptions that Zimbabweans have on the emotive theme of the land issue in the country. Shona authors are at the forefront of demonstrating that, within the discourse on land, Africans are struggling among themselves not only to have access to this land, but also to name it in different ways. The writers refuse to fully endorse the nationalist view that projects Africans as having equal access to the land under the controversial land reform.

This essay re-reads three Shona novels that span Zimbabwe's literary history: Solomon Mutswairo's *Feso* (1956), Raymond Choto's *Vavariro* (Aim or Purpose) (1990) and D. E. Mutasa's *Sekai, Minda Tave Nayo* (You can laugh, we now have the land) (2005). A juxtaposition of these texts from different historical periods reveals, on one hand, Africans who agree on the necessity to invest the land in their hands, while, on the other, fighting among themselves along class and gender lines for control over the land resource. These struggles fought in the public sphere further marginalize some poor Africans who are considered 'dissident' because they choose to critique the ways in which the land reform is being carried out. These dissident characters in the novels remain in the condition of subalternity, and thereby are regarded as being hostile towards the inversive process initiated by the nationalist struggle. Political slogans such as 'Zimbabwe will never be a colony again' (Mugabe, 2001) became the supervisory ideological discourse of political exclusion of those Africans who did not believe that the land struggle was still necessarily and only threatened by the machinations of the UK, the former colonizer. This essay argues that *Feso, Vavariro* and *Sekai: Minda Tave Nayo* actually in some ways confirm that 'Zimbabwe *can* be a colony again', but this time of the nationalist elites who have grabbed most of the productive land.

Feso: Allegory of an Incomplete Struggle for Land

The theme of land in Solomon Mutswairo's *Feso* has been commented upon from different angles (Kahari, 1990; Veit-Wild, 1993; Vambe, 2004). Critics have drawn attention to chapter 1 of the novel on land, which was excised by the Rhodesia Literature Bureau. The absence of this chapter in the Shona version of *Feso*—and its presence in the English version—fanned speculation that the Shona novel had entered its political and public life as a potentially subversive text. The Shona version analysed in this essay centres on Chief Nya'ngombe of the Vahota people. He likes to live peacefully with his people. His name means 'owner of many cattle'. The metaphors of 'wives,' 'cattle' and 'land' are meant to be metonyms of the convenient and stable imagery of '*Guruuswa*' and '*pasichigare*' depicted in *Feso*.

In *Feso, Guruuswa* is a mythical time frame in which the Shona people are depicted living harmoniously on their land. *Guru* means big/tall and *uswa* means grass. Another mono-myth of stability in the land of the Vahota people in *Feso* is captured in the traditional idea of *pasichigare*, which means the distant past when the Shona people are assumed to have had collective and intact identity. *Pasichigare* also conveys the meaning of times of plenty, when land gave fulsomely to its owners. And in *Feso* this moral economy of the imagery of stable identities, and of plentiful land, sustained the ideology of African cultural nationalism in the 1950s when the novel was written.

However, the mythopoetic narratives that link land to rain, to stable identity and to the privileging of the ascendancy of Shona people to power in *Feso* is ironically fractured from within. From the perspective of the historical context of the 1950s in which *Feso* was published, it had become redundant, if not outright reactionary to depict the Ndebele people and some whites who participated in the nationalist struggle as being outside the processes of nation building. Within the narrative interstices of *Feso* the discourse of land and political exclusion that validates Shona ascendancy to power which the novel rehearses is questioned and undermined by a war between two Shona polities, of the Vahota people under Chief Nya'ngombe and of the Vanyai people under Chief Pfumojena ('white spear'). The depiction of these two warring parties is initially meant to allegorize the struggle for the control of land between the African people and the white settlers of Rhodesia.

In *Feso* the political pain that Pfumojena unleashes on his people gives the land he controls a different signification: he kills those he does not agree with and banishes into the forest—land—those dissidents he cannot vanquish. In Pfumojena's narrative, land is both a political signifier and a physical space where he stages violent acts of suppressing his own people. It is not surprising that the Old Man from the Vanyai people conjures images of land, hunger, harassment and a desire for freedom when asking the spirit of Nehanda to intervene on behalf of the persecuted Vanyai. Mutswairo so effectively uses the black voice of resistance to land alienation implied in the phrase "*venhaka dzedu...voshaya nzvimbo dzokurarama*" (Those of our people are denied land to stay) (p. 56). In the 1950s African land was appropriated by colonialism in ways that transformed its African owners to slaves. In the novel Pfumojena takes land from those who defy him. Inside *Feso* the banning of dissent by Pfumojena turns the forest into a space of political resistance to Pfumojena. Inside *Feso* the persecuted Vanyai people join hands with Nya'ngombe soldiers and use forest land as the military base from which to attack Pfumojena. The armed struggle by the dissidents opposed to Pfumojena is born, bred and executed in the forest space that is considered to be the margin.

Similarly, in the 1950s white settlers feared the allegorical potency of *Feso*. They banned the novel from use in African secondary schools because militant black nationalists appropriated its subversive poem on Nehanda and recited it at public political meetings to stage oppositional politics. The banning of the novel by the white settler government in Rhodesia pushed its discourse into the centre of the 'margin' occupied by Africans and this helped African nationalist politics to thrive in the forest, at political rallies and at *Pungwes* (night vigils).

Feso ends with the defeat of Pfumojena and the restoration of Nya'ngombe's lands and that of the Vanyai people to their rightful owners. Inside *Feso* Mutswairo resolves the land question in a harmonious way. Outside the novel this preferred ending was undercut by land struggles among Africans that are depicted as taking place in post-independent Zimbabwe. The theme of struggle for land among Africans at independence is explored by Raymond Choto in *Vavariro*.

Vavariro and The Enigma of Arrival

Vavariro (1990) identifies as its provenance the quest to understand the main aims of the independence war and to measure them against the results of the war after 1980. *Vavariro* is a novel about the Zimbabwean liberation war fought intensely between 1977 and 1979. The story centres on Comrade Tumirai who has brought a group of Zimbabwe African National Liberation Army (ZANLA) guerrillas to fight the Rhodesian Front soldiers from the backyard of Mr Charira's village. However, despite the terrible loss of African land, cattle and lives occasioned by the war, the results of the struggle do not measure up to the contributions that the peasants put up or to what Africans expected. Instead, in *Vavariro* ex-combatants carve out swathes of land and push out the peasants from formerly white-owned land. The ex-combatant, Nhamoyetsoka—now Member of Parliament—uses the police to evict the peasants from Derek's farm. In his new language of acquisitiveness—he now possesses a Mercedes Benz—Nhamoyetsoka shifts from referring to the peasants as '*makomuredzi*'(Comrades) to the anonymous designation '*pane vanhu*' (there are people). This discourse marks the ideological de-linking between the aspirations of the people and those of the nationalist leaders. Nhamoyetsoka accentuates the processing of de-linking from the mass politics of struggle for land when he suggests that African peasants are illegally occupying Derek's farm, which Nhamoyetsoka wants for himself. For him, "*vanhu vari kugara papurazi pano zvisiri pamwero*" (People are staying at this farm illegally) (p. 150).

In *Vavariro* the African peasants initially refuse to move out of the farm they have occupied. However, they are subsequently bundled away from the farm by the police sent by Nhamoyetsoka, their wartime commander (pp. 150–151). What Raymond Choto successfully captures here is the struggle to control land that is now between the peasants living in the overcrowded sandy soils and the black elites. The fact that the novel came out in 1990, long before the land take-overs that characterized the period 2000 to 2003 in Zimbabwe, suggests that the land question was one of the unresolved issues of independence. In a sense, then, the peasants' resistance against the new elites demonstrates that postcolonial Zimbabwe is politically volatile with new struggles waged along class lines.

The conclusion of the novel, where the peasants are whisked back to their sandy soil (p. 151), suggests that the masses were betrayed by those whom they fed during the struggle. In fact, Tumirai is being cynical when he thanks VaChimoto for helping the guerrillas to win the war and enjoy the fruits of independence (p. 156). At the end of the novel, Tumirai is happily married and lives in the very low-density (i.e. privileged) suburb of Chisipiti in a house with a phone in the bathroom, while VaChimoto and other peasants eke out a living in the dusty reserves of Murehwa.

The peasants in *Vavariro* do not opt for open revolt against the politics of deception and betrayal of the goals of independence by the new elites; rather, the novel uses the discursive technique of the questioning mode to measure the distance between the war promises and the reality of the unfulfilled aims of that war of liberation. VaChimoto, the village elder, exposes the hypocrisy of the liberation leaders such as Tumirai when VaChimoto reminds him that it was the guerrillas who told the masses that after the war the masses would be allowed to settle on white-owned farms. In *Vavariro* VaChimoto insists that the peasants' involvement in the struggle justifies their occupation of white-owned land which their leaders also covet: "*tisuka tanga tava kugara kupurazi kwaDereki…asi takazobvako tomhanya*" (We are the ones who had occupied Derek's farm but we were thrown out by the police) (p. 154). With this last remark VaChimoto has passed moral judgement on the ideology of nationalism and revealed that the leaders cheated the masses when they created a binding mythology of collective aspirations of the black people.

Vavariro is a complex novel in its treatment of African subalterns depicted as fighting for land. The novel suggests that at some moments the subalterns align with dominant political formations. At others times, the subalterns seek autonomy. This complex and mobile combination of cultural and ideological elements is not surprising: the subalterns do not wish to remain in a condition of subalternity. They aim to take control of state power and thus become the dominant force. In this process the subalterns reveal uneven levels of consciousness. Those who are dissatisfied with independence, such as VaChimoto in *Vavariro*, can remain in a condition of rebellion against their fellow strugglers, with whom they previously had a relationship of alliance. But these new 'rebelling' subalterns are now considered new enemies to be vanquished (either through force, assimilation or consent) by their erstwhile comrades.

The rewriting of history and re-imagining of the struggle for land from the point of view of the subalterns is therefore not a given, in which there is always mutual consensus. In *Vavariro* VaChimoto's account of the betrayal of the aspirations of the masses to acquire land differs from that of Nhamoyetsoka's—a new member of the emerging class of the rich—in whose discourse the masses are gullible and do not observe the rule of law. The novel shows that the subalterns can authorize emancipatory discourses. Credit is due to Choto for having revealed that, within the subalterns fighting for land, "any of their members in the insurgent community who chooses to continue in such subalternity is regarded as hostile towards the inversive process initiated by the struggle and hence as being on the side of the enemy" (Guha and Spivak, 1988, p. 14).

Sekai Minda Tave Nayo: Land and the New Politics of Appeasement?

Sekai Minda Tave Nayo (2005), by D. E. Mutasa, shifts the reader's ways of imagining the struggle for land and shows that, after 2000, the land invasions which had begun in *Vavariro* became acute. *Sekai Minda Tave Nayo* redefines resistance politics of the ordinary people by depicting how African subalterns in Zimbabwe after 2000 embraced economic opportunities offered by the nationalist government. The novel shows that a conceptualization of the ruled as always resisting some domination fails to open up the question of how power is engaged, contested, deflected and appropriated (Cooper, 2003, p. 24). This paradoxical reality that the novel narrativizes should not come as a surprise, because those who rule can only do so if they are prepared to satisfy some of the interests of the ruled within the same system of capitalist political economy. *Sekai Minda Tave Nayo* shows that subaltern narratives can graduate into variations of the master narratives in which African masses also take part in the massive land invasions of white-owned land in Zimbabwe. One way to understand why this is so is to take into account Antonio Gramsci's view that "the fact of hegemony presupposes that account be taken of the interests and the tendencies of the groups over which hegemony is to be exercised . . . . the leading group should make sacrifice of an economic corporate kind" (1971, p. 216).

Sekai Minda Tave Nayo renders visible the complicated ideology of the nationalist government and how it appeases the masses with land so as to guarantee its continuation in power. The novel is about a young girl called Sekai,[1] who is initially denied an opportunity to attend school. Her father believes in the Shona patriarchal ideology of female silence and subordination. In a letter to her aunt Sekai writes that "*Zvanzi Sekai ngaadzoke izvozvi azorima. Vati ndiani murume angazoroora simbe isingagoni kubata badza. Baba vati kana Sekai achida kupinda chikoro achapinzwa nomurume wake*" (Father said I should come back to till the land. If I want school my future husband will send me) (p.13).

Sekai Minda Tave Nayo does not tell a story of the 'absencing' of women in Zimbabwe's fiction. The female characters are present in the novel but silenced by African males through acts of belittling women, giving them negative or marginal roles in society. Although Mutasa's novel is written against the silencing of rich women, it also recounts the silencing of poor women. In the novel Sekai is taken against her father's wish to school by her two aunts, Tendai's mother from

Mbumbwa and Rose's mother from Makomba. In school Sekai is a smart girl (p. 4), and is good in debates over the necessity of the controversial land reform that the Zimbabwean government engendered after 2000.

Sekai convinces her school mates that land reform is a necessity and that women could begin to own land in their own right. "*Madzimai zvisina kuti mudzimai akaroorwa here kana kuti kwete ngaapiwe pokurima kana achida. Izvi zvinoita kuti tiise upfumi mumaoko oruzhinji*" (Whether a woman is married or not she should get her own land. This ensures broad-based and democratic ownership of wealth by many) (p. 19).

Sekai articulates the aspirations of the ordinary people that land as the means of production should not be monopolized by a few whites or by black elites. She emphasizes the need for trained personal to make land reform a success. This explains why she chooses to do a degree in agriculture and environmental studies in America. When she returns, Sekai acquires land and becomes one of the few prosperous farmers in Zimbabwe. However, other women are not so lucky as Sekai. They remain marginalized in land redistribution carried out by young men and some ex-combatants, all of whom are willing to concentrate good farming land in their hands. The young man, Tirongo, is determined to prevent old women from getting land when he says "*Kuno ndokwemakomuredi*" (This fertile land is for comrades) (p.34). The irony is that Tirongo was only a baby when the war for land was waged. Yet these are the youths who are empowering themselves in ways that disempower poor women who are in need of land. Female ownership of land is publicly promoted by Sekai, who tells people that they now have the land: "'*Minda,*' Sekai akadaidzira. '*Minda tave nayo,*' Ruzhinji rwakadaidzira" (You can laugh but we now have the land *or* Sekai come and celebrate, we now have the land) (p. 103).

The strength of the novel at this point in the narration is its boldness in openly supporting the government-sponsored land reform. This close link between Sekai's narrative and the official nationalization of land is not necessarily an aberration. Stuart Hall argues that the relationship between the ordinary people and authority in different social contexts is not necessarily adversarial. Ordinary people will go along with the government policies that they deem favourable. The same ordinary people will also protest against government policies considered inimical to their material interests. For Hall, "there are lines of alliance and cleavages" (1994, p. 460) between the ruled and those that rule them. In fact, Jean-François Bayart (1993) provides a more broadened theoretical explanation of the seeming contradictory relationship between those who rule and the rulers. He says that in the nationalist struggle, "the small men also work at political innovation and their contribution does not necessarily contradict that of 'big men'" (Bayart, 1993, p. 249). The paradox is that the 'big' men soon forget the contributions of 'small men' and in *Sekai Minda Tave Nayo* this is the root of the betrayal, silencing and marginalization of some women not only by men but by women too.

In *Sekai Minda Tave Nayo* the authorial ideology is very close to the government stance on the land issue. Sekai tells those in charge of distribution to be fair over land: "*Musapa minda muchitarira bato rake*" (Do not give land to people according to political party affiliation) (p. 36). Sekai's narrative of a graduate-cum-farmer silences the reader's curiosity in wanting to know the contradictions of the land reform. By virtue of her education Sekai has entered into the elite class of those with money and resources to farm. The poor unnamed woman who wanted rich farmland found herself receiving exhausted land at the periphery of the farming area, behind the intractable rocks (p. 34). Sekuru Gwariro ironically doles out instructions to the workers at his farm in Zimbabwe, while working in South Africa. To get land is one thing. To possess capital, expertise, and fertilizer and farm that land from the 'spot' is another thing. In *Sekai Minda Tave Nayo* this important dimension of the land reform has been silenced by the constant refrain, "*Kana tapinda mumapurazi ticharima todyara fodya yakawanda tobva tatengesa*" (If we get the land we will grow tobacco and sell it) (p. 25).

The assumption here is that shifting from being peasant farmers to being commercial farmers is automatic, rather than problematic. This silence about the practical dimension of the land reform reflects ideological innocence on the part of Sekai's vision. This is so because the novel makes it clear that the beneficiaries of the land reform do not have adequate capital, labour and expertise to run the new farms (p. 104). An agrarian reform that occurs through a 'confisticatory redistribution' of land may politically satisfy one aim of the national liberation struggle. *Sekai Minda Tave Nayo* suggests that owning land is the first phase, which has to be followed by careful planning in terms of building dams. Otherwise it is not totally true that, if the rain falls, Zimbabweans will fill the silos with maize. Viable commercial farming cannot rely solely on God's will or seasonal rainfall. In the novel this dimension of planning for productive land use is smothered and silenced through the use of a nationalistic discourse whose overriding concern is celebrating the taking over of land.

Sekai Minda Tave Nayo is a welcome creative effort, imaginatively capturing the struggles over control of land in post-2000 Zimbabwe. The novel is, however, blighted by the fact that it insists on a pastoral revolution unmarked by serious internal problems. Mutasa's novel sometimes consciously silences other discourses of the nation that could tell the story of land reform in a different and non-partisan way. The several voices used in the novel have all been made to reach a consensus on the desirability of the land reform. The problem arises when the novel erects and attempts to sustain a mono-myth that the problems in implementing land reform in Zimbabwe are solely ideological. The practical issues, such as availability of labour to run the new farms, expertise, fertilizers, and water needs, related to a potential successful reform have been marginalized, and yet these too matter significantly. The point is that, although land reform was inevitable, its goal has been limited to owning land. Unless land is put to productive use then the reform is undermined. Unless there is a marked cultural revolution that undercuts male chauvinistic attitudes towards those who want to farm, then women will remain bonded to the new land as laborers and not controllers of land and producers of their own wealth.

Conclusion

This essay has focused on images of struggles for land in *Feso, Vavariro* and *Sekai Minda Tave Nayo*. In *Feso* the struggle for land between the Vahota and the Vanyai has been depicted as an allegory of the struggle for land between Africans and white settlers in Rhodesia. If the defeat of Pfumojena in *Feso* can be taken as a consummation of the actual armed struggle for land in Zimbabwe, in *Vavariro* this struggle has been depicted as developing tendencies towards silencing other discourses on land. In *Vavariro* the coming of independence to Zimbabwe introduces new struggles over the control of land between the black elites and the masses of people in whose name the war was fought. *Sekai Minda Tave Nayo* is the first novel in post-independence Zimbabwe to show openly the nationalist government and the masses working together to take control of formerly white land. Although the novel emphasizes the political importance of taking land, its vision is a desire to see Africans producing from the land. Sekai, the female heroine, is there to emphasize that the new social revolution does not silence the voice of women during the land reform processes.

Unfortunately, many poor men and women have been sidelined in the ownership of land. A majority of Africans still remain silenced, because it is mostly the elites who possess more than one farm. The three novels show that land struggles are likely to continue in Zimbabwe to ensure full democratic ownership of land by all, irrespective of race, class and gender.

Note

1. Her name is the plural imperative form of the Shona verb 'to laugh'.

References

Bayart, J.-F. (1993) *The State in Africa: The Politics of the Belly* (London: Longman).

Choto, R. (1990) *Vavariro* (Harare: Baobab Books).

Cooper, F. (2003) Conflict and connection: rethinking colonial African history, in J. D. Le Sueur (Ed.), *The Decolonization Reader*, pp. 22–44 (London: Routledge).

Gramsci, A. (1971) *Selections from the Prison Notebooks*, ed. Quintin Hoare and Geoffrey Nowell Smith (New York: International Publishers).

Guha, R. and Spivak, G. C. (1988) *Selected Subaltern Studies* (New York: Oxford University Press).

Hall, S. (1994) Notes on deconstructing the popular, in J. Storey (Ed.), *Cultural Theory and Popular Culture*, pp. 455–466 (London: Harvester Wheatsheaf).

Kahari, G. (1990) *Aspects of the Shona Novel* (Gweru: Mambo Press).

Mugabe, R. G. (2001) *Inside the Third Chimurenga* (Harare: Department of Information and Publicity Office of the President and Cabinet).

Mutasa, D. E. (2005) *Sekai Minda Tave Nayo* (Pretoria: Simba Guru Publishers).

Mutswairo, S. (1956) *Feso* (Gweru: Mambo Press in association with the Literature Bureau).

Vambe, M. T. (2004) *African Oral Story Telling Tradition and the Zimbabwean Novel in English* (Pretoria: Unisa Press).

Veit-Wild, F. (1993) *Teachers, Preachers, Non-Believers: A Social History of Zimbabwean Literature* (Harare: Baobab Books).

'Deviant' Innovations in Zimbabwean Writing: From the Racial Divide to Same Sex Desire

DREW SHAW
Roehampton University, London, UK

Introduction

> If speaking is too difficult to negotiate, then writing has created a free space for most women—much freer than speech. There is less interruption, less immediate and shocked reaction. The written text is granted its intimacy, its privacy, its creation of world. (Vera, 1999, p. 3)

Writing is a precious space because it can help empower the disempowered. An important function of writing in Zimbabwe has been to challenge oppressive structures, and many authors still do so under tough conditions. The Zimbabwe Women Writers union continues to encourage women to write. Even the most marginialized, the most castigated of groups—prostitutes and homosexuals, for example—are now writing their stories, articulating their experiences, registering their place and plight in the fabric of Zimbabwean society. Virginia Phiri's *Desperate* (2002) tells the stories of women who resort to prostitution through social and economic pressures. The second edition of *Sahwira: Being Gay and Lesbian in Zimbabwe* (GALZ, 2002) is a collection of testimonies and commentary from a diverse community.

Promising new talent often comes in the wake of tragedy. For the second time Zimbabwe has lost a great writer in tragic circumstances. Dambudzo Marechera died of AIDS in 1987, aged just 35. Now, in 2005, we have lost Yvonne Vera, aged just 40. Marechera and Vera can be considered towers in the literary landscape, taking the national literature to new heights. Vera, with her feminine/feminist aesthetics, her willingness to confront taboo issues such as abortion, infanticide, child abuse, rape and atrocity, has blazed a trail. Marechera, meanwhile, continues to haunt Zimbabwean literature and culture with his profound identity questions, his exposure of uncomfortable truths, his exploration of the unconscious, his radical non-conformity.

There is a long tradition of resistance and resilience in Zimbabwean writing—first, in the colonial era, against the tyranny of the Smith regime and now against the tyranny of the Mugabe regime. Some writers continue to speak out fearlessly and have suffered the consequences. Chenjerai Hove has described George Mujajati as "the most tortured writer in the country" (2002, p. 11). Hove himself, unrelenting in his own critical poems and political commentary, has now been forced into exile. On the other hand, many writers have remained, and keep writing, as is witnessed by *Writing Still* (Staunton, 2003) and *Writing Now* (Staunton, 2005), short story collections showcasing extraordinary talent, tenacity and imagination amid harsh conditions. For his short story, *Seventh Street Alchemy* (2003), Brian Chikwava won the Caine Prize in 2004. Despite difficult conditions, Zimbabwean writing continues to flourish—both at home and in the growing diaspora.

In my research I have been particularly interested in transgression in Zimbabwean literature—writing that breaks rules and pushes the boundaries, writing which challenges old assumptions regarding race, gender and sexuality. This has taken me from canonized writers such as Doris Lessing, Dambudzo Marechera, Yvonne Vera, Tsitsi Dangarembga, Stanley Nyamfukudza and Shimmer Chinodya to a whole range of less well known women's writing and, more recently, gay, lesbian and transgendered writing.

In this article I will look at four examples in Zimbabwean writing—two dealing with interracial relationships, one feminist text and one text exploring sexual diversity. The authors I consider—Dambudzo Marechera, Shimmer Chinodya, Melissa Tandiwe Myambo, and Nevanji Madanhire—all court controversy in different ways, yet broaden the concerns of the Zimbabwean national literature in an engaging, revelatory manner.

Marechera's *Mindblast* (1984)

With *Mindblast*, in 1984, Marechera set a benchmark for experimental writing in post-independence Zimbabwean literature. One of his concerns was to upset the prevailing racial ideology. In the 'Journal', an autobiographical addition appended to the miscellany of fiction, drama and poetry, Marechera criticizes reactionary attitudes: "A black man in arms with a white woman was still something of a miracle in Harare. The acid comments and bitter glances spat at us from both black and white people" (Marechera, 1984, p. 131). We learn from the Journal that animosity towards interracial relationships affected the author on a personal level, since many of his intimate relationships were with white women.

It is the early 1980s, and despite the 'liberation' of newly independent Zimbabwe, little seems to have changed in the public mindset, or in the daily lives of 'the povo'—the impoverished majority. The first section of *Mindblast* is entitled 'The skin of time—plays by Buddy' and it is made up of three short plays which expose post-independence corruption and hypocrisy. In order to ruffle the status quo, Marechera deploys the trope of interracial sex as well as stinging Menippean satire—a hybrid, dialogic mode of writing rooted in classical antiquity and marked by fantastical elements, structural contrasts and sudden reversals which ridicule conventional viewpoints and attitudes (on this, see Bakhtin, 1999). In a lecture delivered in 1986 Marechera explained that, in Menippean writing, "Scandalous and eccentric behaviour disrupts 'the seemly course of human affairs' and provides a new view of 'the integrity of the world'. Society is unpredictable; roles can quickly change" (quoted in Veit-Wild, 1992, p. 364).

In 'The Coup', first of the plays in the trilogy, a business takeover is staged in military fashion by Norman Drake, who deposes his brother-in-law, Spotty, from the managerial position of an influential company with close links to the government. In the second play, the Honourable Comrade Minister Nzuzu, a collaborator in the coup, hosts a party to celebrate with friends and allies. However, he is anything but honourable and neither is the behaviour of his guests. ('The Party' doubles in meaning as a comment on corruption in the ruling party). The stage is abuzz with bed-hopping, bribery and corruption. Interracial sexual relationships become commonplace and the colour bar erodes into oblivion as taboos are flouted and double standards exposed. In all there are at least five different interracial couplings: Louise (white secretary to Drake) is married to Alfie (a black Rastafarian); Spotty (a white racist) is having an affair with Arabella (a black housekeeper); Jane (white wife to Spotty) is dating the new Reserve Bank Manager (who is black); Lydia (black wife to the Minister) is having an affair with Drake (who is white and unmarried), and Dick (the white son of Spotty and Jane) is having frequent sex with Raven (the black daughter of Lydia and the Minister).

The interracial sex trope functions to mock political pretensions. Some of the relationships symbolize political and economic alliances in newly independent Zimbabwe. 'Comrade Ministers' and their relatives, who supposedly represent the interests of the oppressed black majority, are literally hopping into bed with white business tycoons and their relatives. When Jane and Drake discover Louise is "Married to an African" (Marechera, 1984, p. 32), they burst into laughter. However, Drake, the crooked business opportunist, quickly says, "Come, come Jane. It's the year of transformation. We are all Comrade-In-Laws these days" (p. 32). One sex scandal leads to another as Jane then admits that she also has a "comrade up [her] sleeve...He's something high in the Reserve Bank" (p. 32). Money and power are the ultimate goals in this game; and interracial affairs as well as marriages of convenience consolidate the privileged position of a new multiracial elite, who have no real concern for the impoverished majority. This echoes Ruth Weiss's (1994) observation that a single multiracial elite class was being established in Zimbabwe shortly after independence, politicians striking deals with business opportunists.

The Honourable Comrade Minister Nzuzu is supposed to be an upstanding representative of the new socialist government, but he takes bribes and does deals with the unscrupulous white business tycoon, Drake. Nzuzu's wife, Lydia, also has a vested interest of her own in Drake. In one episode, shortly after the minister leaves the stage, she "assaults [Drake's] lips forcefully and lingeringly" (p. 34) (significantly subverting the stereotype of the submissive black woman and the dominant white man in the popular imagination). This happens just as Lydia's daughter, Raven, and Drake's nephew, Dick, emerge from the toilet with "clothes rumpled and bedraggled" (p. 34) (obviously having had sex there). There can be no more keeping up appearances when the adulterous parents and delinquent children all stumble upon each other awkwardly outside the toilet (which is centre-stage and symbolic, in general, of degradation). At first Lydia is upset by the idea of Raven's having been 'seduced' by Drake's nephew; but later she warms to the prospect when Drake proposes a lucrative 'marriage of alliance' between the teenagers. This will no doubt involve a generous financial settlement—which will accrue to Lydia—and solidify a corrupt alliance between the families.

Another function of interracial relationships in these plays is to expose hypocrisy and ridicule racist attitudes. Even the most hardened of racists—the comical character Spotty—is having an affair with a black woman, Arabella, who is his housekeeper and mistress. Hypocritically, she rebukes Alfie for marrying a white woman: "What have they got which we black girls haven't got?" (p. 39). But Alfie discovers she is "the black girl who was going to take the gap with Spotty Down South" (p. 39). She had planned to emigrate to South Africa (then still under apartheid) with her white (apparently racist) lover—which is of course an outrageous contradiction.

Hypocritical interracial affairs are nevertheless juxtaposed with moments of openness and honesty. For example, Dick wonders why he and Raven "can't have our sex without locking doors... we are not corrupt businessmen (p. 32). Louise and Alfie arrive at the party as a couple, making no secret of their marriage. But they suffer abuse because of it. When Alfie emerges from the toilet and leaves the stage with his white wife, a group of white men, queuing for the loo, are infuriated. The 1st Man says, "I always said that what these black bastards mean by liberation is just to screw white pussy" (1984, p. 40), to which the 2nd Man declares, "There's gratitude for you. For seventeen years we fought to protect our women and at the drop of independence the tarts jump into bed with the very bastards we were protecting them from. Tsk... Tsk... Tsk" (p. 40). This, the only honest interracial relationship at the party, is not respected as such either by whites (including 'liberals' such as Drake and Jane) or blacks (for example Arabella). Racist colonial discursive structures, Marechera shows, remain stubbornly resilient in the supposedly liberated new Zimbabwe.

A lynching is planned but Alfie and Louise escape and macho white male colonial culture is subsequently ridiculed. One man "bursts into tears and in the sight of God and the whole queue starts to wet his pants" (p. 41). The aggressors thus become the victims of public humiliation. Marechera effectively mobilizes such reversals, typical of the Menippean genre, for satire in the post-independence context. Refusing to observe the colour bar, he transgresses it time and again in this drama, sending up nonsensical racist attitudes. The interracial sex trope is used to mock hypocrisy, expose corruption and overturn oppressive hierarchies.

Shimmer Chinodya's 'Play Your Cards' (1998/2001)

Shimmer Chinodya shows an affinity with Marechera in that his writing has become increasingly experimental, particularly in its investigation of masculinity, sexuality and psychosexual realities (which Marechera explores, in detail, in his novellas *The House of Hunger* (1978) and *Black Sunlight* (1980)). Chinodya is best known for his liberation struggle novel *Harvest of Thorns* (1989), written in the realist mode that resists dichotomous views and instead highlights elements of contradiction. The short story collection *Can We Talk and Other Stories*, first published in 1998 and which was short-listed for the Caine Prize in 2000, begins to effect a break with the predominant genre of social realism. It is Chinodya's most experimental text to date.

The exploration of deceit and infidelity in one of the stories, 'Play Your Cards', reflects on desire between a black man and a white woman. Timothy, husband to Chipo and father to Tapiwa, has an affair with Maria, a wealthy European woman who in the end discovers his lies and turns the tables on him. "He would sleep with her till 2 am", we are told, "then return home because Tapiwa (his four-year-old) would want to see him before he left for work" (Chinodya, 2001, p. 73). The relationship seems purely exploitative on Timothy's part: he makes numerous phone calls from Maria's house and burns out her Jaguar's exhaust with excessive travel. Stories about being under siege from the extended family system are in fact a cover for other illicit activities.

The metaphorical framework of their relationship is cards—"a game of life or death, a ferocious contest" (p. 72) but one where—for a moment—they are equal players. Within the card-playing games desire is intertwined with the will to dominate:

> Often when she won he felt the urge to subdue her in his hot manly way. The razor-sharp vengeance with which they played each other, was almost childish, a sweet but cruel delight. (He adored her face, her neat mouth and her fresh smile. He cherished her plump body for its corpulence, and it made him feel good to be slim.) (p. 73).

Later there is anger and jealousy in Maria's tone when she questions him about other mistresses: "Do we all give you our cars to do as you please? Do we all surrender our telephones, our booze, our bodies to you?" (p. 80). There is suspicion and distrust when Timothy alleges mutual exploitation—that she has been trying to get pregnant by him without his consent. She admits, "Yes, I wanted your baby. But I wasn't going to force you into anything" (p. 80). He then says, "You played your cards so well. I was your guinea-pig all along" (p. 80). The acrimony, however, belies an element of real intimacy and passion between the two. But the flipside of this intimacy is fear. Maria has acted compliantly, until now, but in their last encounter she moves to assert herself as the dominant partner: "She had a steely strength which he had never realized, never imagined. He was afraid to touch her—for the first time since he had known her, she terrified·him" (pp. 80–81). There is a sudden destabilization of roles, in which Chinodya highlights both intimacy and terrifying uncertainty.

Traditionally Zimbabwean literature has upheld the idea of a fundamental rift between black and white, and therefore treated interracial sexual relationships with scepticism or contempt. Chinodya, like Marechera, moves to problematize this notion through the depiction of undeniable desire across the colour bar, and the expression of a real range of emotions—love, anger, jealousy—that accompany it.

Melissa Tandiwe Myambo's 'Deciduous Gazettes' (1999)

From relationships across the colour bar we move now to gender transgression. Melissa Tandiwe Myambo's short story, 'Deciduous Gazettes' (1999) demonstrates an innovative new feminist writing talent, showing an affinity with Marechera in its use of Menippean satire. The title indicates a loose and changeable structure, an annual or periodic shedding of news (like a tree shedding leaves) about current affairs and events which is open-ended and renewable, not sealed off. As Abrams emphasizes, Menippean satires are "held together by a loosely constructed narrative":

A major feature is a series of extended dialogues and debates (often conducted at a banquet or party) in which a group of loquacious eccentrics, pedants, literary people and representatives of various professions or philosophical points of view serves to make ludicrous the attitudes and viewpoints they typify by the arguments they urge in their support (Abrams, 1993, pp. 188–189).

This form is appropriate to the theme of social change—in this case transforming conventional gender relations, for example polygamy.

The central character in Myambo's story is the eccentric Saru, a feminist who is married to Hans, an Austrian professor. She divides her time between the social set of Frankfurt and Harare, usually advising her married female friends not to accept any form of male domination or infidelity. She is a charismatic, messianic figure and this garners her a large following of women who seem to bask in the afterglow of her outrageous patriarchal subversions—her 'feminist miracles'.

One of her friends is Hannah Ncube. Hannah's husband, Mr Ncube, who represents the voice of patriarchy in the narrative, does not like Saru and describes her, as "a loose firecracker":

He constantly complained about her reckless smoking in public; her disregard for womanly dignity; he doubted whether she was legally married. What kind of a woman, if she is natural, normal, does not produce offspring? The word 'whore' was scratching his throat but he didn't spit it out because he feared her (Myambo, 1999, p. 21).

Since Saru is a devout church-going Christian it is difficult for Mr Ncube and others to pin that label on her. She is always a step ahead in the battle against patriarchal stigmatization. Before invading cocktail parties and barbecues, where she performs her subversions with such confidence and ease, Saru first establishes her legitimacy according to the rules of middle-class multiracial Harare society. The main criterion is marriage, which she fulfils quite easily, although she also feels free to leave her husband behind in Frankfurt and has no particular reverence for him or his friends. Saru refuses to be bound by the terms of a patriarchal concept of marriage.

She shares the following anecdote, indicative of her ingeniously subversive powers: "Hanna, my friend, did I ever tell you about the Africans in Frankfurt?...One day Hans came home with an Algerian, a Senegalese and a Malian—countries you and I have never seen. They, all four men, sat down and began to discuss the Islamic faith and whether it was oppressive to women. All four sat and agreed it wasn't...According to the Quran, a man may take up to four wives. All four vociferously discussed the value and historical reasons for this tradition. Then my fellow Africans turned to me and said: "How do you do it in Zimbabwe?"

> I looked at each of them, glowing with the exertion of intellectual exercise, and I told them, this: "In Zimbabwe, it is the inverse situation. One woman may marry up to eight men." They were completely taken aback, nausea flitted across their faces, their hands trembled with self-righteousness and they sputtered out simultaneously: "But how do you know who the father of the child is?" said one. "That's filthy. One woman cannot sleep with so many men. It's disgusting," said the other, and the third: "Whose surname does the child take?"

> Calmly, I explained that we did not mind who the father of the child was: all my husbands would live together in harmony and nurture that child who would, naturally, take my family name, as did my husbands. We, I stated clearly, did not think of this as filthy but it was our tradition, our culture, our heritage—any woman who had the economic means was able, if she so wished, to take up to eight husbands. (pp. 29–30)

Saru intelligently disrupts the naturalization of patriarchy wherever she encounters it. Refusing to accept supposedly 'timeless truths' in a male-dominated continental culture, she imagines instead the possibility of a matriarchal society in Zimbabwe and asserts this quite confidently as a reality, a long traditional practice and a cultural difference, which should be respected. The same arguments of cultural conservatism legitimizing patriarchal polygamy are ingeniously used to legitimize the concept of matriarchal polygamy. In the Menippean tradition, this "serve[s] to make ludicrous the attitudes and viewpoints" (Abrams, 1993, pp. 188–189) of Saru's opponents. In *Deciduous Gazettes* Myambo deploys wit and irony in reversing standard gender roles, and destabilizing patriarchy's claims to 'natural' authority.

Nevanji Madanhire's *If the Wind Blew* (1996)

In his political thriller, set in the 1990s, Nevanji Madanhire breaks new ground by integrating the theme of homosexuality. In *If the Wind Blew*, Isis, an investigative journalist, suffers the effects of brutal male domination in her place of work and on the political scene, as she uncovers a plot to assassinate the leader of the opposition (in a fictitious country closely resembling Zimbabwe). When she is nearly eight months pregnant, she discovers that her husband, Hebrew, is more than just a friend to their Swedish houseguest Christiaan. Towards the end of the novel, late at night, Isis is "dazed" to discover that Hebrew and Christiaan are not playing chess, as she imagines, but sleeping together in the spare room—with the door wide open as if to emphasize the disclosure:

> It had been an intense love act . . . Later in the night, she walked like a ghost to take another look. The moon filtered more intensely into the room. Hebrew lay peacefully on Christiaan's breast. Christiaan himself breathed deeply in and lengthily out. (Madanhire, 1996, pp. 97–98)

Isis cannot believe her eyes, goes into premature labour, and loses the child. But she is not so much shocked by her husband's homosexuality as she is by her own blindness towards it. Later in the hospital, Hebrew breaks down and the truth comes, belatedly, from his own mouth. Once renowned as an incorrigible womanizer, he admits he is actually gay: "I tried to suppress it, but its [sic] my preference. I am convinced now that it's what I always wanted. All those girls were just cover-ups" (p. 98). This articulation of gay sexual preference on the pages of mainstream Zimbabwean literature is a milestone. Moreover, it confounds stereotypes because Hebrew is not only black and gay but also classically masculine: good-looking, fit, strong and virile—an 'ordinary' man. Also, although his lover is European, he seems quite clear in his mind that his gayness is quite independent of 'European influences'.

The gay affair is a brief but astounding revelation with seismic consequences: Isis is prompted, after the divorce, to set about redefining her concept of womanhood and making fundamental changes to her life. Named after the ancient Egyptian goddess, Isis discovers parallels between her life and that of her namesake. She hears a feminist revision of the Isis myth on the radio, by chance, discovering her namesake was "the goddess of justice" and "the most powerful deity . . . [but] . . . [s]he had to be destroyed because men could not stand to be ruled by women", so "they married her off to Osiris, thereby transferring all her powers to a man"—and she was thereafter "reduced to a devoted wife" (p. 101). The parallels with Isis Ndlovu's experiences of male domination become clearer and clearer. This awakens a dormant part of her consciousness to the possibility that, like her namesake, she may be immensely gifted herself, and need not live in the shadow of her husband, or depend, for her success and sense of identity, on men. The sub-plot of Hebrew's gay love affair seems to emphasize, for Isis, that playing the dutiful wife or any other circumscribed social role is ultimately untenable and absurd.

The gay episode awakens not only Isis but also the reader to an unconcealed image of desire and intimacy between men. Noticeably, against the grain of mainstream fiction, Madanhire's non-judgmental narrator does not condemn the gay affair as 'deviancy' but instead offsets it within a broader context of transgression. If we consider the significance of the names, Hebrew (i.e. Jewish) and Christiaan (i.e. Christian), who are black and white respectively, the affair is not only homosexual but interracial, and interreligious at a symbolic level. Moreover, if Hebrew and Christiaan, like Isis, are read as representing deities, their sexual congress is also radically transgressive in a cosmological dimension.

Relevant to an analysis of this novel is the fact that the crime of sodomy under Roman Dutch Law in colonial Zimbabwe was originally defined as "sexual congress *per anum* between a man and woman, or between a man and a man, self-masturbation, mutual masturbation, oral intercourse and lesbian acts and even heterosexual sex of any sort between a Jew and a Christian" (Propotkin, 1998, p. 3; for a more detailed account, see Phillips, 1997). In short, it used to encompass a broad range of sexual transgressions, some of which are no longer considered criminal acts. Hence Madanhire's text can be read as implying that interracial and inter-religious sexual relationships, once stigmatized and even illegal, are now quite acceptable in many societies. It is not clear whether Hebrew and Christian will eventually find such acceptance because they subsequently disappear from the narrative. Madanhire nevertheless allows the unpredictable gay episode to permanently destabilize automatic assumptions of heterosexuality and to reverberate with implications both inside and outside the text.

Conclusion

I have tried to show how the four texts discussed above can all be considered transgressive and controversial, and yet also innovative and insightful in their treatment of race, gender and sexuality. They show how Zimbabwean literature has begun to shift in its consciousness and move into new and uncharted terrains. In the wake of Marechera and in defiance of current political realities inside the country, Zimbabwean writing is developing a capacity to embrace changing realities in an increasingly complex modern world.

References

Abrams, M. H. (1993) *A Glossary of Literary Terms* (London: Harcourt Brace).
Bakhtin, M. (1999) *Problems of Dostoevsky's Poetics* (Minneapolis, MN: University of Minnesota Press).
Chikwava, B. (2003) Seventh Street Alchemy, in I. Staunton (Ed.), *Writing Still*, pp. 17–30 (Harare: Weaver Press).
Chinodya, S. (1989) *Harvest of Thorns* (Harare: Baobab Books).
Chinodya, S. (1998/2001) *Can We Talk and Other Stories* (London: Heinemann).
Chinodya, S. (1998/2001) Play Your Cards, in Chinodya, *Can We Talk and Other Stories*, pp. 53–60 (London: Heinemann).
GALZ (Gays and Lesbians of Zimbabwe) (2002) *Sahwira: Being Gay and Lesbian in Zimbabwe* (Harare: GALZ).
Hove, C. (2002) *Palaver Finish* (Harare: Weaver Press).
Marechera, D. (1978) *The House of Hunger* (Oxford: Heinemann).
Marechera, D. (1980) *Black Sunlight* (Oxford: Heinemann).
Marechera, D. (1984) *Mindblast* (Gweru: College Press).
Madanhire, N. (1996) *If the Wind Blew* (Harare: College Press).
Myambo, M. T. (1999) Deciduous Gazettes, in Y. Vera (Ed.), *Opening Spaces: An Anthology of Contemporary African Women's Writing*, pp. 14–42 (London: Heinemann).
Phillips, O. (1997) Zimbabwean law and the production of a white man's disease, *Social and Legal Studies*, 6(4), pp. 471–491.
Phiri, V. (2002) *Desperate* (Harare: Virginia Phiri).
Propotkin, P. (1998) Getting to the bottom of sodomy in Zimbabwe, unpublished paper, Faculty of Law, University of Zimbabwe.
Staunton, I. (Ed.) (2003) *Writing Still* (Harare: Weaver Press).
Staunton, I. (Ed.) (2005) *Writing Now* (Harare: Weaver Press).
Vera, Y. (Ed.) (1999) *Opening Spaces: An Anthology of Contemporary African Women's Writing* (London: Heinemann).
Veit-Wild, F. (1992) *Dambudzo Marechera: A Source Book on his Life and Work* (Harare: University of Zimbabwe Publications and London: Hans Zell).
Weiss, R. (1994) *Zimbabwe and the New Elite* (London: British Academic Press).

Democratization in Southern Africa: Barriers and Potentialities

KENNETH GOOD
Nordic Africa Institute, Uppsala, Sweden

Introduction

Southern Africa is the most advanced region in Africa in economic terms, and the most developed democratically, in its recent past, the present, and in its potentialities too. It is on these intertwined economic and political factors, and on both their positive and negative aspects that this article concentrates. Southern Africa is a definable region,[1] where there are nonetheless huge differentials of power and potentialities between, say, a South Africa, Angola and Zimbabwe, on the one hand, and Malawi, Lesotho and Swaziland, on the other. Consideration of the barriers to democratization, furthermore, embraces of course the big problems of Africa, and the author stands with African luminaries like Wole Soyinka, Chinua Achebe and Ngugi wa Thiong'o who believe that the key problem for Africa is the failure of its leaders. Soyinka's Old Toad Kings are power-hungry, incompetent and unscrupulous, and their approximations, even in a few cases replicas, are found today in southern Africa. I begin therefore with the barriers to democratization.

Presidentialism and Predominance

This baleful combination is the outstanding feature of South Africa, Namibia and Botswana, although they exist together, in part and tendency, in one or two other places as well. Presidentialism basically entails the centralization of power in one office and person, and the predominance of a single party, under reasonably democratic conditions—different parties compete, but one always wins through the ballot-box—involves, not only the dominance of the executive and legislature, but also a command of the voters' support gained through the presentation of effective policies in repeated elections.[2]

Botswana became a liberal or electoral democracy from the outset, and it is in many ways a 'best case' example. Presidentialism developed under first Seretse Khama and then Ketumile Masire, accompanied by the triumph of the ruling Botswana Democratic Party (BDP) in all nine general elections over 40 years. Characteristically of presidentialism, Seretse Khama readily altered the country's constitution (with the willing approval of parliament, in which his BDP predominated) in favour of the indirect election of the president. His biographers report that he had found the democratic rough-and-tumble of a constituency-based election process tiring. He also sought to centralize power in the office of the president, one of the first steps on the road to autocracy, they recognized. Altering the constitution has never been a serious problem for a predominant Botswana president.[3] When Sir Ketumile Masire wished to stand down in the 1990s, following a series of corruption scandals and intense factionalism in the BDP, the constitution was again changed to allow for the automatic succession of his Vice President, i.e. over the heads of the party in parliament as well as of the people. Meantime, all three BDP presidents to-date, Khama, Masire and his successor Festus Mogae, have manipulated constitutional provisions allowing for the appointment of four specially (un)elected members of parliament; only BDP-aligned figures were appointed, sometimes even BDP MPs democratically rejected by their constituencies. Sometimes these appointed MPs acquire (or re-acquire) immediate ministerial positions too.[4]

The intensification of presidentialism in South Africa is a conspicuous characteristic of Thabo Mbeki's, African National Congress (ANC) government, especially after 1999. While Mbeki has centralized increasing powers in the Office of the President, this was earlier no inevitability. During the 1980s a world-historic participatory democratic process developed, involving at its height perhaps some three million people in newly created, internally based organizations like the United Democratic Front (UDF), Mass Democratic Movement (MDM) and the Congress of South African Trade Unions (COSATU), only to be terminated (with the significant exception of COSATU) soon after 1990, with the release of the established nationalist elites from jail and the return of others from exile.

The transition from apartheid to a conventional form of electoral, representative democracy was achieved in largely exclusive negotiations between a formerly apartheid-supporting political elite and the elites of the vanguard ANC. Those who marginalized and dissolved the UDF-MDM were those whom Zakes Mda terms "the aristocrats of the revolution". Men who could be plausibly seen to have given their lives to the struggle, like Nelson Mandela, Thabo Mbeki and Joe Sloyo, elite figures who, as Bantu Holomisa noted—in the wake of an ANC-fund-raising scandal involving President Mandela—the people venerated too highly and uncritically.[5] Today, the effects of the ANC's predominance are such that voters have in reality no choice—opposition parties have no chance of winning power, and voters must support the ANC or 'spoil their ballots'.[6]

The most egregious examples of presidentialism today, regionally and perhaps elsewhere, are in Angola and Zimbabwe. In the oil-rich country, a 'shadow' or parallel state has been created by and for 'the president's men',[7] which enjoys complete non-accountability and impunity. Oil and military expenditures were exploited to the extent that, in 2001 alone, one-third of the state budget, or some $1.4 billion, was unaccountable.[8] Messiant emphasises that power in Angola lies with the person "occupying all the central institutions of the state". What she terms "tenure of actual power", rather than institutions *per se*, has been "increasingly centralized" on and in the president. He and his *nomenklatura* have brought about a "privatization of the state", and established a patronage and security system "endowed with complete impunity". People have been bound to the president by patronage and privilege available at his discretion.[9]

The Eduardo Dos Santos Foundation (FESA) is perhaps the highest manifestation of "this system of clientelist domination and...the reinforcement of presidential power". As the institutions of the state have abandoned "all pretense of performing public services", the president, through FESA, has arrogated a part of these "to his own person". A self-styled "Engineer Jose Eduardo dos Santos" appears through FESA as "the number one leader of civil society", while being also through official office the head of government and ruling party, commander in chief of the military and controller of the police. He "receives oil dollars which do not appear in any official accounts and determines how they are spent, and is the prime beneficiary of the competition between foreign companies and...governments for Angolan resources and markets". Like Global Witness, she notes that the "utter misery of the people" is combined with the impunity of the powerful.[10]

In ways no less unscrupulous and crude, Zimbabwe in 2005 displays the "emergence of a predatory authoritarian state which is highly personalized and [actually] owned by [President Robert Mugabe]".[11] It has become "ever more authoritarian" and destructive.[12] Anna Tibaijuka reported on the origins and consequences of "Operation Murambatsvina" ('Restore Order' or 'Drive Out Rubbish') to the UN Secretary General. It was a nation-wide demolition and eviction campaign carried out by the police and army with speed and ferocity, "a massive military-style operation". She reports that some 700 000 urban people lost their homes, their livelihoods, or both, and indirectly "a further 2.4 million people have been affected in varying degrees".

A militant nationalism, based on the use of force, had been a mark of Mugabe's rule, through the agency of his party ZANU (PF), the military and the police, and a relatively strong bureaucracy, from the very beginning. As early as 1981 – 82 Mugabe himself had planned, launched and directly controlled Operation Gukurahundi in Matabeland, a protracted military campaign against supposed dissident elements, which saw the deaths of some 20 000 people. Zimbabwe too was "led by a Founding President, a towering and influential political personality, viewed with respect...in all of Africa for his historical role in the...liberation struggle", as Tibaijuka has it. A "combination of this reverence and the inherited colonial administrative structures contributed", she says, "to a heavily centralized government". When the seizures of commercial farms began in 2000, war veterans were mobilized as key "political shock troops" of ZANU (PF) and its leader. In elections during this time, "intimidation and violence" were in "systematic use".[13]

Namibia established a progressive constitution in 1990, but experienced throughout the decade thereafter a "constant gain in and consolidation of political power and control by the former liberation movement" the South West Africa People's Organization (SWAPO). No "numerically meaningful opposition party could firmly establish itself", as SWAPO gained 74% of the votes in national elections in 1994, increased that to 76% in 1999, and maintained that predominance in November 2004. A critical bridge to autocracy was crossed in 1998, when parliament amended the constitution, with the necessary two-thirds majority, to allow President Sam Nujoma a third term in office. In the same year Namibia entered the war in the Congo "as a result of the personally ordered intervention" of the president—he is constitutionally empowered to decide alone for the protection of national security.[14]

Critical voices on these big issues and on others became seen as unpatriotic; "loyalty to Namibia [was] equated with loyalty to SWAPO's policy and in particular to the party's President". Dissenting views were marginalized.[15] The capacity for predominance, here as elsewhere in the region, had its origins in the liberation struggle, which fostered presidentialism in equal measure. As Saunders encapsulates it: "The centrality of the armed struggle in the years of exile meant that SWAPO became dominated by a military culture, strongly hierarchical, authoritarian and closed".[16]

Angola and Zimbabwe are obviously very different from, say, Botswana. And South Africa, despite President Mbeki and the ANC, retains a strong civil society, as a structural feature of its advanced capitalist economy. But there is a core similarity between all the countries described above. Presidentialism and predominance is common, and they facilitate and express very wide social control focused on a single person. People may vote—not since 1992 in Angola and under heavy duress in Zimbabwe—but they are. denied meaningful choice;[17] and free speech faces severe limitations in many places.

Elite Corruption

While Messiant and Global Witness show that kleptocracy is as immense as it is systemic in Angola, elite corruption is also present elsewhere in the region. Corruption is generally understood as the misuse of public office for private gain, and the duopoly of presidentialism – predominance offers enhanced opportunities for the personalized enrichment of a ruling elite. If corruption is theft from the public realm, it follows directly that it is ethically wrong and anti-democratic, even if it happens not to be an offence under national law.

Botswana's authoritarian liberalism is a case in point. Combining wealth and political power was characteristic of the country's economic and political development from the 19th century, as rising Tswana elites participated directly in cattle production. The Setswana word for a chief was the same as that for a wealthy man, and it was deemed natural or preordained that the BDP should be formed and led by so-called cattle-barons who became the leaders of the new nation state. Unlike a Kaunda, Nyerere or Nkrumah elsewhere, these men were 'steakholders' in every sense of the term.

With rapid growth, this continued well enough for a quarter century, but the process went badly wrong with a series of highly visible corruption scandals in the early 1990s. The near bankruptcy of the National Development Bank, a flagship state institution, highlighted the role of President Masire and leading ministers in this debacle. They had awarded themselves generous loan funds and neglected to repay their borrowings. While Sir Ketumile attempted to explain that successful venture capitalism contained inescapable, risks, further public scandal followed in critical institutions like the Botswana Housing Corporation.[18] The ideology of the growth economy in Botswana, that returns in profits, wages and services would go to those who made the biggest contribution to that growth, took a possibly irreparable knock. Vice President Mogae fought to establish an anti-corruption agency, Sir Ketumile eventually stepped down, Mogae succeeded to the presidency, and General Ian Khama, the other supposed new broom, began his rise to power. But the BDP remained faction-riven, a level of crony-capitalism continued,[19] and the BDP's share of the popular vote declined during 1999 and 2004 as that of a weak and divided opposition rose.

Affirmative action or black economic empowerment (BEE) were emphasized by President Mbeki in particular but, when they were associated with the award of government contracts, and specifically with access to an arms procurement programme worth some US$10 billion, these otherwise justifiable initiatives became the source for the private enrichment of the political elite and their associates. As the gap between rich and poor blacks visibly widened in the statistics and on public display, talk of 'fat black cats' and their greediness became rife. Archbishop Desmond Tutu had observed, not long after 1994, that the gravy train had stopped only long enough for the new guys to get on. Tony Yengeni, former MK commander and prominent ANC parliamentarian, was forced to resign, Defence Minister Joe Modisi left office tainted with allegations of profiting from earlier arms deals, and Mbeki finally sacked Deputy President Jacob Zuma in 2005 when evidence of his wrongdoing in the same field was overwhelming.[20] At much the same time a top ANC official publicly revealed that he for one 'hadn't struggled to be poor'.

While opportunities for elite corruption are fewer in Namibia, Melber is clear about the problem. "Self-enrichment by higher ranking officials and politicians utilizing their access to the state is tolerated", regardless of public morale. He notes that the Namibianization of the fisheries sector showed how "national wealth is privatized for the benefit of a privileged few".[21] Namibia is no Angola either, but ex-President Nujoma remained head of SWAPO, and is supported today by an Office of the Founding President,; and a Sam Nujoma Foundation too.

If the main functions of the rapid land seizures that Mugabe initiated in early 2000 were to hold on to presidential power and punish white farmers, the consequences of the redistribution included the self-enrichment of the ruling elite. Anna Tibaijuka's carefully phrased report notes that "the major beneficiaries turned out to be senior ruling party officials, ministers and their families", although not all of them bothered to use their acquisitions productively.[22]

Neglect of the People and their Problems

Mere neglect is too soft a word to use against the ruling elites in both Zimbabwe and Angola. The former country once possessed the second most advanced capitalist economy in Africa. With a diversified economy, it was the region's breadbasket, and its importance here was directly brought home to Mugabe by Presidents' Julius Nyerere and Samora Machel, in 1980—in their famous admonition, "you have inherited a jewel of Africa, don't tarnish it". Yet, he purposefully did the opposite. In a present day summation: "Land grabs have crippled commercial agriculture and irrigation systems. Hyperinflation and lack of foreign exchange makes it hard to buy seeds and fertilizer, while fuel shortages stymie transport. . .the government has [even so far] refused to endorse the UN's emergency programme to help those affected".[23] Renewed farm invasions followed instead, forcing the Governor of the Reserve Bank, Gideon Gono, to declare the obvious in October: "If you invade a coffee, tea, wheat or fruit farm. . .you undermine the productive capacity of the economy". According to IMF data, GDP fell by 4% in 2004 and by another 7% to-date in 2005. The once surplus-producing country was importing at least 37 000 tons of maize a week just for survival.[24]

At the start of the 21st century Angola is awash with oil revenues, yet the people are in the deepest misery. The system of clientelist control established by President dos Santos both operates at the people's expense and accords impunity to the ruler while doing so. Global Witness reports on the "progressive impoverishment" of the country, as a ruling MPLA elite, and a (once) competing elite led by Jonas Savimbi, fought for control of Angola's huge oil and also diamond resources over decades.[25] Conflict was "deliberately exploited" to enrich the rulers through increasing oil revenues, foreign investment and profits from big arms-procurement programmes.

The condition of the people in the oil-rich country is manifest. The population living in absolute and relative poverty was 82.5% (of an estimated total of 12.4 million) around 2000. The population without access to drinking water was 62%; those without health care totalled 76%; some 3.2 million people were known to require food-aid, which, as noted, was not forthcoming from the Angolan government. Unemployment was some 80%.[26] What care the common people received was being provided by churches, international agencies and voluntary groups.[27] The "logic of theft and predation", combined with the depth of the misery, was extreme and aggravated. While the opulence of the *nomenklatura* was ever more visible, there was, "growing among the population, especially in Luanda (home to over a quarter of the country's people), a deep resentment of their condition and of the people held responsible for it".[28]

Botswana was not Angola, and people had voting rights. But it was nonetheless a rich country with many poor people, to borrow from a comment by Vladimir Putin about Russia. Botswana is an Upper Middle Income country where, thanks to a heavy reliance on diamonds, inequalities are rife.[29] According to recent United Nations Development Programme (UNDP) data, the richest 10% got 56.6% of national income, 1989–2000, and the poorest 10% only 0.7%. The ratio between the two was 77.6. The Gini coefficient, a comparative measure of income inequality, was 63.0; only Lesotho and Namibia were worse.

In a rich country, precisely because of these inequalities, poverty and its affects were bad. About 23% of the people lived on less than a dollar a day around the same time, according to the World Bank, and some 50% got below two dollars. The numbers of undernourished people, i.e. those experiencing chronic food insufficiency, had been rising, from 18% in 1990–92, to 24% in 1999–2001.[30] The country's Human Development Index was falling, from 0.675 in 1990 to 0.589 in

2002, even at a time when the country was enjoying high economic growth. While 21 countries in the world also recorded a drop in HDI over the period 1990–2001, Botswana was the only one to do so while experiencing rapid growth.[31]

Diamonds dominated the economy and much else: they constituted 80.7% of exports; some 45% of total GDP; and 65% of government revenue in 2003HD104. Simultaneously, manufacturing was only 4.1% of GDP, while agriculture was 2.3% of total production. Agriculture had been declining on average by 1.2% per annum since 1980, as a result of low government investment.[32] The World Bank also reported that 97% of those existing on less than two dollars daily lived in rural areas. Inequalities in cattle ownership were not dissimilar to those in income. Two-and-a-half per cent of farming households owned 40% of all cattle, said the Botswana Human Development Report 2005, and unofficial estimates indicated that around 70% of rural households had no cattle. Agriculture was in a sense being hollowed out, economically and socially. Cullis and Watson noted that, in 1981, about 29% of rural households were not actually engaged in agriculture, and in 1991 some 42% of people were in this position. Towards the end of the 1990s many poorer households were effectively excluded from agricultural production and obliged to rely on "itinerant casual labouring for their subsistence".[33] In Ghanzi and Kgalagadi districts particularly, poverty was endemic and structural, and many survived only on frugal state destitute handouts.[34]

Not unlike in Angola, there appears to be a causal connection between the national wealth of Botswana (based today on diamonds but historically and culturally in cattle too), inequalities in distribution, and the comparatively deep poverty of the many.[35] The UNDP's Human Development rating is notably higher in poorer African countries than in richer but deeply inequitable Botswana. Wilkinson argues, with a wealth of historical, comparative data, that big inequalities are bad for a person's health and welfare.[36] Botswana's rulers have the capacity to reduce poverty and inequalities, but they are yet to try seriously to do this. Festus Mogae was not the first BDP leader to observe that it would be wrong to give money to the poor by taking wealth from those who were already enjoying it. But either that, or new broad-based and equitable development, is precisely what is required. As the World Bank observed: "High aggregate growth, in itself, will not reduce poverty. The pattern of growth must also benefit the poor, either directly through increased employment and incomes or indirectly through improved social services".[37]

While President Mbeki's ANC government won 70% of seats in national parliamentary elections in April, and majorities in all nine provinces, socioeconomic problems, and consequent popular discontent, existed. The UNDP reported in May that more than 10% of people were living in extreme poverty, and there was a worsening rate of income inequality. Later in the year, and in the wake of Zuma's dismissal from the deputy presidency, COSATU highlighted the policy failings of the government. They include Mbeki's very personalized policy of 'quiet diplomacy' towards Robert Mugabe, where failure was writ large in the collapse of the Zimbabwean economy and the consequent appearance of a visibly failed state on South Africa's doorstep; HIV/AIDS, where, again, highly idiosyncratic policies and beliefs persistently upheld by Mbeki, had led to an adult HIV prevalence rate in excess of 20%, and about 600 AIDS-related deaths a day; and BEE, which had benefited a black bourgeoisie not workers. The country's new black managerial class profited from BEE but added little in productive value to justify their huge salaries. The ANC government was accused by the unions of failing either to create jobs or to save those threatened by market forces—over 130 000 formal jobs were lost in the non-farming economy in the January–March quarter, according to Statistics South Africa.[38]

COSATU took its criticisms further soon after, accusing President Mbeki and his health minister of a "failure of leadership" and a "betrayal of our people and our struggle", in presiding over a situation where six million people were infected with AIDS, on the government's own figures.[39] In the middle of the year popular discontent had broken out, sometimes in violent demonstrations, in townships across the country, expressing anger at the government's failure to deliver services to poor people in key areas like health and sanitation—newspapers carried stories of school girls forced to walk great distances daily to try to find an available, usable toilet. The ANC acknowledged in September that there was "a real danger of steadily but surely eroding public confidence in the [party]". When a lengthy and expensive drive to encourage voter registration ended in early September, fewer than 300 000 out of an estimated five million to seven million unregistered voters had come forward.[40]

South Africa is not in crisis as is Angola and ever more Zimbabwe, but Mbeki's presidentialist, predominant party regime is responsible for serious policy failures which relate directly to the autocratic elements in the system. And there is popular awareness of the scope and cause of these problems.

Intolerance of Criticism

With the suppression prevailing in Angola and Zimbabwe, and the intolerance in Namibia already alluded to, South Africa and Botswana will be focused on here. While South Africa was the cockpit for a great participatory democratic impulse in the 1980s, and it retains an organized civil society, President Mbeki appears to have a loathing of criticism. When it is expressed by black academics and intellectuals, he tends to portray them as disloyal, and when a white critic has the temerity to speak out, Mbeki labels him or her racist. The result in both cases, according to Mamphela Ramphele, speaking when she was Vice Chancellor of the University of Cape Town, is silence, and silence is a "threat to South Africa's infant democracy". Other informed observers have noted that what the Mbeki elite hates most is the white intellectual or activist who tries to speak out in the name of the poor black majority on the big issues concerning them like jobs, the non-delivery of public services and corruption. Vocal critics like Holomisa earlier and Dale McKinley more recently have been publicly hounded from party membership. The governing elite is often supported here by black professionals and business leaders. Christine Qunta is an articulate legal figure, with a regular newspaper platform, who apparently believes that any white who raises the issue of corruption is necessarily, if perhaps subliminally, racist. These restrictions on free speech can be and are resisted. But resistance, as demonstrated by the vivid example of Zackie Achmat and the Treatment Action Campaign (TAC), requires cause, organization and considerable determination.

Democracy is constrained in Botswana, not only at key institutional and structural levels, but in the expression of opinion too. While opposition parties may compete, they must do so on an unfair playing field where the BDP commands the necessary resources of money, mobility and access to the media. Deference remains important in the society, upheld as the desired norm by the ruling elite in their admonitions that even questioning authority constitutes abuse. A bold local critic, such as the lawyer Duma Boko, may obtain a platform for his views; but retaining it is another matter. Criticism can endanger one's career in journalism, teaching, academe and law, to be replaced by self-censorship, and a prevailing 'battered-wife syndrome', where journalists and others scramble to find excuses for authority's mistakes.[41] Incorporation into the established system also ensures uniformity and closure. A number of independent thinkers gained prominence in Gaborone during the 1990s, speaking out critically on women's rights and on economic problems, but the people concerned were fairly quickly accorded high places in the bureaucracy and judiciary. Representation gained, and the modernizing image of the BDP was improved, but critical thought, and those who might have benefited from it, suffered.

Free speech exists in late 2005 if one has nothing too serious to say. Vice-President Ian Khama frankly declared in May that: "I believe one has to have democracy but with discipline".[42] The discipline he perhaps had in mind was exerted over the writer on 31 May, when he was snatched from the portals of the High Court in Lobatse by security personnel, and put on a plane out of the country seven hours later. The author had been declared to be a Prohibited Immigrant in February, and President Mogae had claimed that he was a threat to national security. The writer was resident in Botswana for 15 years, and had been teaching and carrying out research, as Professor of Political Studies at the University of Botswana. His job functions included the responsibility of providing 'service to the community', and he had written, as part of that, on issues such as corruption, poverty and presidential power. The author was a member of no organization other than the university. During the 14 weeks when he appealed against the order in the courts, people frequently approached him in the street saying "we support you, prof," "hang in there" and "you're saying just what we're thinking".

Mogae's drastic action, in the assessment of South Africa's leading financial daily, turned a difference in opinion "into an international *cause célèbre*". The president had apparently acted in a fit of pique against an elderly foreign academic who "dared to mention that the emperor was stark naked". Festus Mogae was clearly "from the same mould as Africa's other 'Big Men'—happy to pay lip service to democracy when the going is good, but autocratic to the core".[43]

Not long after this expulsion two foreign journalists working for Botswana newspapers had their work and residence permits cancelled and were forced to leave the country.[44] Students have written latterly about a stultifying atmosphere prevailing at the University of Botswana and of "silence among those most able to speak [out]".[45] The need for criticism is present across the region, and it exists in reverse proportion to its acceptability to the ruling elites of the various countries. Here lies perhaps the basic failure of Soyinka's Toad Kings. If the people were actively engaged—not merely consulted—both the socioeconomic and the political weaknesses might begin to be corrected.

Potentialities for Democratization

While President Mogae continues to proclaim, as on 29 September 2005, that Botswana is the "longest established multiparty democracy in Africa", the accolade for a functioning liberal democratic system actually lies with Mauritius. With a population of 1.2 million, it is smaller than both Namibia and Botswana, but its economy is sound. Its GDP was $6.3 billion in 2004, it was diversified, with a relatively large manufacturing sector: agriculture (plus construction and electricity) at the same time represented 14.5% of total production, financial and business services were 19.2%, trade was 11.3%, and manufacturing represented 20.8% of GDP (the last sector being roughly five times larger than Botswana's). While the value of the country's sugar exports was significant at $355 billion, that of 'EPZ products' (goods manufactured in the special export promotion zones) was almost $1.2 billion. Real growth was just over 4% then, and GDP per capita was the region's highest at $12 800 (purchasing power parity—PPP).[46] There is no military force, and defence is chiefly entrusted to a special mobile force located within the police and answerable to the prime minister. Expenditure in this area represented just 0.2% of GDP in 2004.[47]

These economic strengths had social and political dividends. Life expectancy, in a region devastated by HIV/AIDS, was 72 years in 2005. The unemployment rate was 10.8% in 2004, the population living below the poverty line, measured a few years earlier, was only 10%, and the Gini coefficient was a mere 37.0 (on 1987 data).[48] Such admirable social statistics were the result both of physical and political factors. While almost half the country's land was arable, the country's leadership had played a very positive role too. Successive governments had invested heavily in education and social welfare, and had subsidized basic foodstuffs and fertilizer. Cawthra recognizes a "political consensus around the social dimensions of democracy". The political elites, he says, have shown "a willingness to sacrifice personal gain for the good of the country" and, with per capita GDP high and relatively evenly distributed, economic growth and democracy are mutually reinforcing.[49]

The political and governmental system is broadly exceptional. The president is appointed by the National Assembly, and the president's role, notes the Economist Intelligence Unit, "is largely ceremonial". The country's liberal, representative democracy is functional and, unlike Botswana's, truly established. Cawthra notes that it is "the only consolidated democracy" in the region, using Samuel Huntington's accepted criterion of two turnovers of elected government.[50] Eight national elections have been held as of July 2005, resulting in four transfers of government. Turnout at the latest was as high as 81.5%, the campaign was fought "largely on economic issues", and the defeat of the sitting prime minister, Paul Berenger, was followed by his immediate resignation.[51]

The national assembly is comprised of 20 three-member constituencies, with the parties fielding multi-ethnic slates in each, and with the island-province of Rodrigues electing two MPs. An additional eight are appointed, on what is termed a 'best-loser' system—those who gained the most votes immediately behind the actual winners—to ensure ethnic representation. In 2005 four of the eight went to the winning Social Alliance (AS) coalition, two to the losing Mauritian Militant Movement-Mauritian Socialist Movement (MMM-MSM), and two to Rodrigues.

The system produces multi-ethnic coalitions, excludes tiny parties and, with its basis in first-past-the-post, produces 'strong governments' simultaneously vulnerable to alternative coalition building—in 1987 a difference of 2% of the votes separated the two major alliances, which translated into a 37% difference in parliamentary seats.[52] Thus, no presidentialism, no predominance, a liberal parliamentary system based closely on ethnic realities, where voter participation is high, and voters change governments regularly. The economy is diversified and dynamic, and development has not been accompanied by poverty and inequalities. Leadership appears attentive to the needs of the people,[53] and it is answerable to the voters at elections—in July, 10 ministers in the outgoing government lost their seats as well as their office.[54] Liberalism functioning unusually well, in a small and relatively wealthy country.

Change away from predominance is possible in Botswana by 2009. Forty-eight per cent of voters supported a divided opposition in 2004, and the electoral trends over a decade disfavour the BDP. People appear to want change, given the ruling party's long neglect of their needs as reflected in the levels of poverty and the depth of inequalities, and the failures in agriculture, manufacturing and diversification. The arrogance often displayed by this presidentialist regime constitutes a further aggravation and weakness. The language emanating from the presidency often expresses contempt and violence. Bushmen were notoriously characterized by Vice-President Mogae, in the mid-1990s, as "stone age creatures", who were "doomed to die out like the dodo" if they did not fall in with the government's development plans.[55] External criticism is readily labelled by the President as "ignorant and malicious comment", or alternatively, as the "regurgitation of ignorance and innuendo".[56] The London-based advocacy group, Survival International, a registered charity, was demonized as a "terrorist organization", after it criticized the government's removal of Bushmen from their homes in the Central Kalahari Game Park.[57] Robert Masitara was the person endorsed by the BDP to run against a combined opposition candidate in a key Gaborone by-election in October 2005. He was known to have a charge of rape pending against him in court, and he displayed "flamboyant and ostentatious conduct" throughout his campaign.[58] And by 2008 or earlier, General Ian Khama will succeed to the presidency, despite his seeming authoritarianism and inexperience, in a process entirely over the heads of the voters.

But the neglect of the people, elitist arrogance, and the urge for change will not be addressed and dealt with without opposition unity. The leading opposition parties, the Botswana National Front and the Botswana Congress Party, must display a unity of programme, purpose and leadership to establish themselves as a credible alternative to BDP predominance. Turnout of eligible voters at national elections in Botswana is more like 50% than the 80 per cent of Mauritius. Participation will only increase if people can see that a change of government is at last a realizable possibility. This process received a boost in the by-election in Gaborone on 15 October 2005, when a combined opposition candidate (the leader of the BNF), supported actively by the BCP, was fielded for the first time against the BDP. The election was doubly historic, as the local *Mmegi* newspaper informed its readers the previous day, when "ever more people are beginning to voice disquiet over the future of Botswana's democracy". The ruling party "shows worrying signs of intolerance for dissent", and it "increasingly comes across as impatient with the democratic process". There was concern too about the "independence of the judiciary" when "key posts were seen to be reserved for individuals known to be close associates of those in power". The unity candidate, Otsweletse Moupo, won convincingly.

Despite Mugabe's tyrannous regime, it is in their structural and organizational strengths that the potentialities of Zimbabwe and South Africa are outstanding.

Although infrastructure has been seriously damaged in the former since 2000, the socioeconomic strengths remain latent in both. The jewels of economic diversification and integration have been more than tarnished by Mugabe, but the fundamentals may still remain. It was the relatively advanced capitalism that produced a diversified and strong civil society, and specifically a trade union movement at its head, which together created a new political party, the Movement for Democratic Change. It was this profound development that seriously challenged the despot for the first time in 2000. The urban-based trade unions have been purposefully weakened by the denuding of the towns in actions like Operation Murambatsvina, but long-term reconstruction would draw them back. On a depth and scale much greater than in Mauritius, there is a mutually supportive interrelationship between advanced capitalism, the formation of civic groups and trade unions, and the formation of a political party representative of those popular interests. They showed their potential capacities in 1999 and early 2000, and they might do so again.

Similarly, but much more so, in Africa's most advanced economy. The participatory democratic experience of the 1980s is only two decades away. Not only did a wide range of popular organizations grow up in efforts to democratize the daily lives of many people, but highly relevant norms were adopted by the UDF—"principles of our organizational democracy"—to combat elitism and strengthen the people. Leaders should be criticized, they must be accountable, they would report back regularly to the rank and file, collective leadership was preferable to that of the single great man, and no one was immune from criticism.

If elites are to be controlled, it is through popular organizations upholding similar values that it will be done. It is unlikely that other means exist to combat the overweening ambitions and arrogance of the aristocrats. No Mbeki can seriously undermine the complex and advanced structures of South Africa's economy and society. The country has one of the highest levels of unionization (members as a percentage of the work force) in the world, and COSATU remains large, self-financing and active. In the TAC and in a social movement like the Landless People's Movement, the nucleus of a politically engaged civil society is present. The power of presidentialism and predominance obviously appears large today, and the consequences of elitism are vivid. But the decade of the 1980s also showed that democratization is a process, where the participatory future is built in the democratic practice of the day. Achieving a more participatory democracy is certain to be slow and incremental, but structural capacities and organizational resources are present in South Africa, and gains might still be made in areas like poverty, landlessness and HIV/AIDS through the agency of the unions and activist civics. Needs are critical,[59] they are unlikely to be satisfied in any other way, and in addressing them democratization is furthered. And criticizing elitism, as the TAC does so trenchantly, is of great value in itself.

Conclusion

The duopoly of presidentialism and predominance poses huge institutional barriers to change, worsened in many places by the arrogance and aggrandizement of individual rulers. Undiversified economies, especially in the form of dependence on minerals in Angola and Botswana, constitute further structural difficulties. Dos Santos and Mugabe are outstanding examples of rapacious, destructive presidentialism in continental terms.

South Africa and Zimbabwe offer the greatest, long-term hope for the future. Socioeconomic structures, and popular organizations, are favourable. The development of diversified economies, and the growth of strong civil societies were the larger part of this, and the formation of a trade union movement, and of a popular, social-democratic party, were essential further steps towards democratization. These were partially realized in South Africa during the 1980s, where dramatic change involving millions of self-organizing people, stopped short of fruition. The fuller process appeared less vividly and briefly in Zimbabwe in 1999 – 2001. And, in both, the potentialities remain, economically and socially, in the awareness and organizational experience of the people.

Botswana displays the limitations of the electoral democratic model, located in a rich but diamonds-dependent economy with big inequalities and debilitating poverty; these problems, neglected by the rulers, begin to stimulate change from the bottom up. On similar, orthodox dimensions, Mauritius represents existing success: the region's only established liberal democracy, in a small and wealthy country, with a leadership associated with, and regularly answerable to, the people. The regional barriers to democratization are big, but the potentialities are at least as strong.

Editor's Note

The April edition of *The Round Table* will be mainly dedicated to papers on conditions in a number of Southern African countries, concentrating on Zimbabwe. This paper serves as a curtain-raiser for that issue.

Notes

1. Gretchen Bauer and Scott D. Taylor, Introduction in Bauer and Taylor, *Politics in Southern Africa*, Boulder and London, CO: Lynne Rienner, 2005.
2. The idea of one-party predominance within a democracy stems from Pempel, and it is considered, among other places, in K. Good, *The Liberal Model and Africa: Elites Against Democracy*, Basingstoke: Palgrave, 2003.
3. He is head of state, head of government and leader of the ruii ng party, and his office has direct control over the bureaucracy, military, police, broadcasting and information, and the anti-corruption agency.
4. Appointed MPs enjoy the full voting rights of their elected parliamentary confreres. Namibia and Mauritius also have provision for specially appointed parliamentarians, but they administer the appointments differently, and deny the appointees voting privileges.
5. The complexities of the transition are considered in Good, *The Liberal Model*. Biographies of Nelson Mandela sometimes reveal his preference for the company of the rich and famous, and the discomfort he experienced when meeting younger and more boisterous UDF members in the late 1980s.
6. It is said that at the last general election 'spoilt ballots' totalled enough votes to have elected three MPs. This was not necessarily a negative or 'apathetic' choice. A few observers had recommended this limited option, which might accurately be seen as 'positive abstention' under the prevailing political circumstances.
7. Another term for this ruling, highly exploitative elite is the 'oligarchy'. Their coin is arms purchasing and currency devaluation as well as oil.
8. Global Witness, *All the President's Men*, March 2002, pp. 3, 59 – 60. All amounts in US dollars.

9. She describes the membership of the *nomenklatura*, and indicates the kind of patronage and preferment which dos Santos wields. While most official salaries are no higher than $200 to $300 a month, and Luanda is one of the most expensive cities in the world, the *nomenklatura* receive "a Christmas bonus of between $25 000 and $30 000". Also available, or unavailable, are "simple gifts in cash of tens, hundreds or thousands of dollars given to individuals". Overall privileges are "favours granted by the Prince". Christine Messiant, 'The Eduardo Dos Santos Foundation: or, how Angola's regime is taking over civil society', *African Affairs*, 100, 2001, p. 294.

10. *Ibid.*, pp. 289–291, 294–297, 301–302.

11. Tendai Biti, in Commentary, *Africa Analysis*, 477, 9 September 2005, p. 15. He quotes George Ayittey: "The nationalists who won freedom for their respective countries were hailed as heroes, swept into office with huge Parliamentary majorities and deified…Criticising them became sacrilegious", and promised freedoms and development were "transmogrified into a melodramatic nightmare".

12. Augusta Conchiglia, 'Zimbabwe's political evictions', *Le Monde Diplomatique*, September 2005, pp. 4,7.

13. Anna Kajumulo Tibaijuka, 'Report of the fact-finding mission to Zimbabwe to assess the scope and impact of Operation Murambatsvina', 18 July 2005, pp. 7, 15, 17–19.

14. Henning Melber, 'Limits to liberation', in Melber (Ed.), *Re-examining Liberation in Namibia: Political Culture Since Independence*, Uppsala: Nordic Africa Institute, 2003, pp. 16–19.

15. *Ibid.*, p. 19.

16. Christopher Saunders, 'Liberation and democracy: a critical reading of Sam Nujoma's "autobiography"', in Melber, *Re-examining Liberation in Namibia*, p. 94.

17. President Mandela utilized his immense stature to achieve reconciliation in South Africa, but did nothing to promote a democratic party system, and instead lampooned the weak opposition as 'Mickey Mouse parties'.

18. Detail is found in Good, 'Corruption and mismanagement in Botswana: a best-case example?', *Journal of Modern African Studies*, 32(3), 1994.

19. Chiefly in 'bail-outs' to citizen-owned companies, in government tenders and in land acquisitions in and around Gaborone.

20. The case is underway. But when Judge Hilary Squires sentenced Zuma's close aid and financial advisor, Schabir Shaik, to 15 years jail for corruption, he said: "His corporate empire's progress and prosperity was plainly linked to the possibility that Jacob Zuma would finally ascend to the highest political office". Shaik's role in the government's multibillion-dollar arms procurement programme, "was a typical example of a privileged treatment to a selected political figure in a situation redolent with lack of transparency and subversion of administrative fairness and integrity". BBC News online, 8 June 2005.

21. Melber, *Re-examining Liberation in Namibia*, p. 19.

22. Tibaijuka, 'Report of the fact-finding mission to Zimbabwe', p. 18.

23. *The Economist*, 8 October 2005.

24. BBC News online, 12 October 2005.

25. When Savimbi's UNITA entered national elections against dos Santos in 1992, the popular perception of the choice offered them was; 'UNITA kills, the MPLA steals'.

26. Global Witness, *All the President's Men*, p. 4.

27. Messiant, 'The Eduardo Dos Santos Foundation', p. 302.

28. *Ibid.*, p. 302.

29. Botswana is the world's most 'Non-fuel mineral dependent' country, and Angola is the world's most oil-dependent state. Michael Ross, 'The natural resource curse: how wealth can make you poor', in Jan Bannon and Paul Collier (Eds), *Natural Resources and Violent Conflict*, Washington, DC: World Bank, 2003, p. 21.

30. UNDP, *Human Development Report 2005*, New York: UNDP, 2005.

31. Jenny Clover, 'Botswana: future prospects and the need for broad-based development', Situation Report, Institute for Strategic Studies, Pretoria, 2003.

32. *Ibid.*

33. A. Cullis and C. Watson, 'Winners and losers: privatising the commons in Botswana', Briefing Paper, International Institute for Environment and Development and RECONCILE, 2003, pp. 12, 17.

34. Clover, 'Botswana'.

35. The ramifications are deep and extensive. See K. Good, 'Resource dependency and its consequences: the costs of Botswana's shining gems', *Journal of Contemporary African Studies*, 23(1), 2005.

36. Richard Wilkinson, *The Impact of Inequality: How to Make Sick Societies Healthier*, New York: New Press, 2005.
37. World Bank, *Taking Action to Reduce Poverty in Sub-Saharan Africa*, Washington, DC: World Bank, 1997, p. 8.
38. *Africa Confidential*, 46(18), 9 September 2005.
39. BBC News online, 26 September 2005.
40. BBC News online, 12 September 2005; and *African Analysis*, 447, 9 September 2005.
41. Term used by Outsa Mokone when he was editor of *The Botswana Guardian*.
42. Christina Lamb, 'In sickness and in wealth', *The Sunday Times Magazine*, 3 July 2005.
43. Editorial, *Business Day*, 2 June 2005. An experienced journalist observed at this time that African democracies are democratic until they are criticised.
44. One, Rodrick Mukumbira, a Zimbabwean, was news editor of the *Ngami Times*, where he had worked for two years. *Bocongo News*, 10 August 2005.
45. Personal communication, 29 September 2005, author's name withheld.
46. Economist Intelligence Unit, *Country Report*, London: EIU, August 2005; and CIA, *World Factbook: Mauritius*, Washington, DC, August 2005.
47. Gavin Cawthra, 'Mauritius', *Africa Insight*, 35(1), April 2005, p. 18; and CIA, *World Factbook: Mauritius*, p. 10.
48. CIA, *World Factbook: Mauritius*.
49. Cawthra, 'Mauritius', p. 15.
50. *Ibid.*, p. 14.
51. An estimated 66% of Mauritians are of Indian origin, of whom 52% are Hindu and 17% Muslim. Berenger was the first European (or Franco-Mauritian) prime minister. EIU, *Country Report*, p. 13; and Cawthra, 'Mauritius', p. 14.
52. Cawthra, 'Mauritius', pp. 15, 16. In Botswana, too, the BDP got just 4% more votes than the combined opposition scored, but under first-past-the-post this won them 77% of Assembly seats.
53. An Independent Commission against Corruption was established in 2002, and a minister resigned the next year, following his arrest over the fraudulent sale of state-owned land. However, corruption remains a problem, says the EIU. *Country Profile*, London: EIU, 2004, p. 6.
54. EIU, *Country Report*, p. 14.
55. Bushmen are a sizeable ethnic minority in Botswana, and their subordination is a defining failure of Botswana's democracy, the more jealously guarded for that reason.
56. State of the Nation address, 8 November 2004; and Press Circular no. 10 of 2005.
57. K. Good, *Bushmen and Diamonds: (Un)Civil Society in Botswana*, Uppsala: Nordic Africa Institute, 2003, Discussion Paper 23. By contrast, Nicky Oppenheimer, chairman of De Beers, sees Survival International as "a reputable NGO". *The Guardian*, 2 July 2005.
58. The group Women and Law in Southern Africa labelled this endorsement as "belittling the seriousness" of the charge of rape, and an "abuse of the integrity of public office". There was further criticism from Emang Basadi, *Mmegi*, 11 and 12 October 2005.
59. The country has over 800 000 people in need of AIDS treatment, but only about 100 000 of them are getting it. *The Economist*, 8 October 2005.

Reflections on the Opposition in Zimbabwe: The Politics of the Movement for Democratic Change (MDC)

BRIAN RAFTOPOULOS

Institute for Justice and Reconciliation, Cape Town

ABSTRACT   *The Movement for Democratic Change split in an almost slow-motion manner over 2005/6, although it was the Senate elections that finally put paid to the idea of a single MDC opposition. The stakes in being the opposition are discussed here – not just the stakes in opposing a ruthless government, but in remaining itself democratic under external and internal duress. The author was a key mediator in the effort to bridge the rift between the two MDC factions and draws upon first-hand knowledge and documentation – after first giving a detailed account of the rise of the MDC in the first place. This is an expanded version of a paper published by the Institute for Justice and Reconciliation, to which the Editors give thanks.*

KEY WORDS: Democracy, opposition, Movement for Democratic Change, factions

Introduction

The dramatic schism and implosion in the Movement for Democratic Change (MDC), Zimbabwe's main opposition party, in 2005/2006, has once again raised major questions about the future of opposition politics not only at national level, but also on the continent. The MDC represented the hope of millions of Zimbabweans searching for a way out of the deep political and economic crisis that characterises contemporary Zimbabwe. For a short period the party pointed to the possibilities of creating an alternative, democratic non-violent, post-colonial politics, while confronting the enormous legacy and legitimacy of a former liberation movement and its enigmatic leader. Founded on the basis of a strong civic movement, enunciating the need for both political and economic reforms, the MDC captured the growing disgruntlement of Zimbabwe's citizens over eroding economic conditions and the political arrogance of the ruling party. The energy of a younger generation of civic activists, no longer paralysed by the fear of confronting the 'party of liberation' and the ideological baggage that accompanied it, brought a vibrant energy into Zimbabwean politics, and expanded the subjunctive mood of the post-colonial milieu. The combination of the politics of constitutional reform and trade union activism provided a national organisational reach and an expansive discursive opportunity that radically challenged the increasingly moribund exclusivity of Zanu PF's nationalism. The politics of possibility dominated the discussions of thousands of activists around the country, and the sense of imminent victory, often of Panglossian dimensions, was everywhere apparent. The huge weight of a political monolith appeared to be lifting, and opportunities to pose new questions not only about the present and future, but also about the legacies of the past, began to appear.

For some analysts the emergence of this opposition was merely an 'anti-Mugabe reaction', a counter to the glaring shortcomings of the ruling party. In short it represented no positive alternatives. One response to this accusation is that of course it was such a reaction; all opposition movements begin in such ways. However it also generated the release of new energies and possibilities and the construction of a novel democratic discourse in the Zimbabwean context. The ruling party and its intellectuals have been loath to admit this, because in the discursive world of Zimbabwe's liberation politics the politics of freedom can only emanate from the former liberation movement. This form of ideological closure has been a central part of the authoritarian politics that has marked the most recent period of Zimbabwe's politics.[1] Despite the repressive response of the state to these challenges such questions continue to be asked.

Notwithstanding the possibilities and hopes that the emergence of the MDC created, the opposition has also been marked by very serious shortcomings that have reflected, both the ways in which dissenting politics often take on the aspects of the political culture they are seeking to displace, and the organisational and imaginative limits of the MDC challenge. These are the issues that this paper will attempt to explore, as well as to point to some of the challenges that are likely to confront any future opposition initiative in Zimbabwe. However before tackling these central concerns the paper will first provide a brief historical context to the emergence of the MDC.

Historical Trends in Nationalist and Opposition Politics

Several studies of African opposition politics in Zimbabwe during both the colonial and post-colonial periods stress the importance of a triple legacy in undermining the growth of a democratic tradition. This legacy includes the influence of 'traditional', subject politics[2], the authoritarian structures of colonial rule and the commandist politics of the liberation struggle with its attendant view that only liberation parties could represent the 'will of the people' for the foreseeable future.[3] Thus while nationalism provided a contingent discursive unity, usually marked by tensions and cleavages, this mobilisational force also carried with it a series of unpropitious tendencies undermining future democratic politics. During the colonial period nationalist politics was often characterised by violent ruptures both between and within nationalist parties. The 1963 split between Zapu and its splinter organisation Zanu, was marked by a series of violent clashes and mutual demonisation that continued until the formation of the Patriotic Front on the eve of the 1979 Lancaster House Conference. The rivalry between the two parties continued in the aftermath of the post-1980 settlement, punctuated by the *Gukurahundi* violence of the new state in Matabeleland and the Midlands in the mid-1980's. This massive deployment of state violence effectively led to the formal subsumption of PF Zapu to the ruling Zanu PF in the form of the 1987 Unity Accord, and thus the demise of a formidable opposition party. Within the nationalist parties themselves, a number of violent power struggles occurred in both Zanu and Zapu in the 1970s that consolidated the leadership of the 'old guard'[4], setting the precedent for the violent marginalisation of dissenting voices within nationalist politics.[5] Ndlovu-Gatsheni describes the effects of these legacies on post-colonial politics as follows:

> The new Zimbabwean state under Zanu PF failed miserably to make a break with the tradition of nationalist authoritarianism and guerrilla violence as well as colonial settler oppression. The ruling party itself failed to de-militarise itself as a militarised liberation movement, not only in practice, but also in attitude and style of management of civil institutions and the state at large. The new Zanu PF government readily assumed the resilient colonial and equally military oriented structures left by the retreating settler state, with serious implications for democracy, human rights and human security.[6]

For most of the 1980's the political milieu was characterised by a combination of repression, in particular the brutal state response to opposition in Matabeleland, and a general deference to the authority and liberation legitimacy of the new state. Most emergent civic bodies and NGOs regarded their activities as complementing the developmental programmes of Zanu PF, and the state could draw on a considerable amount of ideological capital because of its liberation history.[7] By 1987 the ruling party had disposed of two opposition groups, the first, in 1986, by constitutionally removing the entrenched white seats in parliament agreed to at the Lancaster House Constitution, and the second through the brutal *Gukurahundi* campaign against Zapu in the mid 1980s and the pursuant 1987 Unity Accord between the two major nationalist parties which effectively incapacitated Zapu. Through these measures, the introduction of an executive president in 1987 with immense power, and ready access to the repressive legacies of the settler state, the outlook for opposition politics appeared dismal.[8]

However the combination of a contracting economy, the erosion of state legitimacy through the exposure of corruption in the ruling party, and the emergence of critical social forces such as the labour movement, the student movement, along with critical intellectual and media responses, led to the emergence of another opposition party in 1989. Led by former Zanu PF stalwart, Edgar Tekere, the Zimbabwe Unity Movement (ZUM) fought the ruling party's attempts to impose a one-party state in Zimbabwe, and performed favourably in the 1990 Presidential election. Though the party did not survive for long in the 1990s, and was largely confined in terms of its support base to a small urban and student base, particularly in Tekere's home area in Mutare, the ZUM both fractured the seeming unity of Zanu PF and fought for the necessity of multi party politics. The various attempts at opposition that followed in the 1990s, such as the Zanu *Ndonga*, the Democratic Party, the Forum Party and the Zimbabwe Union of Democrats, were largely unsuccessful in constructing national constituencies and in providing popular alternatives to Zanu PF. Moreover in the face of determined state repression and an electoral system that provided little space for them to score electoral victories, these parties, with limited capacity to develop viable structures, remained little more than political amusement for the ruling party.[9] In sum by the mid 1990s opposition politics were largely built around individuals, prone to fractious outbreaks, and unable to develop both a popular message and a national reach. As Masunungure notes, these parties 'appeared to be more aggressive in attacking each other than in directing their firepower at Zanu PF.'[10]

By the latter half of the 1990s the fortunes of opposition politics took a different turn. In to an apparent barren field of dissent emerged the most formidable opposition party of the post-colonial period. In 1999 the Movement for Democratic Change (MDC) was born, the product of a combination of labour struggles, constitutional politics and a generation of human rights struggles, and built on the failures of previous attempts at opposition politics. The new movement also attracted the support of the mainly white large scale commercial farming sector. Constructed in the era of debilitating structural adjustment programmes, the MDC drew on and fed into a growing wave of political and economic disenchantment, and provided a message of 'change' which found resonance through nationally based structures. Through the language of political rights, constitutionalism and economic reform, the MDC and its social partners confronted Zanu PF with its first mass opposition party, and the threat of imminent defeat.[11] Carried on the wave of the constitutional movement's referendum victory in 2000 against a Zanu PF imposed constitution, and backed by the threat of popular mobilisation, the MDC gained nearly 50% of the parliamentary vote in 2000 in the face of enormous electoral obstacles, and state violence. Moreover as Laakso points out, the organisational base of the MDC 'was not merely one of popular discontent with the executive, but an explicit agenda to democratise the state through a peaceful transition.'[12]

Since its dynamic ascension onto the Zimbabwean political stage in the 1990s the MDC has had to face the difficult tasks of building accountable party structures, developing policy positions and peaceful political strategies, and projecting a regional and international profile, against an authoritarian state that has consistently closed down the spaces for opposition politics in the country. Moreover the MDC has had to confront the effects of the country's authoritarian political legacies on its attempts to develop an alternative political culture. It is to the analysis of these issues that we now turn.

The MDC: Confronting the challenges of opposition politics in an authoritarian state

Soon after its launch in September 1999 the MDC had to confront a number of organisational and structural party problems. At a strategic meeting in early 2000 the leadership outlined the following challenges:

- The lack of coordination of policy committees.
- Lack of coordination between the Presidents's Office and the Secretariat.
- Lack of accountability and procedures in the disbursement of funds.
- Need for clearer procedures in the appointment and discipline of the security officials.

- Insufficient consultation between the President and the Vice President.
- Lack of coordination between the party Chairman and other departments.
- The need for more clarity on the functions of the Deputy Secretary General.[13]

The meeting also noted that the 'President's office should provide leadership for the entire party, while facilitating the strengthening of particular departments.'[14] In order to deal with these problems the leadership agreed to rationalise the functions of each position and improve the communication within the leadership, as well as between the leadership and the various levels of the party structures. In addition to these problems the violent land occupations following the NCA (National Constitutional Assembly)/MDC victory in the February 2000 constitutional referendum confronted the MDC with three major strategic problems: The cordoning off of the rural areas by the ruling party; the elimination of MDC structures and personnel; and the lack of alternative sources of information in rural areas.[15] In the face of these challenges the MDC set itself the following objectives:

- To facilitate the reduction of levels of political violence and the creation of more peaceful conditions for electioneering.
- To shift the mode of mobilisation to a low profile campaign,
- To provide information on the election process that would increase voter confidence and the assurance of voter secrecy.
- To raise the profile of the MDC campaign message on the economy, particularly land, jobs, indigenisation and investment.
- To re-engage the civic organisations that provided the bedrock for the formation of the MDC.
- To isolate President Mugabe within his own party, at national level and in the regional and international spheres.
- To pressure the police to carry out their duties.
- To maintain the international media focus on the primary goal of the elections, and the monitoring of election violence.
- To minimise the security threat to the leadership of the MDC.[16]

A number of issues emerge from these early assessments. Firstly the problems of organisation, responsibility and accountability in party structures that would later take on such explosive forms were already apparent. Secondly the party was aware of the central strategic challenge that confronted it, namely the commitment to a peaceful, electoral process of change, while understanding the growing limitations of this approach in the face of the ruling party's intransigence. As a strategy update paper noted, while the 'strongest weapon' of the MDC was 'public adherence to the principles of democracy and the rule of law', the party 'must not lose sight of the fact that we may be in for a much longer and harder race than we first envisaged.'[17] Thirdly the MDC, as part of its commitment to peaceful politics, was still optimistic, many would say naïve, in its belief that it could hope for a certain minimum level of professionalism from the organs of the state. Fourthly, as the ruling party was in the initial stages of reorganising its party and state structures in the face of the MDC threat, the opposition party believed that it was possible to work on the divisions in Zanu PF and to isolate Mugabe. Attention was paid particularly to the fractious Masvingo province where there were long and well publicised differences between the Zanu PF provincial strong man, Edison Zvobgo, and Mugabe. In 2001 it was believed that Zvobgo's position could be summed up as, 'We don't want Mugabe but we are not MDC.'[18] Lastly, in addition to the difficulties faced in attempting to develop its media capacity, the MDC was clearly unsure of how to deal with the problem of rural penetration given the enormous obstacles presented by the land occupations led by the war veterans and supported politically and logistically by the ruling party and state machinery. Some of its suggestions included engaging the support of churches and approaching traditional leaders, but there was little substance provided for the proposed strategies.[19]

Looking at the problem of structures more closely provides some idea of the organisational problems faced by the MDC in 2000. At an MDC District Workshop in August 2000, a number of problems were registered. It was noted that while structures were in place at district level they were weak at branch level. Conflicts were also reported by some of the committees over poor time-keeping, lack of protocol and the influence of alcohol. A request was made for a code of conduct to be passed on to the Secretary General of the party. There was also a 'strong feeling' that all MPs must communicate with their electorate, 'even if they have made promises that they cannot fulfil in the short-term.' The meeting warned that if the MPs 'do not become visible any further campaigning will be difficult.' The members recommended that in order to strengthen the party there was need for training in a number of areas: The procedures for running meetings, minute taking; public speaking; conflict resolution mechanisms; organisation; budgeting and allocation of scarce resources; proposal writing; and writing internal memos.[20] These problems became apparent during campaign periods, when the Party's lack of coordination, strategy and discipline were exposed. A report on the Marondera West campaign in late 2000, revealed a series of operational problems. Youths and security were brought into the area and 'hijacked the campaign as a means to giving employment.' The Provincial Chair 'was allowed to use the campaign for his personal campaign.' In the end the party spent two million dollars 'dealing with youth and security problems and logistics instead of winning votes and getting voters to the voting stations.' The report on the campaign concluded that:

> The bulk of the youth are bad mannered, undisciplined, uncontrollable and only in it for the money. They left the premises and vehicles they used in a disgusting state and when asked to clean up said- 'I am not the one'.[21]

In a recent, useful study of political parties in Zimbabwe LeBas has analysed the context in which these organisational problems developed. She notes that given the changed political environment from 2000–2003 and the increased ruling party violence that characterised it 'violence drove party activists into the cities, and formal party structures subsequently collapsed.' Furthermore she observes that the 'most immediate response to this problem was a turn from visible party structures to more amorphous, socially embedded networks.'[22]

Assessing the state of the party in the aftermath of the 2002 Presidential Election LeBas writes:

> In a post-election report, the MDC's organising department noted that party structures had 'disintegrated'; further there was 'very little or no activity' by provincial structures, due in some cases to misappropriation of funds. Nor could the national executive remain well-informed about conditions outside Harare: an audit in late 2002 found that most provincial leaders were passing along false information about party structures and membership. Members of the national executive pointed to these problems to explain the failure of the planned post-election mass action, saying that it was simply lost in the party structures.[23]

This problem of adapting organisational structures to deal with state violence was not only faced by the MDC but also by key civic movements such as the NCA many of whose members also belonged to the MDC. Assessing the 'mass action' strategy adopted but the National Constitutional Assembly (NCA) after 2000, and the violence that was sometimes used by its membership, McCandless concludes:

> In the case of the NCA the research. . .indicates that the use of violent strategies (even if only by some of their members) undermines their message, which causes disaffection of important NCA constituencies. Moreover, it is ineffectual given their weak position vis-à-vis the violent capacity of the state.[24]

The major organisational response of the MDC to the repressive political environment was to create a parallel structure within the party. LeBas describes this as a 'shadowy party structure, which would be designed to facilitate top-down organising and speedy response to orders from national leadership.'[25] The activities of this structure not only resulted in major problems of accountability and violence within the party structures, but became a central site of struggle for the control of the party between the President and the Secretary General. The first major sign of the problems that were being caused by this parallel structure was the violence that occurred at the Party headquarters in 2004, specifically the beating up of party officials. One of the party officials that was affected by these disturbances, the Director of Security, testified to an internal Commission of Inquiry that this structure was formed by two of the Party Presidents' aides, 'as part of the mass action,' and that over time this structure had 'become a reliable source of force or militia for use in party struggles by unscrupulous politicians.' The official also believed that there was a 'tribal clique of people from Masvingo' who were in control of the parallel structure and who, during the period of Morgan Tsvangirai's treason trial,

> . . .strongly believed that the President would be convicted, leaving a vacuum which in their view must never be filled by a Ndebele person contrary to the MDC party constitutional provisions. Their argument was that even if the Vice-President were to take over, the fact that he stays in Bulawayo, the effective job

of President would fall into the hands of Prof. Welshman Ncube. This imagination frightened them because for a long time they have been working on a programme to eliminate the Secretary General and those deemed as his surrogates.[26]

Others who gave evidence to this commission accused the Secretary General Welshman Ncube, of wanting to sabotage the project of removing Mugabe, and claimed that Ncube had a secret agenda to divide the party.'[27] The report also implied that there were conflicts between the 'professionals' in the Secretary General's department and the 'quasi-professionals' in the President's office who believed that the Secretary General was 'insubordinate to the President and is working to launch a new party.'[28] Among the major findings of the report was the view that there is a 'strong anti-Ndebele sentiment that has been propagated, orchestrated and instilled into the innocent party members' minds by a senior party leader under the guise of sheer hatred for the Secretary General at a personal level.'[29] One of the recommendations made by the commission was that:

> An investigation into the plot by high-ranking officials around the President's treason trial and the build-up to congress be put in place without delay with a view to establishing the extent to which ethnic hatred and division has damaged the party. Throughout this inquiry direct reference was made to senior leaders being involved in the promotion of tribalism. It is this commission's conviction that those leaders mentioned must be given the opportunity to respond to such disturbing allegations and appropriate action taken without fear or favour.'[30]

The findings of this Commission were not made official within the party as the commissioners failed to agree on the final report. The factionalism that emerged in the party was reproduced on the Commission and effectively debilitated the finalisation of the report. Notwithstanding the draft nature of the report it did reveal the emergence of very serious cleavages in the party, around the President, Morgan Tsvangirai and the Secretary General, Welshman Ncube. Moreover these differences were being fed and exacerbated by the parallel structures within the party and constructed in both ethnic and at times 'anti-intellectual' terms.

In May 2005 new outbreaks of party violence took place at the Party Headquarters in Harare, the Bulawayo Provincial Office and in Gwanda, and another Commission was set up composed of the Management Committee. The new Commission noted that the 2004 Commission had 'failed to reach a consensus and therefore no punishment had been meted out to the offenders.' As a result most of the youths who led the disturbances from 12–17 May 2005, had previously, by their own admission, been responsible for the assault on the Director of Security in 2004. Once again aides in the President's office were accused of directing the activities of the youth, and the objective of the violence was alleged to relate to the political battles leading up to the forthcoming national party congress. The allegations of the youth were that the 'Secretary General, the Deputy Secretary General, members of staff were working to replace the President.'[31] An important point made in the report was the danger of party functionaries mobilising unemployed youth to carry out party violence. It was further admitted that the party 'has no capacity to satisfy youth welfare needs' and that there is a 'general lack of education and orientation on party objectives and values.'[32] This point needs to be situated within the broader context of the culture of violence established and perpetuated by Zanu PF. The central findings of the report were:

- "It is common cause that the greater majority of our youths in our structures are activists and unemployed."
- "They have no source of income, therefore they are destitute. This makes them vulnerable to political vultures who are cash driven."
- "Staff, some party leaders and the external forces are using the youths for various political ambitions and devious goals."
- "The party goal and values for which the MDC was founded have been abandoned in pursuit of narrow selfish, self-satisfying ambitions and greed."
- "The congress agenda has hijacked the party focus."
- "The issue of ethnic affinity is also being abused in the party to form divergent groupings."
- "The notion that there are some who are more equal than others and falsely believe they are the only founders of the party, is a divisive issue."
- "Competing interests of politicians are a threat to the very existence of the party."[33]

As with the 2004 report there was little action taken on the issues raised, apart from the expulsion of several youth believed to have been responsible for the violence. There was no attempt to hold to account the senior party figures alleged to be the 'handlers' of these youth. The party's legal spokesperson David Coltart complained about this failure in the report. In a statement to the National Executive of the party Coltart noted:

I cannot believe that the youths involved in these despicable acts acted independently. It is common cause that they were unemployed and it is equally clear that they had access to substantial funding. That money must have come from people with access to resources. The instructions to act must have come from people within the Party as no-one else would have the detailed knowledge the youths had access to. In expelling the youths and relatively low ranking members of the security team we have only dealt with the symptoms of the problem, not its root cause.[34]

Coltart also charged that it was 'abundantly clear...that the Management Committee either did not manage to find out who instigated these acts of violence or it chose not to reveal those responsible', and that whatever the case 'there has been an inadequate investigation into who was behind the violence.' Coltart then stated his explanation for the compromised nature of the report:

It is common cause that the principle reason behind the violence was an alleged power struggle within the Management Committee. For that reason alone the Management Committee should not have conducted the investigation. They were in fact judges in their own cause.[35]

Finally Coltart attempted to reassure Tsavangirai that his Secretary General, Welshman Ncube, had no ambition to replace him as President.

> Within the MDC only Morgan Tsvangirai has sufficient stature to contest the presidency. Welshman Ncube knows that; I know that. Those within the party who seriously suggest that Morgan Tsvangirai's presidency is under threat are either being deliberately mischievous or simply do not understand basic political reality within Zimbabwe.[36]

Discussions on these problems continued amongst the leadership at a management committee retreat in July 2005. Once again the issue of the parallel structure was raised and the allegation was made that a 'kitchen cabinet', made up of Presidential aides, had formed around the President and undermined the decisions of the elected leadership:

> Members of the Management Committee explained that they felt decisions that were taken by the team were changed after the President consulted with members of his staff, or that staff counteracted their decisions, or took decisions that were beyond their 'brief' or job descriptions.[37]

It is important to note that these allegations were made by four of the six members of the Management Committee, namely the Vice President Gibson Sibanda, the Secretary General Welshman Ncube, the Deputy Secretary General Gift Chimanikire and the National Treasurer Fletcher Dulini. Tsvangirai disagreed saying that these concerns over the 'kitchen cabinet' 'were unsubstantiated...due to rumour and miscommunication.'[38]

The Chair of the party Isaac Matongo, after some equivocation, lined up behind his President. Thus the division within the leadership appeared to be, and was constructed as, an ethnic divide with Tsvangirai's critics, except for Chimanikire, coming from Matabeleland. At the July retreat the leadership were also fully aware that the party was losing political ground, and that 'deep concerns about the MDC's ability to lead itself, let alone compete effectively against the ruling party exist and are growing monthly.' The leadership then agreed on the need to devise a programme of activities that would 'demonstrate unity, build relationships amongst members of civil society, and create PR opportunities which contradict the consistent negative image of a fractured party,'[39] The Management Committee also noted the central need to focus on the defeat of Zanu PF, because in the absence of this,

> ...members are worrying about consolidating existing positions, and any future positions that maintain prestige or financial income. Although the situation internally is precarious, members can stilt derive status and income from positions within the MDC. The focus of maintaining these positions is distracting from commitment to the political struggle.[40]

While the MDC leadership had to deal with a growing factional struggle, it also had to continue to contend with the strategic difficulties of confronting the Mugabe regime. In the run up to the 2005 general election the leadership resolved that the election message had to change:

> The debate on participation has revolved around the issues of governance. However, experience had shown that elections are won by focussing on bread and butter issues hence jobs and food had been put at the forefront of issues to be addressed by the Party. The immediate challenge was in essence to send the right message to the people that the MDC not only focuses on human rights and intellectual liberties but day to day issues.[41]

Moreover, given the limitations of electoral participation as a political strategy in the repressive political climate, the party needed to 'strike a balance between voter expectations and the real situation on the ground' Messages had to be communicated which did not create a 'crisis of expectations' and people had to be 'psyched up for a bruising fight.'[42] These statements represented the tension at the heart of the MDC strategic dilemma: A commitment to participate in elections, while recognising the limitations of this option, and preparing its support base for the limits of electoral politics while preparing for an alternative strategy based on mass action. However, the problem has been that as MDC supporters have grown increasingly disillusioned with electoral politics, the party has been unable to develop a sustainable strategy for mass action. This problem has also been true of its civic partners such as the Zimbabwe Congress of Trade Unions (ZCTU) and the National Constitutional Assembly (NCA). In April 2005, soon after the MDC defeat in the general election Morgan Tsvangirai and his Deputy Secretary General, Gift Chimanikire met with leaders from the NCA, the ZCTU and the Crisis in Zimbabwe Coalition to discuss the way forward after another electoral defeat. The NCA in particular argued at the meeting that the MDC should not take up its seats in parliament, but instead concentrate on extra-parliamentary struggles, and stop sending confused signals to its support base. The MDC leadership pointed out that there was a strong lobby within the MDC advocating the importance of 'occupying the democratic space in Parliament', notwithstanding the limitations o the electoral process. While the MDC was still unsure of how to proceed, it was also clear that the civic groups had no clear alternative strategy beyond the broad call for mass action.[43]

In addition to these strategic and organisational challenges, the MDC has faced the problem of developing an inclusive, non-tribal and non-racial post-nationalist ideology, which was not a vulgar neo-liberalism. This has proved an exceedingly difficult challenge with the hazards of tribalism, as noted above, already apparent in the factional struggles within the party. The problem of developing a non-racial party has also proved extremely challenging. The 'white face' of the MDC has been heavily exploited by Zanu PF in a country and region where the memories of settler colonial rule are still fresh. This factor has also been an impediment in the mobilisation and media strategies of the MDC. In a post by-election campaign report in 2000, one party secretary made the following observation on the role of white members in MDC campaigns:

> They must not involve themselves physically on the ground as has been the case. They should occupy the back seats so that Zanu (PF) does not see them. Zanu

(PF) captures seats because it tells the people that the MDC is for the whitemen. Through ignorance the people believe and they vote Zanu (PF) in.[44]

While this problem was certainly not the same in all areas of the country, it is safe to say that it represented a general challenge for the MDC. White political participation in the politics of independent Zimbabwe was for most of this period marked by the racist legacy of settler politics, and the unofficial pact of the ruling party's Reconciliation Policy. This provided for whites to continue playing a key role in the economy, while having to vacate the political sphere, aside from participation through their various economic lobbying groups. The emergence of the constitutional movement and the MDC, and the major challenge these represented to the ruling party, provided new spaces for the involvement of whites in the political arena. The land occupations and their direct threat to private property rights certainly provided a strong impetus for involvement. However the inclusive language of the opposition, which appeared in stark contrast to the exclusive racialised discourse of Zanu PF, also provided an invitation to non-racial politics. The following extract is an example of how one individual responded:

> The advent of the No Vote was a watershed in the history of Zimbabwe. Zanu PF and its agents pitched a massive Vote Yes campaign along racial lines with prominent newspaper advertisements like a photograph of two elderly whites with the question "Are you going to allow them to continue to tell you what to do?" The people, the overwhelming majority of them blacks, rejected this propaganda, and in doing so showed just how politically mature they have become, but most importantly to me, sent out a clear signal that racism is not the burning issue that Zanu PF wants it to be. Being part of the white minority which is constantly used as a punch bag by the President when things go wrong, and with it the ill feeling, the No Vote came as an emotional triumph.[45]

This euphoric embrace of the politics of the opposition demonstrated both a lack of historical perspective on the continuing resonance of race in a post settler society and the sense of victim-hood which had begun to mark the narratives of white discourse after 2000, in particular. Harris describes this aspect of white narratives in Zimbabwe as follows:

> Mugabe's revocation of the discourses of reconciliation has allowed for a white re-imagining of the past that . . . exculpates white Zimbabwean involvement in racial tensions through dehistoricising that white identity.[46]

Dealing with the weight of such racial legacies in the MDC structures has been immensely difficult. While the MDC has been the party most committed to non-racialism in Zimbabwean politics, the deepening crisis within the party has resulted in less inclusive forms of politics. This has been the result both of the withdrawal of white, particularly white farmer, involvement in the party following the increased violence of the state, and an attempt to deal with the labelling of the MDC as a 'white controlled' party. There is also an important sense in which Mugabe's anti-white message resonates with members of the MDC in the context of the legacies of racism in Zimbabwe. In a critique of the party structures carried out in 2005, the MDC leadership itself viewed the party as having 'moved away from its social democratic, all inclusive, non-tribalistic foundations.'[47] Thus it is clear that one of the responses of the MDC to the authoritarian nationalism of Zanu PF has been a more guarded approach towards its public racial profile,[48] and a greater sensitivity to the ruling party's accusations of foreign domination of opposition politics.

As the organisational and strategic problems deepened in the MDC, the factional struggles within the party intensified. For those in the leadership who were connected to or controlled the parallel structure, the latter became the means for isolating the members of the leadership opposed to Tsvangirai in the run up to the proposed national congress in 2006. Most of the energies of these structures have thus been turned on those perceived as enemies within the party, rather than to developing a strategy to confront the Mugabe regime. The last attempt to organise a mass Stay Away on the 9–10th June 2005 by the MDC and its civic partners, constituted as a Broad Alliance, proved a dismal failure. Commenting on the role of the MDC in this action, Atwood has written:

> The MDC's involvement in the action was. . .half-hearted. In the run up to June 9 and 10, MDC President Morgan Tsvangirai issued a statement urging the people to "mobilise themselves," and warning government that if it continued with Operation *Murambatsvina*, the people's reaction might be unpredictable. When questioned MDC Secretary General Welshman Ncube distanced the organisation from the activities of the Broad Alliance. Like the ZCTU, the MDC was at the time mired in its own internal commission of inquiry regarding cases of indiscipline and fracturing party unity. It did not take a strong leadership role in coordinating the call to mass action.[49]

This failure was particularly apparent in the light of the government's Operation *Murambatsvina* in May 2005, which constituted a brutal attack on the livelihoods of a large section of urban workers, the major constituency of the MDC. Thus for Ncube and his supporters the use of the parallel structures within the party has been understood as largely a means of isolating and pushing them out of leadership positions at the next congress. It is against this background that the fateful debate over participation in the Senate elections in 2005 took place.

The Senate Debate and the Split in the MDC

The issue that brought matters to a head in the MDC was the decision on whether or not to participate in the Senate election in late 2005. Mugabe's major reasons for re-introducing the senate into the political sphere were, both to accommodate those in the ruling party who had lost in the parliamentary elections, and to exacerbate the divisions within the MDC, divisions that had been actively cultivated by Zanu PF. To many observers the Senate debate first appeared as a fairly innocuous issue which would be resolved within the MDC's top six and National Council. However, given the growing conflict and division within the MDC, the Senate question became the central battleground of the leadership for the control of the party. On October 12th 2005, after the top six leadership had failed to find a consensus on the issue, the

MDC National Council voted 33–31 (with 2 spoilt papers) to participate in the Senate elections. Tsvangirai's response to the vote was:

> Well you have voted, and you have voted to participate, which as you know is against my own wish. In the circumstances I can no longer continue...No I cannot let you participate in this Senate election when I believe that it is against the best interests of the party. I am President of this party. I am therefore going out of this and (will) announce to the world that the MDC will not participate in this election. If the party breaks so be it. I will answer to congress.[50]

The MDC President then left the National Council meeting and soon after held a press conference at which he misinformed the media that the National Council vote was deadlocked at 50-50, and that he had then used his casting vote to decide against Senatorial participation. Following this meeting the Deputy President of the party, Gibson Sibanda, wrote to Tsvangirai summoning him to a hearing of the National Disciplinary Committee on the charge that because of his actions at and after the National Council meeting of October 12th, Tsvangirai had wilfully violated clauses 4.4 (a), 6.1.1 (a) and (d) of the MDC constitution as well as clause 9.2 of the Party's Disciplinary Code of Conduct. Sibanda's letter also stated that Tsvangirai had further violated the above clauses after the meeting of the 12th by:

- "Writing to all party provincial chairpersons on the 13th October 2005 instructing them to ignore a letter written by the Party's Deputy Secretary General instructing provinces to commence selectivity of candidates."
- "Writing to the Zimbabwe Electoral Commission on 14th October 2005 falsely advising that the MDC had resolved not to participate in the Senate elections and calling upon the Commission to register as Independents all MDC candidates that would offer themselves to contest the election."
- Addressing numerous rallies and meetings in various places throughout Zimbabwe urging members and supporters of the party to boycott the Senate elections, contrary to the resolution of the National Council."
- "Instructing the party secretariat to re-employ Nhamo Musekiwa and Washington Gaga after they had been dismissed pursuant to a National Council resolution. In doing so you acted in violation of a standing resolution of the National Council contrary to clauses 4.4 (a) and 6.1.1 (d) of the party constitution."[51]

On the same day another letter was written to Tsvangirai informing him that the National Disciplinary Committee had met on the 20th November and resolved to suspend him from his position as President of the party with immediate effect pending his appearance before the Disciplinary Committee on misconduct charges. The letter also instructed Tsvangirai that he was barred from holding, addressing or attending any meetings, rallies or functions organised under the name of the MDC, that he should not visit the party headquarters, regional, provincial or district offices and that he should surrender all party property except the two vehicles issued for his use.[52]

In response to these events Morgan Tsvangirai stated that the pro-Senate group had 'already prepared the votes, the ballots and they had bought a lot of people,' and also accused his opponents of not carrying out legitimate provincial consultations.[53] Moreover in response to the legal arguments of his opponents, and accusations that he had 'refused to respect the founding values of the party'[54], Tsvangirai pitched his arguments at a populist level, arguing that his position on the Senate expressed the will of the people:

> Even if I am left alone, I will not betray the contract I made with the people. The issue that is there is not about the Senate only. It is about whether you want to confront Mugabe or you want to compromise with Mugabe. Some of us are now working towards a new unity accord. We are saying 'no' to unity accord number two. With us there is no unity accord ... we will not do what Nkomo did.[55]

In this statement the MDC leader was not only identifying his views with 'the people', he was also appealing to the sentiments of the people of Matabeleland by distancing himself from the possibility of another unpopular 'Unity Accord', and portraying the pro-senate faction as betraying the people of this region. This message was emphasised by the MDC party chair, Isaac Matongo, who accused the Ncube faction of complicity with Zanu PF, stating that the latter wanted to 'see Tsvangirai out and then put someone who could play to the Zanu PF tune.'[56] The debate over the Senate became an ugly public spectacle carried out in the state-controlled and private press, and characterised by disturbing levels of character assassination on both sides. Accusations and counter-accusations of corruption,[57] violence,[58] tribalism[59] and complicity with the ruling party were thrown about liberally. Moreover in a further ironic twist the internal battles in the MDC have ended up in the courts of the Mugabe regime.[60] As the leadership struggle continued Tsvangirai expelled the 'Senate rebels' from the party[61] and convened another National Council meeting which passed a resolution to nullify the disciplinary proceedings instituted against the MDC leader, and 'dissociating the rest of the party from Gibson Sibanda and others.'[62] The response from the major civic groups to the party struggles has largely been in support of the Tsvangirai position. The boycott of elections coincided with the long-term position of the NCA, while the ZCTU denounced the 'creation of the Senate and urges all workers to oppose it with all their might.'[63] The ZCTU paper *The Worker* made its editorial position clear:

> Now the onus is on the opposition, the Movement for Democratic Change (MDC) to reject taking part in the Senate election. All civic organisations have rejected the constitutional amendments. The MDC did reject them in Parliament and if they want to be taken seriously, they should not take part in elections. Zimbabweans should also stay home during elections to show their displeasure over the government action.[64]

Thus for both factions in the MDC the Senate debate took on a wider and more intense significance. For Tsvangirai and the anti-Senate campaigners, the boycott campaign was important for several reasons. Firstly Tsvangirai's political base within the party was increasingly organised through the parallel structure and the 'kitchen cabinet' against those in the top six of the leadership who were thought to be contesting his leadership. These structures had been built, outside of the control of the Management Committee of the party, both to develop alternative mass action responses to Mugabe's rule and to avoid having to deal with the Secretary General's office. There was thus a reluctance to make them accountable to an electoral strategy under the top six. Secondly, after another electoral defeat in the 2005 general election the MDC was under growing pressure to provide an alternative response to the Mugabe regime, or face the prospect of political irrelevance. Thirdly Tsvangirai felt that his views resonated with most of the party's support base in believing that there was little point in pursuing electoral politics under the present conditions in Zimbabwe. It is in this context that Tsvangirai called for the boycott of the senate elections and stated:

> The Zimbabwean struggle needs a paradigm shift. Parliament cannot be the main arena of our struggle. Our experience in Parliament since 2000 shows that the struggle resides outside ZANU PF.[65]

For the opposing faction the decision to campaign for participation in the Senate election was based firstly on their unwillingness to surrender political strategy to what was thought to be Tsvangirai's 'thuggish' parallel structures, working against Welshman Ncube, Gift Chimanikire and others in this faction. Secondly this group argued both that the people of Matabeleland would not agree to ceding political ground to the ruling party without a fight, and that in any case the anti-Senate argument presented no viable alternative strategy to participation in the elections. Ncube's reluctance to engage with mass action strategies was thus based not only on the belief that the parallel structures were working outside of party accountability through parallel funding, but also that they were not able to develop organised mass action activities in any coherent form. In short they were both unaccountable and ineffective and only ended up exposing the party's elected structures to state harassment.[66] It was against this background that Ncube declared:

> There is no other way of removing Robert Mugabe except through elections. Anyone who tells you the other way is cheating you. Even if Zanu PF says there is an election for a toilet caretaker we will participate.[67]

By February 2006 it was clear that the division in the MDC had solidified and the split in the party would be formalised at the two forthcoming congresses of the different factions. It is also clear from the analysis in this paper that the Senate issue, that provided the pretext for the party divide, was not in itself the fundamental cause of the problems in the MDC. It was merely the site on which the different factions fought out long-standing problems of organisation, structure, accountability and strategy within the party. At the mediation meeting held in October 2005 to try to resolve the party crisis there was a consensus amongst the leadership that the Senate issue was a 'tactical difference' and 'a symptom of a disease.' In the discussions that ensued at this meetings the issues raised centred around the problem of the parallel structure, the 'mafia kitchen cabinet', the growth of youth violence, attacks on the authority of the President, conflict and competition between the offices of the Presidency and the Secretary General with the resulting lack of implementation of party programmes, Tsvangirai's perception of the 'destructive' effects of President Mbeki's mediation efforts, infiltration by the regime's Central Intelligence Organisation, and the perception that the division over the Senate was based on tribal affiliation in the party. There was of course a different emphasis on which problems had proved to be most destructive, with Tsvangirai stressing the undermining effects of the Secretary General's office and arguing that the 'consensus leadership' at the top was not the most effective way to confront an authoritarian regime. Alternately Ncube and three other members of the top six concentrated on the destructive effects of the 'kitchen cabinet' and the parallel structure on the elected structures of the party.

At the end of the first meeting a compromise position was placed on the negotiation table, which included the following positions: Firstly the pro-Senate faction would withdraw from the Senate election; secondly the Management Committee would deal with the problem of the 'kitchen cabinet' and the parallel structure; thirdly the leadership would draw up a programme on the way forward. Moreover, henceforth the public recriminations from both sides were to cease. These issues were due to constitute the agenda for the next meeting and were to be kept strictly confidential. The day after this meeting full details of the discussion appeared on the front page of the *Independent* newspaper. At the second mediation meeting which lasted forty five minutes, both sides refused to shift from their positions, with Tsvangirai unwilling to make a commitment on the problem of his aides and the pro-Senate faction unwilling to go back on the Senate issue. The lack of trust within the leadership was all pervasive, and it was clear that both sides were at this point committed to a split in the party. However it was also clear that neither faction had developed effective strategies to confront the Mugabe government and also that both would have to face the difficult task of once again developing the national constituencies that the united MDC had once claimed. For the anti-Senate group the challenge would be to win over the Matabeleland region, while for their opponents the lack of a credible Shona leader would constitute a huge limitation in their efforts to develop a national profile.[68]

Conclusion

A great deal of commentary has been dedicated to the break up of the MDC. Within Zimbabwe the state media has wallowed in a sense of glib satisfaction and an endless stream of false retrospective 'wisdom'. The country's independent press and the internet news sources have staked their factional claims in the ongoing controversy. However one of the issues that both the state and independent media have concurred on is that the MDC crisis emerged because of a lack of good leadership and ideological unity.[69] While the opposition has certainly displayed leadership problems and faces a huge challenge in constituting an ideological unity, these are not problems peculiar to the MDC. The history of nationalist politics was characterised by its own leadership deficiencies and ideological struggles. Moreover ideological unity can only be constructed through long-term struggles and the project, though at certain historical moments contingently stable, is never complete. The challenge of the MDC has been to break the disciplinary hold of the nationalist legacy and to develop a more democratic, inclusive and plural discourse that is able to confront both national authoritarianism and international dictat. This is the challenge for any progressive movement in the contemporary world, and it is one on which the MDC made important progress at national level. At continental level the opposition party has had much more difficulty in presenting itself as a progressive force against Mugabe's Pan Africanist rhetorical stance. Its limitations at this level have decreased the terrain on which it has been able to operate and develop its vision. More recently the split in the MDC has bred speculation that the division has emerged because of ideological differences between the more 'radical populist' anti-Senate faction and the pro-Senate 'neo-liberals.' There is little evidence that this is the case with both factions espousing broad social democratic positions and both likely to adopt some form of neo-liberal economic recovery policy. Nevertheless the challenge of developing ideological consistency in the party and the various ideological trends apparent in its pronouncements, have caused problems for both the supporters of the MDC and those commenting on its activities.

Notwithstanding these limitations the central fact of the MDC crisis is that it has taken place in an authoritarian national political culture that has persistently closed down the spaces for democratic growth. The loss of three national elections under these conditions, and the fact that the MDC has not been able to successfully challenge these fraudulent elections has led to increasing frustration in both the leadership and general membership of the party. The corrosive effects of this persistent defeat would be enough to challenge the future of most opposition parties. The fact that Zanu PF has conducted its authoritarian politics under a populist anti-colonial and anti-imperialist banner has provided little solace to those forces in Zimbabwe struggling for more open national political spaces. The broader national and international context of the Zimbabwe crisis has been discussed elsewhere.[70] This dimension has clearly played an important role in shaping the politics of Zanu PF. External forces have also shaped the form of the debacle in the MDC. Ill conceived international alliances and reports of dubious funding by, and advice from, right wing organisations such as the International Republican Institute and Freedom House[71] are likely to have had their effects on the strategies and leadership stances taken in the party. Moreover the impact of South African interventions in the MDC has yet to be fblly explored. What is clear thus far is that the SA presidency has had serious doubts about the capacity of the MDC to develop a national government and to gain the confidence of the Zimbabwean armed forces, and these factors have underlair the push by the SA government for a government of national unity in Zimbabwe. Moreover President Mbeki's dealings with the leadership of the MDC have also contributed to the growing distrust between the two factions within the party, with Morgan Tsvangirai feeling increasingly distrustful of the South African leader's relationship with the Ndebele leaders in the MDC. This paper has not addressed these wider concerns and future discussions will need to penetrate this important dimension. At present there is much speculation but little evidence produced in the discussion of this factor, but clearly there are disturbing questions that need to be answered. This discussion has concentrated on the internal factors in the MDC crisis and both the strengths and weaknesses of the paper stem from this emphasis. Nevertheless it is hoped that the paper has provided a more informed basis for discussion of the crisis in Zimbabwe's major opposition party. At present the future of opposition politics in Zimbabwe appears bleak, with neither side in the MDC offering a viable strategy to confront the ruling party. This current malaise in opposition politics is likely to have a broader dampening effect on the politics of civil society at a time when the major civic groups are themselves struggling t survive state repression and general public despondency. The challenge for opposition forces is now to rethink and reconfigure the organisational structures and strategic interventions that are needed both to confront a repressive regime and build a sustainable alternative, democratic culture. In this difficult process the lessons learnt from the fracturing of the MDC will be invaluable.

Postscript: April 2006

This paper was written prior to the formal split in the MDC which took place after the two factions held their respective congresses in February and March 2006. In the light of the split with Tsvangirai, and given the ethnic dynamic of Zimbabwean politics, the pro-Senate faction was forced to look for an electable Shona leader to oppose both Tsvangirai and Mugabe. Given the lack of a suitable candidate within the existing ranks of the pro-Senate faction, the latter looked to a candidate outside of the existing leadership structure and elected Arthur Mutambara, a university professor and former leading student leader in the 1980s. From his election speech it was clear that Mutambara was keen to appropriate the language of radical nationalism that had been seen as the preserve of Mugabe and his party, and attempt to link it to the discourse of human rights and democratic accountability that had dominated the language of opposition and civic politics since the 1990s. Mutambara set out his vision in the following terms:

> We stand opposed to any form of imperialism, violation of state human rights and unilateralism. We will not accept assistance at the expense of our dignity, values and sovereignty. We make a clear distinction between strategic partners and political allies. We are anti-imperialist, driven by nationalist interest and informed by Pan African ideals. I do not believe in sanctions.[72]

Mutambara was also keen to establish the links between the struggles of the MDC and the legacy of the liberation struggle:

> We are also coining in with the tradition of the liberation war recognising the role played by people like Chitepo, Tongogara, Nikita Mangena and John Nkomo. No one owns the history of the liberation struggle. We are coming in the tradition of ZANLA and ZIPRA fighters.[73]

For the future it will be interesting to assess the ways in which Mutambara is able to manage the discursive and strategic tensions in a political project that requires the need for both a radical anti-imperialist stance and a commitment to the civic struggles around democratisation and human rights. It is however important that this project be attempted given the distortions in Mugabe's severing of the two discourses. At the very least Mutambara's new political language is an important new development on the Zimbabwean political landscape.

For Tsvangirai and his camp the importance of their congress was to show the support of large numbers of the MDC constituency, and to consolidate the power of the presidency in the party structures. In his opening speech Tsvangirai acknowledged the contribution of the pro-Senate leadership:

> Allow me to note the work done by my colleagues who have chosen not to be with us today but who pioneered and contributed to the growth of the MDC and this democracy project with us for many years. Thank you for risking life and limb to try and rebuild Zimbabwe. We have not forgotten that contribution.[74]

Tsvangirai's speech also stressed the importance of 'peaceful democratic resistance'. He declared:

> The options open to us are very clear. We need a short sharp programme of action to free ourselves. The call is made to you once again to intensify the peaceful democratic resistance to the current tyranny. Your resilience to reclaim your rights has shaken Mugabe's corridors of power.[75]

Notwithstanding the declarations of both MDC parties, the strategic, organisational and ideological challenges that have been discussed in this paper remain in different ways for both sides. The hard work of rebuilding an effective opposition to confront Mugabe's authoritarian regime remains to be done, even as the latter puts in place further legislation on communications surveillance of its citizenry, and an anti-terrorist law constructed largely to further criminalise the activities of the opposition.

Notes

1. Amanda Hammar, Brian Raftopoulos and Stig Jensen (Eds), **Zimbabwe's Unfinished Business: Rethinking Land, State and Citizenship in the Context of Crisis,** Weaver Press, Harare, 2003; Brian Raftopoulos and Tyrone Savage (Eds), **Zimbabwe: Injustice and Political Reconciliation,** Institute for Justice and Reconciliation and Weaver Press, Cape Town and Harare, 2004; Terence Ranger, "Nationalist Historiography, Patriotic History and the History of the Nation: the Struggle over the Past in Zimbabwe," *Journal of Southern African Studies,* Vol 30, No 2, June 2004, pp. 215–234.
2. See Mahmood Mamdani, **Citizen and Subject: Contemporary Africa and the Legacy of Late Colonialism,** Princeton University Press, Princeton, 1996.
3. Masipula Sithole, 'Zimbabwe: In Search of a Stable Democracy,' in Larry Diamond, J.J. Linz and S.M. Lipset (Eds) **Democracy in Developing Countries: Volume 2: Africa,** Lynne Rienner, Boulder, 1988; also his "Zimbabwe's Eroding Authoritarianism," *Journal of Democracy,* Vol 8, No 1, 1997, pp. 127–141; Jonathan Moyo, "Civil Society in Zimbabwe", *Zambezia,* xx, (i), 1993, pp. 1–13; Sabelo J. Ndlovu-Gatsheni, 'Putting People First- from Regime Security to Human Security: A Quest for Social Peace in Zimbabwe, 1980–2002,' in Alfred G. Nhema, **The Quest for Peace in Africa,** International Books with OSSREA, Addis Ababa, 2004, pp. 297–327; Eldred Masunungure, 'Travails of Opposition Politics in Zimbabwe since Independence,' in David Harold Barry (Eds), **Zimbabwe: The Past is the Future,** Weaver Press, Harare, 2004, pp. 147–192.
4. David Moore, 'The ideological formation of the Zimbabwean ruing class,' *Journal of Southern African Studies,* Vol, No. 3, 1991, pp. 472–495; David Moore, 'Democracy, violence and identity in the Zimbabwean war of national liberation: Reflections from the realms of dissent,' *Canadian Journal of African Studies,* Vol, 29, No. 3, pp. 375–402.
5. The struggles within Zanu have been well described by the recent autobiography of Fay Chung, **Re-Living the Second Chimurenga: Memories from Zimbabwe's Liberation Struggle,** Nordic Africa Institute and Weaver Press, Uppsala and Harare, 2006.

6. Ndlovu-Gatsheni op cit, p. 306.
7. Sara Rich Dorman, "Inclusion and Exclusion: NGOs and Politics in Zimbabwe". D.Phil. Degree, University of Oxford, 2001.
8. Jonathan Moyo, **Voting for Democracy: Electoral Politics in Zimbabwe**, Harare, University of Zimbabwe Publications, 1992.
9. John Makumbe and Daniel Compagnon, **Behind the Smokescreen: The Politics of Zimbabwe's 1995 General Election**. Harare, University of Zimbabwe, 2000.
10. Eldred Masunugure, op cit, p. 165.
11. Masungure op cit, and Brian Raftopoulos, 'The Labour Movement and the Emergence of Opposition Politics,' in Brian Raftopoulos and Lloyd Sachikonye (Eds), **Striking Back: The Labour Movement and the Post-Colonial State**, Harare, Weaver Press, 2001, pp. 1–24.
12. Liisa Laakso, "Opposition Politics in Independent Zimbabwe", *African Studies Review*, 3,30,2004, p. 13.
13. MDC Strategic Meeting, Harare, 6th January 2000. Present at the meeting were Morgan Tsvangirai (President), Gibson Sibanda (Vice President), Welshman Ncube (Secretary General), Fletcher Dulini (National Treasurer), and Gift Chimanikire (Deputy Secretary General). This became known as the Top Six Management Committee.
14. Ibid.
15. MDC Strategy Paper, April 2000.
16 Ibid.
17 Strategy Update, 8th May 2000.
18. Strategic Planning Meeting, 6th March 2001.
19. MDC Strategic Paper April 2000.
20. MDC District Workshop, 19th August 2000. In attendance were the following branches: Mbare 1, Mbare 2, Mbare 3, Waterfalls, Highfield and Harare Province.
21. Memorandum: Marondera Campaign, from Topper Whitehead to the Election Director, 1st December 2000.
22. Adrienne Lebas, "Polarisation and Party Development: Capturing Constituencies in Democratising Africa," Draft PhD Dissertation, Columbia University August 2005, pp. 183–184.
23. Ibid, p. 186.
24. Erin McCandless, "Zimbabwean Forms of Resistance: Social Movements, Strategic Dilemmas and Transformative Change," PhD, American University, Washington, 2005, p. 584.
25. LeBas op cit p. 187.
26. Commission of Inquiry into Disturbances at Party Headquarters (Draft Report), December 2004, pp. 4–5. The Commissioners were Dr. Tichanona Mudzingwa, the Hon. Miles Mutsekwa and the Hon. Moses Mzila-Ndlovu.
27. Ibid, p. 20.
28. Ibid, pp. 27–28.
29. Ibid, p. 31.
30. Ibid, pp. 32–33.
31. Report of the Management Committee of an Inquiry into the Disturbances and Beatings at Harvest House, Bulawayo Provincial Office and in Gwanda at the late Masera's Funeral. 2005, p. 6.
32. Ibid, p. 12.
33. Ibid, p. 16.
34. David Coltart, "Statement of David Coltart: MDC National Executive Meeting: 15th July 2005."
35. Ibid.
36. Ibid.
37. Report of the Management Committee Meeting, 30th July 2005, Pretoria.
38. Ibid.
39. Ibid.
40. Ibid.
41. Report of the Strategic Planning Meeting, 21–22 January 2005, Cape Town.
42. Ibid.
43. Author's notes from the Meeting between Morgan Tsvangirai and Gift Chimanikire (MDC) and leaders of the NCA, ZCTU and Crisis in Zimbabwe Coalition, held in Harare, 6th April 2005.
44. Report from the MDC Secretary, Mashonaland East, 26th November 2000.

45. "Clear Choice": Letter from Bill Searle a businessman and member of the MDC support group in 2000, support@mdc.co.zw Nd. Another example of this kind of sentiment was a letter from an additional member of the MDC support group, businessman Topper Whitehead: "I have never involved myself in politics because like most whites, I did not believe there was any hope of having an influence on the way I would like to see things. I have now involved myself as I believe I can help change things, and let me state clearly I have no intention of standing for office or to be elected for any post." support@mdc.co.zw Nd.

46. Ashleigh Harris, 'Writing Home: Inscriptions of whiteness/descriptions of belonging in white memoir-autobiography,' in Robert Muponde and Ranka Primorac (Eds) **Versions of Zimbabwe: New Approaches to literature and culture.** Harare, Weaver Press, 2005, p. 107.

47. Report of the MDC Management Committee Meeting, 30th July 2005.

48. One recent vehement assertion of this was made by Job Sikhala, the MDC MP for St. Marys. In the course of a newspaper interview with the government controlled *Herald* Sikhala pointed to the problem of race as one of the consequences of the MDC's broad alliance of social forces. Referring to one of the key white figures in the MDC Sikhala complained that in the MDC alliance 'we had people like Eddie Cross, who is a white supremacist, an ardent follower of Rhodesian fundamentalism who believes that everything begins and ends with Rhodesia.' "Kitchen cabinet destroyed MDC: Sikhala." *Herald*, 7th January 2006.

49. Amanda Atwood, 'Stay-Away 9–10 June 2005: Some Lessons Learned' Unpub. Mimeo 2005, p. 4. "Operation *Murambatsvina*" refers to the government's widely condemned urban 'clean up' campaign carried out in May 2005.

50. Trudy Stevenson, 'MDC's October 12 Meeting-the facts'. *Zimbabwe Independent* 13th January 2006.

51. Letter from Gibson Sibanda, Vice President of the MDC to Morgan Tsvangirai, President of the MDC, 24th November 2005.

52. Letter from Gibson Sibanda to Morgan Tsvangirai, 24th November 2005.

53. Violet Gonda, 'Hot Seat Programme: Tsvangirai says vote buying and self interest swung MDC senate vote.' violet@swradioafrica.com 18th October 2005.

54. This is a statement from the Deputy Secretary General of the party, Gift Chimanikire quoted in Caesar Zvayi, 'Tsvangirai a dictator: MDC faction.' *Herald* 1st November 2005.

55. Tsvangirai says faction working with Zanu PF.' *The Daily Mirror*, 31st October 2005.

56. Walter Marwizi, 'Plot to oust Tsvangirai;' *The Standard*, 20th November 2005.

57. "MDC falls apart: Tsvangirai's financial dealings in ZCTU, Ben-Menashe saga exposed." *Herald* 14th November 2005.

58. "Bid to block Tsvangirai rally flops." *The Daily Mirror*, 10th November 2005.

59. This accusation was fuelled by a report that the Deputy President of the MDC, Gibson Sibanda, was alleged to have advocated an independent state for Ndebele speaking people. At a campaign rally Sibanda is alleged to have said: "Ndebeles can only exercise sovereignty through creating their state like Lesotho, which is an independent state in South Africa and it is not politically wrong to have the state of Matabeleland in Zimbabwe.' "Sibanda calls for Ndebele State", *Daily Mirror* 8th November 2005. Pro-Senate MDC spokesperson Paul Themba Nyati denied the report saying that 'not only is the allegation untrue, it also appears to be a deliberate attempt by the newspaper to fan ethnic tensions in the MDC and the country as a whole.' *The Independent* 18th November 2005.

60. The most recent example is that the pro-senate faction has filed a Z$100 billion dollar suit against Tsvangirai for allegedly accusing them of colluding with Zanu PF to assassinate the MDC leader. Njabulo Ncube, "The saga continues… Tsvangirai files notice of appeal." *Financial Gazette* 2–8 February 2006.

61. "Tsvangirai expels Senate 'rebels.'" *The Sunday Mail*, 13th November 2005.

62. The MDC National Council Meeting and Resolutions, 1st December 2005.

63. "ZCTU Position on Senate Elections." *Sunday Mirror*, 20th November 2005.

64. Comment: "Boycott Senate Elections." *The Worker*, September 2005.

65. Morgan Tsvangirai, "Senate: what is in it for the people?' *The Financial Gazette*, 29th October 2005.

66. Report on the MDC Management Committee Meeting, Pretoria, 30th July 2005.

67. "Elections only way to dislodge Zanu PF: Ncube." *Daily Mirror*, 4th January 2005.

68. This writer was the mediator at the two meeting of the top six and the details of the two paragraphs above are taken from the writer's notes on the meetings of the Management Committee held on the 26th and 31st October 2005.

69. As examples see, Robert Mukondiwa, "MDC death: The post-mortem", *The Sunday Mail*, 20th November 2005, and Dumisani Muleya "MDC's problem is lack of ideology", *The Zimbabwe Independent* 4th November 2005. Jonathan Moyo, one time government critic turned state propagandist and now leader of a new party, the United People's Movement, has made the same point: "...infighting within the MDC was bound to take place ever since the party was formed in 1999 as the ideological question facing it, arising from not having a shared ideology was not whether such a fight would happen but when. The proposition that the root cause of the infighting is because of a lack of a common ideology shared by the MDC leadership is demonstrated by the fact that the infighting is very personalised and when it is not, the issues at stake are procedural and not substantive." "MDC infighting was bound to take place." *The Zimbabwe Independent*, 4th November 2005.

70. Hammar, Raftopoulos and Jensen 2003 op cit; Brian Raftopoulos and Ian Phimister, "Zimbabwe Now: The Political Economy of Crisis and Coercion," *Historical Materialism*, Vol 12, No Issue 4, 2004, pp. 355–382; Ian Phimister and Brian Raftopoulos, "Mugabe, Mbeki and the Politics of Anti-imperialism," *Review of African Political Economy*, 101, 2004, pp. 385–400.

71. The *Herald* reported that Morgan Tsvangirai and eight top officials his faction were deported from Zambia on the 2nd February 2005 after meeting with representative of Freedom House and losing Zambian presidential candidate Anderson Mazoka. "Zambia deports Tsvangirai", *Herald*, 3rd February 2005.

72. Nkululeko Sibanda, "Mutambara attacks Britain." *The Daily Mirror*, 27th February 2006.

73. "Mutambara calls for MDC re-unification". *The Daily Mirror*, 14th March 2006.

74. Foster Dongozi and Valentine Maponga, "15000 attend MDC congress." *The Standard* 19–25th March 2006.

75. Ibid.

Engaging with Mugabe

RICHARD DOWDEN
Royal African Society, London, UK

Introduction

In the late 1980s Douglas Hurd, the then British Foreign Secretary, on his way to Zimbabwe asked me what I thought of Robert Mugabe. I ventured that in his heart the Zimbabwean president was still a one-party state socialist. "His heart?" Hurd scoffed, "Never worry about what is in a politician's heart. Politicians have to do what they have to do."

My inference is that Hurd assumed that whatever Mugabe felt in his heart, he would have to do, whatever he was told by the British and other donors, if he wanted to succeed and stay in power. It is an assumption that still underlies much of Western policy towards Africa: the donors have the power of the aid strings in many African states and therefore can control their politics.

It is wrong. All politics in Africa are local and personal. When African leaders are faced with a choice between appeasing the demands of local politics or international donors, they invariably choose the local. There is also an assumption in Western circles that African politicians would never deliberately impoverish their own countries or their people. If a country is doing well economically, that must boost a ruler's popularity and power. If it is doing badly, the ruler will surely be kicked out. That too is wrong for much of Africa. In country after country in Africa we have seen rulers destroy their economies rather than leave or share power. As long as Africa's wealthy and powerful elites and their families enjoy the fruits of office, they do not worry too much about what happens to the rest of the people. As they say in Kenya: "It does not matter how thin the cow gets if you are the only one on the teat".

Zimbabwe's economy is wrecked but Mugabe has never had more power. In the May 2005 elections he increased his majority in parliament enabling, him to change the constitution. Even in the ludicrously unlikely case of the opposition winning all their electoral challenges in the courts, they would still not have a majority in parliament. That seemed a possible moment for Britain to accept the inevitable and re-engage with Zimbabwe. But the opportunity—if there was one—was missed and Mugabe set about making his political security into a complete dictatorship.

He reintroduced an upper house senate and packed it with his own nominees. Within the party he undermined the position of Emmerson Mnangagwa, a potential successor, thereby strengthening, if narrowing, his hold on ZANU (PF). However, many analysts detect a shift in power from the party to the military. Finally, he swept the poor—potential demonstrators—out of the towns in Operation Murambatsvina, ensuring that there could be no popular urban uprising in view of the media. Unless he chooses to change the constitution again, Mugabe now faces no electoral challenge until parliamentary elections in 2008.

The opposition movement, the Movement for Democratic Change (MDC), which gave so many Zimbabweans hope when it emerged in 1999, has split along ethnic lines over whether to boycott elections for the senate. The party now lies fatally wounded, fought over by lawyers. Its leader, Morgan Tsvangirai, is isolated and discredited. An attempt to create a 'Third Force', between ZANU (PF) and the MDC has gone nowhere.

On the international front the African Union has managed to shrug off criticism that it has not acted on Zimbabwe, despite a fiercely critical report on Operation Murambatsvina by Anna Tibaijuka for the United Nations. South Africa has stayed quiet except for announcing security cooperation with Zimbabwe, which will, in the words of Ronnie Kasrils, South Africa's security minister, let Zimbabwe and South Africa "march shoulder to shoulder". The South Africans also announced a project to cooperate on training air force pilots. However, Billy Masetla, South Africa's security intelligence chief, did express "huge concern" about the numbers of Zimbabweans fleeing across the South African border.

More than 80% of Zimbabweans now live below the poverty line and the economy has shrunk to two-thirds of what it was in 1999. Inflation is now estimated at over 500% and the Zimbabwe dollar, two to the US dollar in 1980, is now 110 000 to the dollar on the streets. The agriculture sector, Zimbabwe's economic driver, has shrunk by more than a quarter. Most worryingly much of the sophisticated, if haphazard, irrigation systems on the commercial farms that allowed Zimbabwe to produce crops even in drought years have been ripped up and sold as scrap metal. This—and the expertise to run those farms—are Zimbabwe's most grievous and lasting loss.

In February 2006 Zimbabwe paid off US$9 million in arrears to the IMF thus avoiding loss of voting rights but that did not prevent the IMF immediately demanding radical economic reform. Between three and four million Zimbabweans have fled the country, mostly to South Africa, where most are forced to do jobs way below their qualifications. Will they go back? Past experience shows that those most successful elsewhere will stay out until they can find equivalent work back home. That is unlikely in their lifetime.

The general picture is that, barring dramatic events such as the death of Mugabe, Zimbabwe is heading for steepening decline which will end, not in an uprising or resistance, but in mass poverty and starvation. There will be no dramatic collapse or meltdown, just a slow return to the Iron Age—with guns.

What does this mean for a policy for the rest of the world towards Zimbabwe? The British—given the nod by other Western nations to take the lead on Zimbabwe because of its colonial connection—got it wrong. British Prime Minister Tony Blair has always feared *The Daily Mail* more than any other political opponent or media voice. He chose to echo its strident line on Zimbabwe, despite the fact that it had always supported white rule in Zimbabwe. Making an assumption similar to Hurd's, the British thought they could warn Mugabe, threaten him, even browbeat him with words. Mugabe relished that treatment and returned the abuse with interest, accruing massive support from other Africans by replaying old anti-colonial tunes. Sanctions, smart or otherwise, did not even make him blink. It is unlikely that any of his loyal cronies have lost a single drop of malt whiskey as a result.

The British went ahead with that policy in the teeth of warnings from African leaders. When the policy broke there was no Plan B and there were no African allies willing to say much in public. One fallback position is to sit and wait either until Mugabe dies or until there is total collapse. But allowing things to get worse will not bring about positive change. People are too busy looking for something to eat to get involved in a political movement. The backbone of the opposition movement, the urban, educated, aspirant professionals, has left the country. Ignoring Zimbabwe will only allow things to spiral on down.

Nothing can be done by the UK or other countries on Zimbabwe without the agreement of South African President Thabo Mbeki. Severe wounds were inflicted on Anglo-South African relations when Mbeki was outvoted on the expulsion of Zimbabwe from the Commonwealth in 2003. But it is clear that the UK, *The Daily Mail* notwithstanding, will not jeopardize its relationship with South Africa further over Zimbabwe. Elsewhere in Africa Western governments and companies have to worry about the Chinese and their search for raw materials and UN votes. Despite their lack of squeamishness about how they secure these elsewhere on the continent, the Chinese are unlikely to prop up Mugabe. In 2005 the Chinese spent some $100 million on a platinum mine in Zimbabwe and sold military equipment. They also agreed to mutual support at the UN but while this helps Mugabe it does not provide him with the sort of aid that he needs let alone a saviour.

The question now is what sort of Zimbabwe might emerge once Mugabe is gone and how could Britain and the rest of the world contribute to rebuilding it. A plan should be drawn up now and made public, offering Zimbabwe a generous reconstruction package when Mugabe goes. It will probably make no political difference—Mugabe does not look like a man about to step down and the opposition is too weak to exploit such an offer. But it would give Zimbabweans hope for the longer term.

My guess is that Mugabe will not resign but prefer to die in office. Previously many assumed that when he went there would be a power shift and the opposition MDC would come to power. With the MDC permanently crippled it is more likely that Zimbabwe's next ruler will come from within ZANU (PF). But will the party survive his death or is Mugabe's rule a one-man dictatorship like that of Sani Abacha's in Nigeria or Mobutu's in Zaire where the power base—and the state—imploded when they died?

ZANU (PF) is now bitterly divided and these divisions are likely to explode when Mugabe goes. At the moment Joyce Mujuru, the vice president, would succeed but it is unlikely that she would be able to hold either the party or the country together for long. If the party were able to agree on a candidate such as Simba Makoni, the technocratic former finance minister, the rest of the world would be able to swing into action with the reconstruction plan. If, however, the party tears itself to pieces in civil war, the army would step into the power vacuum, making it far more difficult for outsiders to support it, particularly since all the army commanders are tainted with atrocities.

Under these scenarios it may seem counter intuitive to argue for greater engagement in Zimbabwe. What, many ask, is there to talk about? True, there is little to be gained directly, but all the alternatives are worse. Ignoring Zimbabwe will not make it go away or get better. Like sitting at the bedside of a delirious patient, remaining engaged and talking does no harm and it would leave Britain well placed to take a lead with African governments and institutions in helping Zimbabwe back on its feet again when the moment arrives.

Index